The Abbé Grégoire

1787-1831

Contributions in Afro-American
and African Studies

The Abbé Grégoire
1787-1831

THE ODYSSEY OF AN
EGALITARIAN

Ruth F. Necheles

*Contributions in Afro-American
and African Studies, No. 9*

A Negro Universities Press Publication

GREENWOOD PUBLISHING CORPORATION   WESTPORT, CONNECTICUT

TO JOHN AND HENRIETTA NECHELES

Library of Congress Catalog Card Number: 75–105987
SBN: 8371–3312–2

A Negro Universities Press Publication

Greenwood Publishing Corporation
51 Riverside Avenue, Westport, Connecticut 06880

Printed in the United States of America
Designed by Harriett Banner

Contents

Prelude

THE JEWS

Part One

THE FRENCH REVOLUTION AND THE BLACKS

Part Two

TOWARDS A NEW IMPERIAL SYSTEM

Part Three

GREGOIRE IN OPPOSITION

Part Four

CONCLUSION

Illustrations

Abbreviations for Notes

AD, L&C: Archives Départementales, Loir-et-Cher
AN: Archives Nationales
AP: *Archives parlementaires de 1787 à 1860* . . .
AS: Vatican, Archives Secrète
BH: Bibliothèque Historique de la Ville de Grenoble
BM: Bibliothèque Municipale (Besançon, Blois, Laon, Lunéville, and Nancy)
BN: Bibliothèque Nationale (MSF: Manuscrits françaises; NAF: Nouvelles acquisitions françaises)
BPR: Bibliothèque de Port-Royal
GS Nancy: Grand Séminaire
HEH: Henry E. Huntington Library
LC: Library of Congress (DBW: David Bailie Warden Collection; TJ: Thomas Jefferson Collection)
MHS: Maryland Historical Society
NYHS: New York Historical Society

Acknowledgments

Many people have helped me complete this study. The friendship and generosity of several French scholars and librarians—foremost of whom are the Abbé Jean Matha of Paris and M. André Gazier, librarian of the Bibliothèque de Port-Royal—opened to me collections which I never would have discovered on my own. The encouragement, advice, and moral support given over so many years by my former advisor, Professor Louis R. Gottschalk of the Circle Campus, University of Illinois, and by my present chairman, Dr. Thomas Stirton of Long Island University, have eased the many traumas and frustrations which such a project entails. Funds from the American Philosophical Society as well as repeated grants and reduced professional obligations from Long Island University have provided the necessary financial assistance and free time. I am particularly indebted to my friends and colleagues, Esther Hyneman, Mary Klein, and Lester Wilson, for their criticism and advice throughout the preparation of this manuscript.

The Abbé Grégoire in 1828.
Medallion by Pierre-Jean David d'Angers.

Introduction

That Henri-Baptiste Grégoire has puzzled men for more than two centuries is not surprising; even contemporary artists could not agree on his external features. At the outset of the Revolution one portrayed him as a slight young man with a long but delicate nose, fine lips, sharp staring eyes, and incongruously heavy jowls. Shortly thereafter another depicted him as a gross Germanic peasant, while to the sculptor Pierre-Jean David d'Angers he appeared tired and lined, an intellectual with a high noble forehead and a strong Roman nose.

Grégoire's various portraits reflect his inconsistent upbringing. Born on 4 December 1750 of petty bourgeois parents in the village of Vého in ducal Lorraine, he identified with the impoverished peasantry but vacationed with a neighboring seigneur. His devout, possibly Jansenist, mother sent him to a Jesuit *collège*; when that order was dissolved, he completed his studies under various lay and religious professors who were engrossed in the mid-eighteenth-century intellectual controversies over the *philosophes'* theories. After his ordination, Grégoire restlessly alternated between literary and religious pursuits, submitting secular reform projects to academic contests while he retraced his father's pilgrimages through Central Europe.[1]

Although, by abstracting their common concern for mankind, Grégoire achieved a tenuous synthesis between the two dominant influences in his life, pietistic Christianity and eighteenth-century enlightenment thought, the anachronistic character of both traditions hindered his legislative career. He hoped to achieve religious goals through political action based on environmental, materialist assumptions, but otherworldly considerations seemed irrelevant in an era of rapid secular change, while the intricacies of revolutionary reform required specialized knowledge. Grégoire avoided the most obvious problem by deemphasizing his religious aspirations, but he remained a dedicated amateur on secular questions, a priest whose theological assumptions and encyclopedic interests prevented him from absorbing enough information to understand his varied causes.

Grégoire's awkward amalgamation of Christian and philosophic principles led to an erratic political career. Combining a pessimistic chiliasm with an optimistic faith in the power of man's reason, he was constantly torn between his desires to hasten the inevitable fulfillment of God's plans through any available means and his belief in man's ability to create his own destiny.[2] Convinced that man must govern himself, he embraced republicanism as the most appropriate political form, yet he became impatient with French conservatism and accepted the Terror dictatorship as a necessary evil. Forced to choose between democracy and authoritarianism, he tolerated the latter because it seemed the only way to institute needed reforms. Thus, for all his belief in reason and peace, a thread of apocalyptic violence ran throughout his speeches and writings. He seemed to demand a ritual purification for France in terms more suited to either an Old Testament prophet or the most bloodthirsty radical rather than to a Christian cleric or a democratic statesman.[3]

Grégoire's Christian universalism also contradicted his

nationalism, but he reconciled these incompatible attitudes by subordinating the latter to the former. He viewed mankind as a family which shared the same rights and which eventually would be united by a common faith in a revitalized Christianity. Local and class privileges separated this family, however, and Grégoire hoped that national authority would transcend all artificial distinctions, thereby creating the environment in which a cosmopolitan society of free and equal men might develop. According to him, this society must rest upon a regenerated universal church within which nations would act as administrative units, or dioceses, entrusted with translating into laws the eternal verities discovered by reason and sanctified by faith.[4]

Early in the Revolution, the first legislature denied to such foreigners as Jews and Africans the rights which it gave to Frenchmen. Sensing that his colleagues had only enlarged their parochialism, Grégoire protested that the Revolution had an international constituency and that national interests must be measured against a transcendant, universal, and Christian morality. Although the other representatives also believed in the family of man, they regarded France as a microcosm of the world. Hence they could not understand Grégoire's vision of an all-embracing church and thought that solving France's temporal problems would save mankind without supernatural intervention.

Throughout the first two years of the Revolution, Grégoire's political program suffered from its subordination to his theological aspirations. Convinced that man's eternal fate depended on rigid adherence to the truth, he could not become a good party man in the modern sense of the term because he had to determine each issue on its own merits. Certainly he could not accept a platform or program dictated by others. Avoiding permanent affiliations, he cooperated with like-minded men on individual crusades but failed to create an effective following for his overall program.

Still Grégoire pursued his reform projects until repeated failures as well as his election as bishop in 1791 and his subsequent experiences during the National Convention convinced him that revolutionary politics contradicted his religious beliefs. Between 1792 and 1795 his self-image and tactics changed. No more interested than before in traditional ecclesiastical methods, he ceased participating in factional feuds and aspired to serve as an impartial mediator above the contending parties. Envisioning himself as a disinterested, dispassionate spokesman for the enlightened conscience, or "general will," of mankind rather than as a legislator, he set rigid standards for himself: he had to be correct, he had to be dignified, and he had to be courageous.

Thus Grégoire deliberately created a legend which had only limited foundation in reality. Striving to be magisterial, he was actually dogmatic. Unable to see any mid-point between good and evil and increasingly certain that he alone possessed the truth, he never analyzed his fundamental assumptions. Consequently, he could not permit others to challenge his faith and attributed all dissent to discreditable motives—a trait that had dangerous implications in the emotion-packed atmosphere of the Revolution.

Although Grégoire believed that his status as bishop should have made him immune to criticism, his unecclesiastical behavior left him open to attack. Under stress he spoke uncharitably and made immoderate, occasionally rude, and at best ill-considered statements which he later had to explain away. He finally learned to control his temper but at the cost of hiding a warm, impulsive soul behind a stilted, pompous mask.

Grégoire also failed to live up to his standard for courage, successfully clouding the record by exaggerating either the seriousness of the threats against him or the firmness with which he resisted danger. When an issue became not only unpopular but also dangerous, like Christianity during the Terror, he declined to defend his faith. Even though he sought amnesty for Roman Catholic clerics late in 1794, he had abandoned his Girondin friends eighteen months earlier, with only an ambivalent statement concerning the pressures which had been exerted upon the National Convention. On the crucial question of judging the king, he penned a deliberately misleading letter condemning Louis to an unspecified punishment. Since the other deputies had to decide between execution, imprisonment, or an appeal to the nation, Grégoire's vagueness merely begged the question.[5]

Still, Grégoire never apostatized or abandoned his Christian faith, and he never supported policies of which he disapproved. He espoused such unpopular causes as civil rights for Jews and mulattoes, republicanism under the Restoration, and toleration for Constitutional priests after the church had lost its official status. In addition, he voted against Bonaparte's major policies —the Concordat, the reinstatement of an aristocracy, and the creation of an hereditary empire.

Blessed with an acute sensitivity toward subtle shifts in his colleagues' opinions, Grégoire knew when he could safely plead for nonjurors or Jews. But he used this sensitivity either for his own survival or for propagandistic purposes. He could not use it to gather an effective following because he so underestimated the value of cooperation that he declined to tailor his statements to his audience's prejudices. In order to remain alive, he might avoid certain topics and gloss over others, but he would not try to gain popularity by catering to man's baser nature.[6]

Sensitivity and sheer accident rather than courage enabled Grégoire to reach the age of eighty-one with only emotional discomfort. He was not interested in and never commented on such divisive questions as diplomacy, fiscal policies, and maximum prices. His absence from the legislature during the debates on foreign policy, the vote on Louis XVI, the months of bitter controversy between Gironde and Mountain, and the Bonaparte coup of November 1799 enabled him to escape commitment at dangerous and decisive moments.

Although not the martyr he claimed to be, Grégoire's steadfast refusal to court either popular favor or political support made him an admirable hero and champion of long-term impossible causes. Because he did not use his short-lived prominence to further his own career, and because he gained so little from his leadership in the Constitutional church, his enemies could not plausibly accuse him of petty personal ambition. His pride and dogmatism were impersonal, in the service of greater causes, and if he created a superhuman image, he did so because his goals transcended individual considerations. By the end of his life in 1831 he represented the best in the Christian and the liberal enlightenment tradition. Like most potential martyrs, he exercised the greatest influence either in direct personal relations or in disembodied form—as an author, a correspondent, or even as a statue.

The man behind this myth has probably been destroyed by his own will; most of Grégoire's personal correspondence was burned either by himself or by his executrix, and he drew a veil of silence over all but the most formal aspects of his childhood.[7] The few remaining letters written simply for friendship's sake are tantalizing hints at a warm, generous, and whimsical man, who loved nature, pastoral life, and the companionship of old and trusted friends.

In fact, Grégoire's friendships remain the best indication of his personality. Their breadth and diversity say more for his generosity and tolerance than all his speeches. He could hate groups abstractly, but he frequently admired and sometimes was genuinely fond of their members. He exercised great tact among his friends by avoiding controversial subjects. Thus the agnostic Lafayette, the Jansenist Degola, and the evangelical Macaulay were numbered among his close friends.

Even when he quarreled bitterly with associates or disillusioned them by his failure to live up to his public image, Grégoire later was able to renew his friendships.[8] In most cases he was the offender and his friends forgave him. Unfortunately this personal charisma, which he could not translate either into prose or into his dealings with larger groups of men, is seldom illuminated in his well-censored record.

The voluminous, but chaotic, revolutionary archives also fail to reveal much about Grégoire's personality. Indeed, they make it exceedingly difficult even to determine what he said during such crucial debates as the 31 May through 2 June 1793 crisis when the Girondins were expelled, or on 7 November 1793 when he was asked to resign his bishopric. The archives are even more obscure on questions relating to post-Terror religious history. In view of these obstacles and the diffuseness of Grégoire's interests, this study has been limited to his egalitarian career and deals with his religious activities only in so far as they shed light upon his crusades for Jews and blacks.

The only complete narrative of Grégoire's career is the one-hundred-and-thirty-year-old introduction to his *Mémoires*. Subsequent historians have ignored Grégoire, and the few who have seriously studied him have been motivated by sectarian or political interests. Orthodox Catholics have concentrated on condemning his schism, neo-Jansenists have glorified it, while socialists have disregarded the theological foundation of his egalitarian career and hence have missed its significance.[9] All of these studies fail to penetrate the legend which Grégoire deliberately created, for only a balanced study which recognizes his complex personality can indicate the magnitude of his intentions and the tragedy of his failure.

NOTES

1. For Grégoire's early life, see chapter 1 of this volume; Dugast, ed., *Histoire patriotique*, pp. 7–8; Arthur Benoît, *L'Evêque Grégoire, vicaire à Marimont*, 1776 (n.p., 1831).
2. Grégoire's religious ideas are described in chap. 1.

3. For example, see Brethé, ed., *Journal inédit de Jallet*, p. 129.

4. For similarities with nineteenth-century radical views of nationalism, see Krieger, "Nationalism and the Nation-State System," pp. 104, 124.

5. Criticism of Grégoire's failure to defend the church: "Réflexions rapides sur la lettre encyclique des évêques," undated, BPR, carton Concile National 1797 I; Necheles, "The Abbé Grégoire and the Constitutional Church," p. 22; summary of evidence on 7 Nov. 1793: James Guillaume, ed., *Procès-verbaux du Comité d'instruction publique de la Convention nationale* (Paris: Imprimerie Nationale, 1891), 3:779–82; vote on Louis XVI: Aulard, ed., *Recueil des Actes*, 1:463; *Annales de la religion*, 1801, pp. 35–41; manuscript draft of Grégoire's memoires, Arsenal 5290, p. 143; *Journal des amis*, 2 Feb. 1793, p. 198.

6. His address to the National Institute in 1796 is a notable exception; see chapter 8.

7. The only exception is Maggiolo's "L'abbé Grégoire, Discours de réception," pp. xxx–cii, which used contemporary and now destroyed documents.

8. Numerous examples can be cited. Grégoire bitterly denounced Lafayette in 1792, fought with LeCoz over Jansenist influence in the Constitutional church in 1797, and alienated his old friends in Lorraine, yet by 1802 he was close friends again with all of them.

9. Carnot's introduction to Grégoire's *Mémoires*; Paul Pisani, *Répertoire biographique de l'Episcopat Constitutionnel, 1791–1802* (Paris: Alphonse Picard et Fils, 1907); Gazier, *Etudes sur l'histoire religieuse de la Révolution*; Grunebaum-Ballin, *Henri Grégoire, l'ami des hommes de toutes les couleurs.*

PRELUDE

The Jews

1

The Making
of an Egalitarian

"Liberty, equality, and fraternity" was the rallying cry of the French Revolution. Yet this slogan was never realized because neither the National Assembly nor subsequent legislatures ever translated it into concrete legislation covering Jews, mulattoes, and Negroes. However there was one deputy, Henri-Baptiste Grégoire, who served as spokesman for the national conscience and who castigated his colleagues when they hesitated to fulfill their revolutionary promises to minority groups.

Grégoire displayed an unusual concern for the welfare of minority groups, but he was not a typical revolutionary legislator. Lorraine, the province in which he spent the first forty years of his life, between 1750 and 1789, was very different from the rest of France. Annexed only in 1766, the duchy had closer ties with rural Rhineland Germany than it had with France. Its intellectual, religious, and social institutions had been shaped by German and Belgian influences. In addition, the region had a backward, impoverished economy. Lorraine had never recovered from the devastation caused by the wars of the seventeenth century, and French tariff regulations isolated the territory from its natural markets in Central Europe. It was particularly plagued by absentee landlordism and a lack of fluid capital.[1]

Different as this intellectual and economic environment was, Grégoire's social background was shared by most French priests. His father was an artisan in Vého, a small village that had close ties with the peasants in the surrounding countryside. Both parents were very devout, and they desired to give their child a clerical education. Still Grégoire received the necessary training only because his precocious intelligence impressed the local curé and a nearby seigneur. He graduated from the seminary when he was twenty-two, too young to be ordained, and taught in a *collège* for three years before assuming his duties as a secular priest. His childhood patrons secured positions for him. For several years he served as vicar and tutor in the seigneur's parish and then succeeded his old teacher as curé in Emberménil.[2]

The years before the Revolution were restless and discontented ones for Grégoire, but he was not the only priest to be unhappy with his lot. Even before he entered the seminary, the Lorraine clergy had revolted against what they called episcopal tyranny. In one respect they were more fortunate than their French counterparts because they had a guaranteed minimum salary, however inadequate. Yet formal regulations prevented them from anticipating promotion within church ranks. The hierarchy made a few concessions in the 1770s, but when Grégoire graduated he could expect to remain the curé of a small village for the rest of his life.[3]

While still a teacher, Grégoire searched for more useful ways of employing his abundant energy. He traveled throughout the Northeast and Germany and devoted his free time to literary activities, submitting poetry and prose compositions to various contests. In 1773 he received an award for his *Eloge de la poésie*. At the same time he joined a philanthropic society. After he was ordained in 1775 he abandoned frivolous occupations for philanthropic, educational, and humanitarian pursuits more compatible with his ecclesiastical dignity.[4]

The question that absorbed most of Grégoire's leisure time before the Revolution concerned the status of Jewish communities in the Northeast. It was a complex problem, but it was largely ignored and received little publicity because the Jews were concentrated in only two regions of France. As late as 1789 they numbered only 34 thousand out of a total French population of 26 million.[5] Even the church took little interest in the Jews. From time to time individual priests recommended more vigorous missionary programs, but most clergymen preferred a policy of isolation, and a few joined northeastern lawyers and government officials in advocating expulsion.[6]

The only area where pro- or anti-Semitism evoked widespread public response was in Grégoire's native Northeast. Yet the problem could not be solved by local officials because Jews elsewhere in France had to be considered. In addition, because northeastern anti-Semitism was rooted in the depressed agriculture of that region and because northeastern agrarian problems were related to national economic difficulties, only the king and his ministers could ameliorate the conditions which aggravated northeastern hostility toward Jews.

The small number of French Jews and their peculiar geographic distribution can be explained by historical circumstances. They had been expelled from the entire country during the last years of the fourteenth century, and various monarchs renewed this prohibition until 1615. A few Jews unofficially entered the country well before the seventeenth century. Their number increased after Henry II issued letters patent granting broad rights equivalent to naturalization to Portuguese "new Christians" in 1550. These Jews, later known as Sephardim, were scattered throughout several southern communities, and their total population remained small.

The southern Jewish settlements avoided serious anti-Semitism or friction. When necessary, crypto-Jews attended Catholic services and had their births, marriages, and deaths recorded by the church. They followed a very modified Jewish tradition in the privacy of their homes but were forced to abandon most of their dietary laws, ritual practices, and marriage and divorce customs. Everyone—neighbors, clergy, bureaucrats, and king— deliberately ignored the Sephardim's failure to become sincere Catholics. The monarchy, taking advantage of the situation, demanded from the "new Christians" the same special taxes that other sovereigns levied on the Jews. The king justified these extractions on the grounds that the Sephardim were foreigners, ignoring their letters patent of naturalization.

In order to assess and collect the special dues imposed on them, the Sephardim formed community organizations or corporations. These bodies also governed their common institutions. They supervised special schools, selected rabbis, allotted charity, and settled internal disputes. Because the southern Jews learned French rapidly, mingled with their Christian neighbors, and participated in community affairs, the corporations played a comparatively minor role in their lives.

A few Sephardim prospered in colonial trade, and one was even known as "one of the kings of Bordeaux."[7] Gradually the Sephardim gave up the pretense of Catholicism and ceased baptising their children. During and after the reign of Louis XIV they held public Jewish services to commemorate victories and the king's recovery from serious ailments. Yet their religious status remained unclear until 1776 when Louis XVI permitted them to live according to their customs anywhere in France. The same decree declared Sephardim to be equal to other French subjects. On the basis of this law, in 1789 some Bordeaux Jews participated in elections to the Estates General.[8]

Before 1789 few Sephardim took advantage of Louis XVI's permission to disperse throughout France. A small number of Jews from both the South and the Northeast lived in Paris, but, contrary to the 1776 decree, even the Sephardim had no legal rights there. Classified as transients and divided by ritual and language, the Paris Jews did not form a community and did not exercise the leadership which their geographic location might have given to them.[9]

The second sizeable Jewish community, and a far larger one, was located in the Northeast. These Jews, who followed the Ashkenazim or German rite, lived under far less favorable conditions than the southern Jews enjoyed. The northeastern provinces—with the exception of the three bishoprics of Metz, Toul, and Verdun which already belonged to France—had been annexed in the late seventeenth and mid-eighteenth centuries. By that time the monarchy no longer cared to impose even superficial religious conformity upon the Jews. The Versailles government confirmed existing religious and economic legislation in the annexed territories, including regulations governing the Jews.

Details varied among the episcopal cities, Alsace, and Lorraine, but the general restrictions were similar. Throughout the Northeast, Ashkenazim were forbidden to own real estate or agricultural land, to follow most professions, and to move freely from one community to another. Although a few prospered despite these restrictions, most Ashkenazim did not. Reduced to abject poverty and subject to extraordinary and onerous taxes, the majority survived by becoming peddlers, rag dealers, money-lenders, and middlemen for livestock and grain. In the cities where they were permitted to reside, they were restricted to certain streets, forbidden to erect synagogues, and denied public welfare and charity. Isolated in ghettos, many could not speak French, the majority were illiterate, and the rest wrote only Hebrew or Yiddish.[10]

Anti-Semitic legislation in the Northeast retarded assimilation and encouraged Jewish conservatism. Rabbis and community leaders selected from the small oligarchy of wealthy merchants exercised a rigid control over members of the community. Aware of the Sephardim's past apostasy and present failure to follow traditional ritual, even the more cosmopolitan Ashkenazim hesitated to establish social contacts with Christians and fought to maintain the integrity of their faith. This conservatism was as much an obstacle to assimilation as was Christian anti-Semitism.[11]

Ashkenazim defensiveness, which amounted in some cases to xenophobia, was intensified by the unpopular but essential functions which they performed in the Northeast. The region lacked adequate banking facilities, and the peasants depended on Jewish middlemen to loan them money on their anticipated crops. Misunderstandings frequently arose because the barely literate peasants could not comprehend the Hebrew or Yiddish contracts which they signed. Such abuses as loans to minors, interest over and above that specified in notarized contracts, and failure to notarize certificates of indebtedness provoked widespread hostility toward the Jews among intellectuals as well as peasants. Yet the peasants' desperate need for funds which no one else would supply vitiated all decrees designed to regulate money-lending. When on rare occasions a peasant managed to bring his complaint before a court, local nobles and royal officials, anxious to preserve their special taxes, defended the Jews. But many well intentioned people, including lawyers and bureaucrats, were more interested in the peasants' welfare, and they urged the king to expel all Jews from the Northeast.[12]

The Ashkenazim possessed limited means of self-defense and did not rely entirely on aristocratic or royal favor. In 1603 the bishop of Metz permitted the Jews to form their own council and community organization. This corporation gradually extended its jurisdiction over Ashkenazim who resided in territories subsequently annexed to France. In 1657 royal letters patent placed Alsatian Jews under the protection of the French king, and this community also formed a corporation.

The Lorraine Jews were the last to organize. Early in the eighteenth century Duke Leopold made a few half-hearted attempts to expel Jews who had settled illegally. When this failed, he invited in some who, he thought, might build textile manufacturies. Leopold's successor authorized the Ashkenazim to form a corporation that would supervise tax collection, educational facilities, and Jewish tribunals. Thus by 1789 the Ashkenazim had three separate corporations of which the Alsatian was the most important.

Most northeastern bourgeois were as anti-Semitic as the peasants, but two decades before the Revolution a few literary figures and lawyers, such as Pierre-Louis Roederer and Pierre-Louis Lacretelle, became interested in the Ashkenazim's plight. While Grégoire lived in Metz, for example, Lacretelle represented some Jews who requested increased trading rights in the land belonging to that city. In 1785 Roederer, as secretary of the Metz Société Royale des Sciences et des Arts, proposed a contest on the topic: "How can Jews be made happier and more valuable members of French society?"[13]

Concern over the Ashkenazim affected even the king. In 1784 Louis XVI abolished the most humiliating tax imposed on the Jews, the *péage corporal*, which was also levied on livestock. A year later he made Ashkenazim eligible for letters patent of naturalization and awarded such documents to a few prominent members of the northeastern community. Yet these two decisions did not help many Jews, and as soon as Guillaume-Chrétien Lamoignon de Malesherbes completed the legislation which granted limited civil rights to Protestants, Louis asked him to revise northeastern regulations concerning Jews. Malesherbes issued a general appeal for information and consulted a number of northeasterners, including some Jews, but he resigned from the Council of State before proposing any legislation.[14]

Louis' interest in the Ashkenazim encouraged public debate on their status during the 1780s. This discussion was more localized than was the earlier controversy over Protestant rights, and not all participants favored the Jewish cause. A few influential eighteenth century writers expressed blatant anti-Semitism and refused to apply to non-Christians the principles of religious toleration by which they justified Protestant liberation.

Sympathetic writers directed their works to northeastern audiences and did not attempt to link philo-Semitism with the Protestant cause. Ignoring Jews elsewhere in France, they dealt with the northeastern situation exclusively. Yet most authors glossed over the economic foundations of anti-Semitism. Because they could not anticipate the economic and social revolution which might make Jewish money-lending unnecessary, most publicists focused on the humane and religious aspects of Ashkenazim liberation. Their suggestions, therefore, were oversimplified and impractical.

Grégoire was attracted to the ethical rather than to the economic side of the Jewish controversy. Coming from rural Lorraine, and probably having known peasants who had had unpleasant experiences with Jewish money-lenders, he regarded the problem as extremely important. While still a seminary student in Metz, he heard about Jewish requests for increased trading privileges. At the same time, he and one of his professors, the Abbé Antoine-Adrien Lamourette, discussed the possibility of converting the Jews. Not long after graduation, Grégoire joined a philanthropic society in Strasbourg which had several Jewish members.[15] Heretofore he had seen how usurers had abused peasants; now he learned that Christians had maltreated Jews.

Grégoire's interest in Jewish affairs was more than humanitarian; it was founded in the unorthodox and eclectic theology which he developed during his early years. Two suspect beliefs, predestinarianism and millenarianism, colored his ideas about Jews. His use of predestinarian terminology and his sympathy with millenarian attitudes led his enemies to call him a Jansenist. And indeed he did exhibit the two traits of piety and puritanism which characterized all those who at one time or another have been called Jansenists.[16] Grégoire's Jansenism went no further. Interested in practical action rather than theological disputes, he refused to avow or deny those doctrines which had led the church to condemn Jansenism in the seventeenth century. His reticence did not silence his conservative critics, but it enabled him to remain aloof from doctrinal quibbles.

In Grégoire's mind, predestinarianism had a peculiar connection with the Jewish question. Like other predestinarians, he believed that he could distinguish those who were saved, but he employed somewhat unusual standards. He thought that salvation was individual rather than racial or national, and he denied that God had automatically excluded any race or nation because it shared "Ham's curse" or responsibility for Christ's death.[17] For him, the only visible sign distinguishing the saved from the damned was adherence to Catholicism. This classification transcended all other earthly distinctions based on race, nationality, or economic status. Yet mere observance of Catholic ritual would not guarantee admission to heaven; it was only a precondition. The saved must also lead a pious life and be called by God. Since all non-Catholics were automatically excluded, Grégoire believed it was his duty both as priest and philo-Semite to help create the conditions under which Jews might become Catholics. Then, whether they achieved salvation was entirely up to God's will.[18]

God's final decision concerning the soul's ultimate destiny would be known only at the last judgment. Throughout the Middle Ages, some sects believed this judgment would take place on earth after Christ had returned and ruled for a thousand years. Condemned as a superstitious aberration in the fourth century, millenarian eschatology had few adherents by the eighteenth century.

Yet some chiliastic attitudes towards secular reform influenced Protestants and Catholics alike. The medieval sectarians, mostly displaced peasants who could not find a place in the growing towns of the high Middle Ages, used eschatological hopes as grounds for demanding immediate social and economic reform. Convinced they were a band of saints authorized by God to create the utopia foretold in the ancient Hebrew prophecies, millenarians attacked the inequities and injustices which personally affected them.[19] During the eighteenth century the heirs of the millenarian tradition in England, especially the Methodists, translated their predecessors' utopianism into such philanthropic programs as penal reform and abolition of slavery.[20]

Preoccupied with their own problems, medieval millenarians did not worry about other people. They either ignored the Jews or identified them with the forces of evil that must be destroyed by the forces of good before Christ would return to earth.[21] In eighteenth-century France a small band of neo-Jansenists adopted a modified millenarian belief that assigned an important role to Jews in the final days. Paying more attention to the Old Testament than Catholics commonly did, they tried to reconcile God's promises to the Jews with their belief in Christ as the Messiah, which led them to some startling conclusions.

According to the neo-Jansenists, because God had promised the Jews a messiah and a kingdom centered in Jerusalem, the true church could not be created by Catholics alone. Catholicism would never become the purified faith prophesied in the Old Testament as long as God's first chosen people, the Jews, remained outside the fold. The neo-Jansenists went even further and insisted that the real Christian church must not only include Jews but must also be organized by them. Thus it was unwise and wrong to persecute or massacre the Jews. Instead they must be persuaded to adopt Christianity through such peaceful means as preaching, prayer, and charity. Otherwise, unlike eighteenth-century English chiliasts, neo-Jansenists accepted the status quo and did not actively pursue the secular utopia.[22]

Grégoire learned of the neo-Jansenists' ideas concerning the Jews even though this sect's precarious position within Catholicism made the members reluctant to publicize their views. He readily accepted their conclusions concerning the importance of the Jews for the future of Catholicism, but he refrained from avowing millenarian beliefs openly and reserved judgment concerning their eschatology.[23] Realizing that he stood little chance of persuading his fellow ecclesiastics, he tried to translate this philo-Semitic attitude into terms that would be more convincing than apocalyptic visions.

Grégoire had another reason for deemphasizing theology in his philo-Semitic writings. Converting Jews might be an important long-range goal, but before this could be attained certain practical problems had to be solved. Raising obscure and questionable theological points would only detract from the real issues. Grégoire thought it more important to improve the conditions under which Jews lived and to reform the church in order to make it more attractive to outsiders.[24]

According to Grégoire, no organization as corrupt and intolerant as the contemporary church could attract nonbelievers. For many centuries Catholic priests had condoned discrimination. Grégoire absolved the church from direct responsibility for the ill treatment of the Jews. Yet he thought the failure of his fellow ecclesiastics to criticize unjust rulers had led to widespread anti-Catholicism among persecuted minority groups. Now the church would have to repair the damage by taking a vigorous stand against all intolerance and by becoming a leading force for social and economic change. Before the church could alter its policy so drastically, it would have to sever its ties with the secular interests of state governments and the Roman administration. Only then would the church respond to popular needs.

The first struggle would have to take place within the church itself where power would have to be wrested from the aristocratic hierarchy. In preparation for assuming broader responsibility, priests would have to receive a better education. Although Grégoire wanted to separate church and state interests, he thought secular officials would have to intervene in order to destroy the aristocrats' monopoly over high offices. Acting on these assumptions, Grégoire devised a new curriculum for seminaries and participated in the lower clergy's prerevolutionary struggle against the northeastern episcopacy.[25] Still, as long as the king supported the ecclesiastical aristocracy rather than the reformers, Grégoire's proposals for regenerating the French church had little chance of success.

With or without internal reform, the Catholic church could not hope to win Jewish converts until Jewish hostility towards Christians subsided. Jews would accept Christ's divinity only if practicing Catholics gave the Jews an opportunity to observe the glories of Christianity. This would require civil emancipation.

During the decade preceding the Revolution, Grégoire developed a program and a rationale for ameliorating the economic and social status of northeastern Jews. He presented his ideas to various scientific and philanthropic organizations of the Northeast which, unlike the church, proved willing to listen to a young ecclesiastic of nonaristocratic background.[26]

Grégoire carefully tailored his arguments to his audience. Addressing intellectuals, he justified philo-Semitism by pointing out the utilitarian value of easing restrictions on the Jews. Using the concepts concerning human nature and society popularized by such writers as John Locke, Claude-Adrien Helvétius, and Jean-Jacques Rousseau, he explained how alleviating the plight of the Jews would make them better subjects and would thereby contribute to the national interest. He optimistically postulated that, if given an opportunity, men would improve their intellect, character, and institutions. Attributing virtue, morals, and intelligence to environmental factors such as diet, health, and occupation, Grégoire discounted theories concerning original sin and innate differences among men. A strong society must be founded on physical liberty and prosperity because, without freedom and economic security, men would be unable to make intelligent decisions concerning any subject, be it religious, moral, or political. Grégoire did not think coercion would alter anyone's mind, but he argued that the government might have to force people to change their environment. Healthy surroundings might then permit people to form more rational beliefs.[27]

Grégoire held anachronistic views of what a healthy environment should be. Raised in a small village and only a casual visitor to the urban centers of the Northeast before the Revolution, he intensely disliked everything connected with urban society. Coming from an underdeveloped region of France, he never understood capitalism in its commercial or early industrial forms. He judged economic questions in ethical terms and tolerated commerce and industry as necessary evils. He condemned as immoral the luxury trade upon which French prosperity rested. Like Thomas Jefferson and Rousseau, he envisioned the good society as one composed of independent, self-sufficient farmers who would be nearly equal in wealth. He therefore regarded the Ashkenazim environment in the most unfavorable light, morally as well as physically.

Grégoire was one of the few prerevolutionary publicists who tried to explain the Ashkenazim's behavior in secular, pragmatic terms. He traced the Ashkenazim's misfortunes and antisocial activities to centuries of persecution and discrimination by Christians rather than to God's wrath or to the Jews' natural inferiority. Attributing the Jewish problem to secular and religious discrimination, he insisted that their way of life and morality could be improved only by concerted action of church and state.

The state would have to take the first steps by imposing new regulations designed to force the Jews out of the cities and into new professions. This would serve the dual purpose of providing them with wholesome surroundings and, at the same time, would break the rabbis' tyrannical hold over them. He compared the power of the rabbis to episcopal domination and thought both should be abolished. Only after individual Jews were free to mingle with their neighbors would they lose their understandable animosity toward Christians and become more honest in their business dealings.

After a period of paternalistic rule during which time Jews would be given an opportunity to earn an adequate living, they would cease relying upon money-lending. They would become stronger physically and more able to contribute to the French economy. In the meantime Jewish children should be sent to interdenominational schools where they would learn French and become assimilated to the dominant culture.[28] All of these changes would result from a carefully devised set of regulations drawn up by a reforming monarch and imposed, if necessary, by force upon the Jewish people.

But dispersing Jews throughout rural France would only partially solve the Jewish problem, according to Grégoire. As long as Jews remained isolated, anti-Semitism was not a serious matter outside the Northeast. Once they began to migrate elsewhere, ignorant Christians probably would refuse to accept them. Thus, even if the Ashkenazim abandoned usury and broke up their large settlements, hostility bred by centuries of anti-Semitic propaganda would not disappear. Grégoire thought that the clergy as the moral leaders of their communities would have to modify their teachings concerning deicide and urge their flocks to be tolerant. Following his own advice, he asked his parishioners in Emberménil to treat the Jews kindly. Eventually he hoped Jews would realize that the church professed "the true religion, that of justice and toleration."[29] On the whole he expected more cooperation from state officials than from his fellow ecclesiastics.

Convinced as he was that secular reform had to precede any missionary activity among the Jews, Grégoire tried to gain a wider audience for his ideas by submitting two or three papers to contests sponsored by various scientific and philanthropic societies. His early treatises, dating from 1779, have been lost. The only one that has survived is his *Essai sur la régénération physique, morale et politique des juifs,* which he entered in 1785 in a competition sponsored by the Metz Société Royale des Sciences et des Arts. In 1788, after some revisions supervised by Roederer, the Metz society's secretary, Grégoire and two other contestants shared the award. This success seemed to be the opening wedge in Grégoire's quest for Jewish rights and—perhaps—personal fame.[30]

The Metz society did not publish award-winning essays, and Grégoire had to find the necessary funds himself. He appealed to some of his friends. He also responded to Malesherbes' request for information concerning Jews and asked the minister for financial assistance or at least official patronage. Malesherbes gave him only moral support, but Grégoire managed to publish his *Essai* in March 1789.[31]

By the time Grégoire received the Metz award, controversy over Louis XVI's decision to convoke an Estates General in 1789 had spread throughout France. Grégoire's *Essai* came too late to influence electoral assemblies. Indeed, it was temporarily lost among the numerous pamphlets concerning such urgent problems as taxation and voting within the Estates which circulated at the same time.

Grégoire himself was distracted by an epidemic among his parishioners and by disputes over whether and by whom Lorraine should be represented in the Estates General. For the first time the Lorraine priests, supported by the bourgeoisie of Nancy, gained admission to the provincial Assembly of the Three Orders. Grégoire belonged both to the Lorraine clergy and the Metz clergy, and he played a leading role in the struggle for the rights of the lower clergy in both dioceses. As a reward for his efforts, the priests of the district of Nancy elected him as one of their two representatives to the First Estate.[32]

Absorbing as the electoral controversy was, Grégoire managed to pay some attention to the Jews. He succeeded in excluding anti-Semitic clauses from the two *cahiers*, or memoranda of grievances to be considered by the Estates General, which he helped to write. Still, he could not persuade his countrymen to include pro-Jewish demands. The proliferation of anti-Semitic articles in other northeastern *cahiers*[33] convinced him that the Estates would not help the Ashkenazim unless he could demonstrate active concern over the Jews' plight. He encouraged the Jews to publicize their own grievances, and he asked Malesherbes to sponsor a Jewish petition to the Estates. But Malesherbes had temporarily retired from public affairs and was unwilling to become involved in current political issues.[34]

In the meantime, independently of Grégoire's suggestion, Cerf Berr, the head of the Alsatian Jewish corporation, appealed to the Council of State. The Ashkenazim wanted permission to write a *cahier* which they would then give to a regularly elected deputy—presumably Grégoire. The ministry only granted part of Cerf Berr's petition. It authorized him to draw up a *cahier*. But rather than designate an official spokesman for the Ashkenazim, the ministry instructed Cerf Berr to present the Jews' grievances directly to the king rather than to the Estates. Evidently the Council preferred to keep the Jewish question out of the assembly.

The Sephardim, for their part, were alarmed by the Council's partial acceptance of Alsatian requests. The southern Jews preferred to leave well enough alone, for they felt little identification with the Ashkenazim whose poverty, ignorance, and xenophobia they feared. Any investigation of Jewish rights and disabilities might place them in the same legal category as the underprivileged northeasterners and might thereby jeopardize their comparatively favored status.[35]

Here matters rested before the Estates General opened. Opposition to modifying Ashkenazim regulations came from educated as well as illiterate northeasterners and even from the assimilated Sephardim in the South. The king and his council might in theory agree to improve the Ashkenazim's status, but more urgent problems demanded their attention, and they wished to avoid any discussion of Jewish affairs by the Estates. Grégoire was virtually alone in considering Ashkenazim grievances to be an important issue, and as a curé from a small village in a peripheral area of France he had very little prospect of attaining a hearing before the Estates.

NOTES

1. Taveneaux, *Le Jansénisme en Lorraine*, pp. 715–18; Parisot, *Histoire de Lorraine*, 2:136; Lionnois, *Histoire des villes vielle et neuve de Nancy*, 2:214–15.

2. Maggiolo, "L'Abbé Grégoire," pp. lv n., xxxiii, lxv, xxxvi-xxxix; Grégoire, *Mémoires*, 2:1–2; autograph note by Grégoire in BM Nancy; Pfister, "Les préliminaires de la Révolution à Nancy," p. 91.

3. For a general summary of the prerevolutionary clergy, see Soboul, *La France à la veille de la Révolution*, pp. 106–7.

4. Pfister, *Histoire de Nancy*, 3:330; Grégoire, *Eloge de la poésie. Discours qui a remporté le prix des belles-lettres, au jugement de MM. de la Société Royale des Sciences et Belles-Lettres de Nancy* (Nancy: Lesure, 1773); *L'Esprit des Journaux*, July–Aug. 1773, pp. 79–80 citing the *Mercure de France; Affiches des évêchés* (Nancy), 15 May 1773, p. 82; Parisot, *Histoire de Lorraine*, 2:316–17.

5. These 34,000 were distributed as follows: 27,500 Ashkenazim, 5,800 Sephardim, and 500 in Paris. See Anchel, *Napoléon et les juifs*, pp. 1–2 and Liber, "Les juifs et la convocation des Etats-Généraux, (1789)," 64:passim.

6. See, for example, one of the essays submitted in 1786 by a Benedictine which was a vicious attack on Jews: Cahen, "L'émancipation des juifs devant la Société royale des sciences et des arts de Metz en 1787 et M. Roederer," p. 93.

7. Elinor G. Barber, *The Bourgeoisie in 18th Century France* (Princeton, N.J.: Princeton University Press), pp. 28–29.

8. Hertzberg, *The French Enlightenment and the Jews*, p. 180; Liber, "Les juifs," 64:248–49 and 65:90–91; Malvezin, *Histoire des juifs à Bordeaux*, pp. 222–31; Sagnac, "Les juifs et la Révolution française," pp. 6–10.

9. Kahn, *Les juifs de Paris*, pp. 2, 12; Liber, "Les juifs," 66:175.

10. Parisot, *Histoire de Lorraine* 2:159, 228–29; Szajkowski, *Economic Status of the Jews in Alsace, Metz and Lorraine*, is the best general study of economic conditions in the Northeast. See also: Liber, "Les juifs," 63:185–92, 194–96, 200–201; Pfister, *Histoire de Nancy*, 3:314–21.

11. Anchel, *Napoléon*, p. 5.

12. Parisot, *Histoire de Lorraine*, 2:136, 199, 205–10; Szajkowski, *Economic Status*, pp. 14–15.

13. Cahen, "L'émancipation," pp. 83–96.

14. Grosclaude, *Malesherbes*, 1:631–44.

15. Antoine-Adrien Lamourette to Grégoire, 9 Sept. 1789, BPR, PQR; Berthe, "Grégoire, élève de l'abbé Lamourette," pp. 40–41; Grégoire to Ehrmann, 1 Sept. 1788 in Ginsburger, ed., "Zwei unveröffentliche Briefe von Abbé Grégoire," p. 205; Grégoire to Ferdinand Dubois de Fosseux, 8 Dec. 1788, and Lamourette, *Decret de l'Assemblée Nationale sur les biens du clergé*, (p. 33) cited in Berthe, "Grégoire, élève," pp. 40, 44.

16. The controversy over the existence of a Jansenist sect or movement is too complex to be summarized here. The term, however, distinguished a significant number of French, Netherlandish, and North Italian Catholics who, if nothing else, "did not like Jesuits." By the eighteenth century, whatever unity Jansen's followers in Belgium or the adherents of Port Royal in France might once have had disappeared, and sympathizers of the persecuted seventeenth-century divines went in several different directions, varying among puritanism, antipapalism, antimonarchism, convulsionarism, and millenarianism. See: Gazier, *Histoire générale du mouvement janséniste*, 1:vii; Taveneaux, *Jansénisme en Lorraine*; Préclin, *Les Jansénistes*.

17. Grégoire to Jean-Baptiste Mouton, 27 Feb. 1798, The Hague, Allgemeen Ryksarchief OBC 3458; for Grégorie on deicide see: *Essai sur la régénération physique, morale et politique des juifs*, p. 25. For his remarks on the "curse of Ham" see: *An Enquiry*

concerning the intellectual & moral faculties, & literature of Negroes, pp. 25–26.

18. In a letter to Scipione de' Ricci, 8 Aug. 1808 (Florence, Carteggi Ricci 101, c. 107), Grégoire said that conversion of the Jews would result from a combination of human efforts and divine providence. He was a member of a group of neo-Jansenists scattered across Europe which on certain hours on prearranged dates prayed together for the conversion of the Jews; "Règlement et supplement," 1802, appended to his *Bréviaire blésois* (1799):1, 5, in Arsenal, 2164.

19. Cohn, *Pursuit of the Millennium,* pp. 31–32.

20. Davis, *Problem of Slavery,* pp. 293–94.

21. Cohn, pp. 49–52, 61–63, 72, 92–94.

22. Max Weber attributed the French Jansenists' apathy towards secular problems to their mystical outlook which encouraged them to ignore problems of this world; see *The Protestant Ethic and the Spirit of Capitalism,* trans. Talcott Parsons (London: George Allen & Unwin, 1930), p. 226, n. 35.

23. Hertzberg, *French Enlightenment,* pp. 258–67. In Dec. 1788 Grégoire hoped to study millenarianism in greater detail; see his letter to Dubois in Berthe, "Grégoire, élève," p. 40. His mature judgment on millenarianism can be found in his *Histoire des sectes religieuses,* 1:207, where he refused to commit himself because the lack of evidence in the Scriptures indicated God's desire to keep men in ignorance concerning their ultimate fate.

24. Grégoire avoided discussing conversion. In his *Essai sur la régénération,* for example, he only once hinted that this might be his goal, but he was more open in his correspondence; see: *Essai sur la régénération,* p. 132; letter to Eustachio Degola, 17 Aug. 1806, AS Vatican, Carte Degola, and letter to Ricci, 8 Aug. 1808, Florence, Carteggi Ricci.

25. Flotte [?] to Malnori [?], 11 Oct. 1783, BPR, MNO; Grégoire to Dubois, 8 Dec. 1788, Berthe, "Grégoire, élève," p. 40; *Essai sur la régénération,* p. 223n; Taveneaux, *Jansénisme en Lorraine,* p. 719; Chassin, *Les cahiers des curés,* p. 268; Parisot, *Histoire de Lorraine,* 2:303–17.

26. Grégoire's membership in the national philanthropic society, the Strasbourg philanthropic society, and the Nancy philanthropic

society, see: Rigault to Grégoire, 22 Messidor Year 9 (11 July 1801), BPR, MNO; Grégoire to Dubois, 8 Dec. 1788, Berthe, "Grégoire, élève," p. 40; Jean Bossu's note in *Chercheurs et curieux* 5 (1955); 204–5; report in *Mémoires de l' Académie de Metz* 55 (1840–41): 164. There has been some debate as to whether any of these were Masonic lodges. Perusal of the Masonic papers in the Bibliothèque Nationale did not reveal Grégoire's name, but two lodges in Strasbourg included men whom Grégoire mentioned as fellow members of the Strasbourg society; see list for Saint-Jean, Parfait Silence, 25 April 1782 and St. Jean d'Hérédon de Ste. Geneviève, 24 June 1789, printed lists naming Fréderic-Jacques Saltzmann and Jean-Jacques Ehrmann as officers: BN, Masonic Collection.

27. Earlier in his career he believed more completely in the influence of environment on character, but by 1808 he admitted that innate talents existed. Compare his *Essai sur la régénération*, pp. 43, 108–9, with *An Enquiry*, pp. 248–9, and his *Mémoires*, 1:445. Environmentalism, according to Winthrop Jordan, characterized much of eighteenth-century revolutionary ideology; see *White Over Black*, pp. 287–94.

28. Recommendations for Jewish legislation were scattered throughout his *Essai sur la régénération*. Twenty years later he placed greater emphasis on integration, especially in education; see his *Observations nouvelles sur les juifs* (1806) and his *Observations nouvelles sur les juifs*, (1807).

29. Cited by Edmond Morse-Levy, *Droit et liberté*, 7 Dec. 1950, p. 1.

30. *Histoire des sectes*, 2:392; "Prix proposés en 1787 par la Société Royale des Sciences et des Arts de Metz," and Cahen, "L'émancipation des juifs," pp. 83–102. Roederer's papers concerning this contest are in AN, 29 AP 101. For Grégoire's earlier efforts, see: *Programmes de la Société des philanthropes* (n.p., n.d.) and his *Motion en faveur des Juifs*, p. iii.

31. Grégoire to Simon von Geldern and to Ehrmann, 1 Sept. 1788 in Ginsburger, pp. 204–5; Grégoire to Malesherbes, 6 Sept. 1788, AN 154 II 136, de Tocqueville Papers, used with the kind permission of M. de Tocqueville. This letter, but neither the subsequent ones nor the minutes of Malesherbes' replies, is reprinted in Grosclaude, *Malesherbes*, 1:647.

32. Grégoire to Dubois, 8 Dec. 1788, Berthe, "Grégoire, élève," p. 40; Pfister, "Les préliminaires," pp. 18–23; records of the various meetings of the Lorraine clergy in GS Nancy, MB 123; [Chatrian], "Calendrier historique de Nancy pour 1789," p. 101, GS Nancy, MC 121.

33. Liber, "Les juifs," 64:92–93, 101. Only three *cahiers* recommended improving the condition of Jews, one urged the Estates to study the problem and forty-five (all from the Northeast) demanded increased restrictions; see Hyslop, *French Nationalism in 1789*, pp. 35–36 and notes.

34. Liber, 64:269–72; 65:96–97. For the *cahiers* see Jérome, *Les élections et les cahiers*, and GS Nancy, MB 123. Grégoire's three letters to Malesherbes and the former minister's notes for replies in AN, 154 AP II 136; Grégoire to Isaiah-Berr Bing, 23 February 1789, "Lettres inédites," *Archives israélites de France*, p. 416.

35. Cerf Berr to Necker, 9 April 1789, in Liber, "Les juifs," 64:269; Hertzberg, *French Enlightenment*, pp. 179, 314, 326. Grégoire evidently knew that the Ashkenazim planned to present a petition to the Estates General; see his letter to Malesherbes, 28 Feb. 1789, AN 154 AP II 136.

2

The Secular Utopia
and the Jews

Grégoire arrived in Versailles in May 1789 determined to fight for the rights of the lower clergy, the Third Estate, and the Jews. Yet he was only a provincial clergyman, and although broadminded and tolerant, he was limited in experience to the boundaries of northeastern France and western Germany. His comparative insignificance, his preconceived ideas, and his ignorance about France seemed to preclude his taking an active role in the Estates.

But the sharp division within the First Estate between priests and members of the hierarchy provided articulate and determined men with an opportunity to attain prominence. As just such a man, Grégoire helped organize the clerics who denounced episcopal domination and wished to form a national assembly. Allying with the most radical deputies, the so-called Breton Club, he published a *Nouvelle lettre d'un curé* a few days before 19 June when the clergy voted to join the Third Estate. Although his name did not appear on the pamphlet, his authorship was an open secret, and the newly formed National Assembly elected him one of its secretaries. In addition, several journals now printed favorable reviews of his *Essai sur la régénération.* Now, he optimistically assumed, the deputies would listen to his pro-Jewish arguments.[1]

Grégoire's experiences in the opening weeks of the Revolution influenced his ideas about Jews. As he learned more about the French nation in general and Jews in particular, he decided to propose the enfranchisement of all Jews regardless of rite, origin, or prerevolutionary status. A public letter addressed to him by several Bordeaux Jews helped him to reach this conclusion. It showed him that southern Jews already lived freely and without friction, and he now hesitated to call the Sephardim's rights into question by proposing new restrictive legislation which would be appropriate for only the Ashkenazim.[2]

By June Grégoire became disillusioned with Louis XVI's failure to devise a reform program for France.[3] Convinced the king would not or could not take the initiative, Grégoire placed his hopes on legislative action. In view of his active role in forming the National Assembly, he assumed that he could transfer his personal popularity within the Assembly to the Jewish cause, but he seriously underestimated anti-Semitic influence in that body. In particular, he did not foresee the formation of an anti-Jewish coalition composed of northeastern radicals and conservative Catholics. Contrary to his expectations, anticlericals and traditional Catholics joined forces to defeat any measure which would improve the Ashkenazim's status.

Paradoxically, anti-Semites were strong because the Jewish problem was a local one. Besides northeastern and conservative Catholic deputies, few representatives had strong feelings about the Jews one way or another.[4] Most deputies regarded Jewish status as a matter that should be left to local officials who understood the issues involved. The anti-Semitic coalition was small in number, but it threatened to filibuster if the Assembly discussed the Jews. In order to justify its intransigent stand, the coalition predicted that northeastern peasants would revolt if the Assembly showed any favor towards Ashkenazim money-lenders. Since rural disorders plagued all regions of France during the summer of 1789, the deputies hesitated to provide rioters with an additional pretext.

Only a small group of deputies saw the broader principle involved in Jewish liberation. Even these men—a combination of moderate aristocrats and secular-minded bishops—cared more about religious tolerance than philo-Semitism, and they regarded the Jewish question as relatively unimportant. Although they recognized Grégoire's unique qualification as a priest to speak for the Jews, they distrusted him because of his radical opinions on unrelated political and social questions.[5] In addition, they did not care whether the Jews converted to Catholicism.

Thus, Grégoire's general political philosophy and his ideas on religious reform were closer to those held by the radicals of 1789. But few of them cared about the Jews, and most did not play a significant role during the first year of the Revolution.

Faced with determined opposition and half-hearted support, Grégoire could appeal only to the deputies' humanitarian instincts. On several occasions he had an opportunity to mention Jews in passing, even though the Assembly did not permit him to present a prepared speech. Briefly, he described recent anti-Semitic outbursts in the Northeast and requested special protection for the Ashkenazim there.[6] His appeals struck the proper cord among influential moderate philo-Semites. Following their advice, rather than Grégoire's, on 28 September 1789 the Assembly removed Jews from local jurisdiction and made royal officials completely responsible for their security.

The 28 September decision did not affect the Ashkenazim's legal status because it did not modify any of the existing restrictions. The representatives refused to listen to Grégoire's requests for further action since they regarded the problem as too insignificant to merit much more time. Moreover, it would be senseless to discuss Jews before the Assembly defined the nature of citizenship. Once it decided who were French, then the status of Jews could easily be clarified.

In the fall of 1789 the Assembly held a series of debates which affected the status of the Jews. While laying the groundwork for the constitution, the deputies tried to transform France's stratified society into a homogeneous body of citizens. In order to merge the innumerable categories of subjects into a unified whole, the Assembly had to remove all special privileges and discriminatory restrictions so that, eventually, all Frenchmen would be subject to one law and would exercise the same rights and privileges.

The first step in transforming the French body politic occurred on 4 August when the deputies abolished the peasants' personal dues as well as an assorted collection of special class privileges. The concept of citizenship was further broadened by the Declaration of the Rights of Man, proclaimed on 27 August 1789, which condemned all distinctions among Frenchmen not based on "general utility."[7] Now, theoretically, the Jewish question focused on whether they, as individuals, were citizens rather than on the revisions that should be made in their status as a group. If the Jews were classified as resident aliens, then their special, unequal status could be maintained because it was useful; but if they were to become citizens, then all discriminatory regulations would have to be rescinded.

The concepts of nationality and citizenship received concrete meaning only during the course of the Revolution. Between 1789 and 1799 Frenchmen gradually transferred their loyalty from the dynasty and their particular geographic regions to a nation identified by territorial, cultural, linguistic, and religious characteristics.[8] In this context, Ashkenazim could be considered French only on the basis of residence. Their culture stemmed from the far side of the Mediterranean, their language was German or Hebrew, and their religion was not even Christian. As Frenchmen increasingly tended to identify citizenship with a specific language and culture, nationalism replaced religious ideology as a basis for anti-Semitism. This new nationalism helps explain the bitter and emotional opposition to Jewish emancipation demonstrated by Protestant and anti-Christian northeastern radical deputies.[9]

Grégoire did not accept the common definition of nationality. He had grown to manhood in a region which became French when he was sixteen. For many years thereafter numerous people in Lorraine still spoke German; yet they regarded themselves as French.[10] To Grégoire cultural unity was a potential rather than an actual bond, and he was less willing to equate citizenship with language and heritage than were deputies who came from the heartland of France. Regarding the nation as an instrument for educating citizens and for introducing reforms, he thought that it must first integrate aliens into its society before expecting them to adopt the customs of the majority. The only other alternative to gradual assimilation was to expel all foreigners, and this he believed would be a mistake. He hoped that French nationality eventually would embrace all people who shared a desire for freedom, regardless of their ancestry, religion, or language. Therefore he defined citizenship on a territorial and ideological basis which transcended prejudices grounded in religious, cultural, and economic differences.

Grégoire was unable to voice his opinions concerning citizenship before the Assembly. Frustrated with his enforced silence, in October he published his *Motion en faveur des juifs*, which discussed both the Jewish question and the broader subject of citizenship. He triumphantly proclaimed the brotherhood of all men. Revolutionary France, he insisted, had a universal constituency. Admitting that Jews were not legally French, he recommended enfranchising them simply because they were human beings. As creatures of God, he said, their rights were determined by a higher, eternal law which distinguished right from wrong in political as well as personal affairs.[11]

The deputies in the National Assembly were not yet ready for Grégoire's cosmopolitan ideas concerning citizenship. Wedded to their parochial prejudices, they ignored his *Motion en faveur des juifs* and failed to enact into law all the implications of the Declaration of Rights. Still, they tried to demolish some of the barriers which separated Frenchmen. Having on 4 August terminated several of the special obligations imposed on peasants, the Assembly subsequently decided to remove some of the distinctions which were based on religious differences.

On 24 December the deputies permitted Protestants to fill municipal offices, but they deliberately excluded Jews from eligibility. This law was ominous for Sephardim and Ashkenazim alike, and its implications were catastrophic for Sephardim because at least those in Bordeaux had voted in the 1789 elections and had regarded themselves as full citizens.[12] The Ashkenazim had not previously participated in French public affairs, and they lost nothing. Yet the new law left them worse off than before because they could not anticipate eventual citizenship.[13]

Moderate pro-Jewish deputies regarded Protestant rights as more important than Jewish emancipation. Thus, when Grégoire tried to speak in favor of the Jews, both anti- and philo-Semites agreed to keep him silent. The moderates calculated that if Grégoire were to speak, he would convince the northeastern radicals to vote against the municipal offices bill; if he remained still, then only conservative Catholics would oppose Protestant enfranchisement and the principle of nonsectarian citizenship would be achieved.

The moderates won full civil rights for Protestants in December 1789, but their strategy provoked criticism from several newspaper editors who thought that Grégoire should have participated in the debates.[14] The moderates hesitated to alienate outside opinion, and when the Jewish question arose a month later, they permitted Grégoire to utter a few words. Yet even then they denied him sufficient time to elaborate his views.

Grégoire's final opportunity to speak about the Jews came

on 28 January 1790 when Bishop Talleyrand, a prominent spokesman for religious and racial toleration, advised the Assembly to enfranchise the Bordeaux Jews who had exercised political rights before 1789. Grégoire objected to Talleyrand's motion because it perpetuated the division of the Jews into numerous isolated communities. He persuaded the Assembly to transcend some of these distinctions by enfranchising *all* Sephardim regardless of where they lived. In addition, he asked the deputies to enfranchise those Ashkenazim who had letters patent of naturalization.

Grégoire's insistence upon discussing the northeastern Jews threw the Assembly into disorder. Unwilling to equate prerevolutionary naturalization with citizenship, the anti-Semitic coalition prevented a vote for over an hour. Finally the deputies, anxious to end the session, approved Sephardic rights and referred the Ashkenazim question to the Constitutional Committee.[15] Thereafter Grégoire found it very difficult to revive the issue because, under the Assembly's standard procedures, once a topic was consigned to a committee, individual members were discouraged from making unauthorized speeches on the subject. In the case of the Ashkenazim, the Constitutional Committee (which included Talleyrand) showed no interest in clarifying their status.

The Assembly enacted other legislation which incidentally affected the Ashkenazim. In February 1790 the deputies dissolved all religious corporations. Even though the law was directed against monastic orders, it could be applied to the Ashkenazim organizations as well. It raised questions about the judicial and taxing powers of the northeastern communities, thereby striking at the roots of the corporations' strength. The syndics, or heads, no longer had the authority to speak for Ashkenazim interests. Because the northeastern Jews had no voice in the selection of local officials, the February law placed them completely at the mercy of locally elected officials who were probably anti-Semitic.[16]

Throughout the remainder of the National Assembly,

Grégoire did not address the members on the subject of Jews. There were several reasons for his silence. His committee assignments left him little time for Jews. None of the committees to which he belonged had jurisdiction over the Jewish question, and the various presidents of the Assembly refused to place his name on the agenda when a relevant topic arose. In addition, since he had very little money, he could not afford to publish pamphlets advocating Jewish rights.[17]

Despite his inability to express his philo-Semitic sentiments, Grégoire advised his Jewish friends in the Northeast as to strategy[18] and made one final attempt to provoke a legislative debate on their status. On 18 January 1791, the first day of his term as president of the Assembly, he permitted a member of the Ecclesiastical Committee to speak about Jewish rights even though the committee had no jurisdiction over citizenship. The speaker proposed enfranchising all Jews regardless of origin and residence who had received letters patent of naturalization before May 1789. This motion would have made citizenship dependent upon a legal rather than an hereditary distinction, but it would have included only a few Ashkenazim.

Grégoire, having permitted a colleague to raise the issue, took no further action. He remained silent when the current president of the radical Jacobin Club, the Prince de Broglie of Alsace, criticized him for admitting such a motion,[19] and he raised no objection when the Assembly referred the motion to the apathetic Constitutional Committee. Grégoire abstained from all debates on the Jewish question during the remainder of the Assembly, even when that body finally enfranchised a limited number of Ashkenazim in September 1791.

Grégoire's failure on 18 January 1791 to defend a motion which he obviously supported seems at first to be an astonishing reversal of his once enthusiastic philo-Semitism, but the reason becomes clear if his religious interests are kept in mind. He probably remained silent because, during the last months of 1790, conservative Catholics began using his philo-Semitism as a way to combat the ecclesiastical reforms upon which his entire religious program rested.

Conservative opposition to church reform was a serious threat to Grégoire's plans. He was certain that unless the church was purified, it would continue to lose its members and would fail to attract converts. Much as he wanted to assist the Jews, therefore, he could not risk identification with their cause as long as conservative Catholics employed northeastern anti-Semitic prejudices to provoke opposition to the entire Revolution, including its program of church reform.

During the period when the ecclesiastical reforms embodied in the Civil Constitution of the Clergy were in the process of development and then while they were being inaugurated, northeastern clerics tried to discredit the changes by identifying them with philo-Semitism. Taking Grégoire as their symbol, they accused him of leading a Free Masonic plot against the church, the monarchy, and the nation. They asserted that a man who favored republicanism, toleration for deicides, and church reform could not be a loyal Frenchman.[20] Appalled by the idea of popularly elected priests and bishops, the conservatives erroneously insisted that Jews had voted for bishops in Grégoire's Constitutional church, and they nicknamed the diocese to which he had been elected in February 1791 a "little synagogue."[21] Grégoire could not combat such deep-seated prejudices singlehandedly, and, preferring to save the new church, he temporarily cut his public ties with the Jews.

The conservative Catholics who organized an anti-Semitic counterrevolutionary coalition against the constitution of 1791 were discredited by the end of the National Assembly. Still, northeastern radicals remained in the legislature. Perhaps Grégoire remained silent during the two days of debate preceding the passage of the 28 September law which enfranchised some northeastern Jews because he feared arousing renewed anti-Semitic opposition. Perhaps the backers of the bill, prominent Feuillants whose desertion from the Jacobin

Club Grégoire recently had denounced, refused to grant him the floor. The exact reason for his silence cannot be determined, but shortly after the Assembly closed he expressed his satisfaction with the law and considered himself at least partially responsible for its enactment.[22]

Grégoire correctly assumed credit for partial Ashkenazim enfranchisement. Certainly if he, as a cleric, dared advocate toleration for deicides, then Catholic laymen could hardly refuse to grant them civil rights. His early philo-Semitic stand contrasted favorably with the bigotry and conservatism of other ecclesiastical deputies who insisted on excluding Jews and who refused to consider much needed church reforms.

Grégoire's identification with philo-Semitism and church renovation temporarily helped achieve revolutionary change. Because he symbolized the revolutionary clergy, his radicalism contributed to the polarization of French politics. In order to fight his religious program, orthodox clerics joined other conservatives on all issues, not only those involving the church, and thereby lost whatever influence they had exerted in the Assembly. As moderates became counterrevolutionaries, more and more drastic changes became possible. Yet the alienation of many Catholics eventually provided counterrevolutionaries with the emotional issue they needed to destroy the reforms for which Grégoire and other innovators had fought.

The philo-Semites' victory of 28 September 1791 proved illusory well before counterrevolution set in. The enfranchisement law covered only those Jews who explicitly renounced membership in their corporations. Because many Ashkenazim could not meet the property qualifications for active citizenship established by the 1791 constitution, they saw little reason to exchange their traditional affiliations for a status which offered them limited benefits and no protection. Only the few who had significant property or who wished to participate in the division of communal lands went through the requisite formalities. Even they encountered numerous obstacles imposed by

"Mr. Jew, will you purchase this Capuchin habit?"—"Keep it, reverend, to make a patch for the seat of your pants, since it is not worth a farthing."

local officials. The overwhelming number of Ashkenazim continued to live much as they had before the Revolution, although the power of their corporations had been seriously reduced. By 1792, for example, their schools and tribunals no longer had legal status, and their taxation power had been removed.

Developments after 1791 temporarily forced the Ashkenazim to emerge from their ghettos. Both the war in the Northeast and the antireligious policies of local republican officials placed increased pressure on the Jews to leave Alsace-Lorraine and to abandon their traditional practices. In 1793 the National Convention enacted a new law specifically abolishing their corporations, and under its provisions many Ashkenazim were expelled from the Northeast. Local officials also used anticlerical laws and fiscal regulations to undermine whatever traditional institutions had survived.

The Terror had no more of a permanent effect on the northeastern Jews than had the 1791 enfranchisement law. After 1794 those who had remained in Alsace-Lorraine still lived apart from their Christian neighbors and still refused to profit from the increased opportunities now open to them.

But the Ashkenazim could not remain isolated forever. Even though they failed to become active citizens, the abolition of special taxes and the removal of residence restrictions placed them in a far better position than that enjoyed by the Jews in the Holy Roman Empire. Thus, as French troops advanced into Central Europe, a significant number of German Jews emigrated to the Northeast and more than replaced the French Ashkenazim who had left during the Terror.[23]

The influx of German Jews had grave effects for the stability of northeastern France. Anti-Semitism, which had been stimulated by the Terrorists' antireligious policies, was intensified by the post-1797 migrations. Peasants and small merchants, faced with potential inundation, again listened to anti-Semitic agitators who used pro-Catholic sentiment to stimulate antirepublicanism. Anxious to stem the royalists' influence, local officials urged the Consulate to reenact prerevolutionary restrictions on Jews and recommended their forceable dispersion throughout the rest of France. The central government, preoccupied with other problems, ignored the prefects' complaints until 1805.

The recent emigrés, in addition to jeopardizing the relationship between the northeastern Jewish communities and the surrounding population, also created tensions among the Jews themselves. The emigrés brought with them a reform program which had been devised several years before in North Italy. This scheme included a new ritual and code designed to enable those Jews who followed the German rite (the Ashkenazim) to modify their practices sufficiently to fit into modern European society.

Reform ideas spread rapidly through some Dutch and German communities which had been influenced by the assimilationist views of Moses Mendelssohn. The French Ashkenazim, however, rejected the new ritual. They had only recently recovered from the Terrorists' assaults on their religion, and the example of the Sephardim's near apostasy alerted them to the dangers of assimilation. The quarrels between the conservative and the reform Jews became increasingly bitter. Anxious to control communal property, both sides petitioned the government to recognize them by including their version of Judaism in the Organic Articles which, after 1802, served as France's religious code.[24]

Grégoire had an opportunity to observe the reform ritual in practice when he traveled to Germany and the Netherlands. He sympathized with the progressives because the North Italian program included exactly those changes which he had long hoped the Jews would adopt. Despite his interest in the reform movement, however, during the Terror and the two regimes thereafter, Grégoire abstained from public involvement in Jewish problems. In 1797, for example, the legislature created a committee to clarify the Ashkenazim's current status. Appointed to this committee, Grégoire neglected to attend its sessions and had to be replaced.[25]

Still Grégoire maintained his private associations with the northeastern Jews. He corresponded with them and whenever possible procured state pensions for them, advised them on legal problems, and encouraged their entry into such new professions as science, literature, and the law. He also wrote one short essay in which he answered racist anti-Semitic arguments by describing the moral, intellectual, and social progress made by acculturated Jews.[26]

Disturbed by the quarrels within the Ashkenazim congregations, Grégoire encouraged the spread of assimilationist ideas among his Jewish friends. Yet he advised French officials to remain aloof from these disputes because he was convinced that religious innovations must be introduced by the faithful.

According to him, the government should limit its activities to maintaining law and order and, if necessary, to providing money for new congregations.[27]

During the first year of the Consulate, Napoleon Bonaparte did not interfere in Jewish affairs. In 1801 he ignored the prefects' complaints concerning increased Judeo-Christian tension in the Northeast, and a year later he omitted Judaism from the Organic Articles. The First Consul's silence raised many questions concerning the status of both emigré and French Jews. Grégoire and others urged Bonaparte to resolve these questions, but for several years he neglected to do so, and friction between northeastern Ashkenazim and Christians continued to mount.[28]

In 1806 Bonaparte—now Emperor Napoleon—called a Jewish general assembly. Less concerned than Grégoire about converting Jews, the emperor summoned Jewish deputies in hopes of terminating northeastern tensions once and for all. He attributed friction there to the Jews' continued reliance upon money-lending. Like Grégoire, Napoleon thought usury was caused by ghetto life—voluntary or otherwise—and by traditional limitations on Jewish economic opportunities. The cure, therefore, lay in broad social and religious reforms. Although Napoleon called the assembly to deal with usury, he planned to present the delegates with a complete program for abolishing ghettos and assimilating the Ashkenazim. In preparing the agenda, which was to include answers as well as questions, the emperor preferred to consult experts on Jewish life rather than rely on the prefects' advice. He therefore summoned a committee which included Grégoire, the Nancy lawyer Thiéry who, in 1788, had shared the Metz award with Grégoire, and the Ashkenazim manufacturer, Isaac Cerf-Berr.[29]

This committee received little publicity, but anti-Semites responded vigorously to rumors about Napoleon's plans. Before the Jewish assembly opened, a spokesman for the revived conservative forces in France, Gabriel-Ambrois-Louis de Bonald, published a scathing attack on the Jews which was as much antirepublican as anti-Semitic. Imitating his revolutionary predecessors, he focused on Grégoire's pro-Jewish reputation and attacked his philo-Semitic ideas. Jews, de Bonald asserted, were and always would be foreigners whose only interest in Christians was to seize their riches for sectarian purposes. If Jews had been as numerous in the rest of France as they were in Alsace, he postulated "would not the Friends of the Jews, just as the *Amis des Noirs,* have had to reproach themselves for the haste with which they admitted [Jews] to freedom."[30]

Grégoire, recognizing the personal character of de Bonald's remarks, hurriedly published his *Observations nouvelles* in which he implicitly answered de Bonald's comments. Grégoire had not written this pamphlet as an argument for Jewish rights. Instead he originally had thought that a glowing description of the reform communities which he had visited in Central Europe would encourage French Jews to adopt the North Italian ritual. Now he hoped these examples would also disprove de Bonald's derogatory statements about the Jews.[31]

Most anti-Semites ignored Grégoire's *Observations nouvelles* while some Jews objected to his intemperate passages concerning rabbinical tyranny. The most serious attacks came from his own friends who disliked his increasingly open sympathy with the assumption that equal rights for Jews might hasten the millennium. The quarrels which developed between Grégoire and his friends hinged on theological quibbles, but they affected his fundamental assumptions. His friends criticized both the content of his eschatology—his ideas that Jews must convert before the apocalypse—and the entire concept of the earthly millennium.[32]

Grégoire cared little about theological disputes because he regarded religious truth as above man's judgment in any case, and he refused to defend his millenarian tendencies.[33] Practical, at least in so far as doctrinal arguments were concerned, he believed it more important that Napoleon hold the projected Jewish general assembly than that a few suspect Catholics or

Protestant pastors accept his version of what the final era of human history would be like.

Napoleon ignored the anti-Semitic sentiments which influenced even his family (his uncle, Cardinal Joseph Fesch, for example) and his Council of State. Preparing for the opening of the General Assembly, in May 1806 he proclaimed a one year moratorium on all debts owed to Jews. He then presented the General Assembly with an agenda that covered religious and social questions as well as the crucial problem of usury.

The deputies were nonplussed by Napoleon's broad program because the emperor covertly threatened to expel all of the Jews unless they devised suitable regulations. Grégoire, when asked for advice, warned them against assuming responsibility for instituting drastic changes in Jewish life and tradition. Urging them to consult their home congregations, he refused to offer any specific recommendations as to how Jewish ritual, family laws, and ecclesiastical organization should be revised so that Jews might participate in modern European society. He did not need to; the delegates had only to look at his *Essai sur le régénération* and his *Observations nouvelles* if they wished to know his opinions. Grégoire gathered information regarding specific points raised in the assembly, and, departing from his practice of avoiding proselytization, he gave one of the delegates a book on the life of Christ. "This grain," he hoped, "will fall on fertile soil."[34]

In January 1807 Napoleon approved the General Assembly's modified Jewish ritual. Then, fearing that most Jews would ignore regulations drawn up by a predominantly lay assembly, he convoked a traditional Jewish religious council, a Sanhedrin, to ratify the Assembly's work.

This new council included Jews from the Empire as well as from France, and the more assimilationist attitudes of Central European Jews won over the conservative French Ashkenazim. The Sanhedrin drew up a uniform rite and organizational scheme that transcended the differences between Ashkenazim and Sephardim. Thereafter, Jews gradually merged into a homo-geneous group composed of French citizens rather than remaining separated into individual communities of Iberian or German descent. The Sanhedrin helped abolish traditional and heredi-tary distinctions among Frenchmen. It was, therefore, one stage in the revolutionary process of creating a unified French society. Still, the Sanhedrin did not satisfy anti-Semitic critics or silence their agitation, and its sudden closure was attributed to increasing pressure from the so-called devotés, led by the em-peror's uncle, Cardinal Fesch.[35]

Because the Sanhedrin had not resolved the problem of usury, which had led Napoleon to call a Jewish assembly in the first place, the emperor postponed promulgating its de-cisions. Shortly after it disbanded, the Council of State pro-claimed another moratorium on debts owed to the Jews. In 1808 Napoleon imposed new limitations on the residence, commercial activities, communal organization, and military exemptions of northeastern Jews. Annulling preexisting Jewish legislation in conquered German territory, he extended the northeastern regulations to the Imperial Jews. The 1808 re-strictions were to be removed when the prefects regarded them as no longer necessary.

Napoleon's Jewish legislation provoked strong protests from all French Jews. But they improved the civil status of the Central European Jews who had been subject to harsher regu-lations under the now defunct Holy Roman Empire. They also eased tension in France because German Jews no longer had to migrate if they wished to become citizens. By the end of the Empire the practice of usury was significantly curtailed in the Northeast, and this, too, improved Judeo-Christian relations.

The second, less controversial part of Napoleon's 1808 Jewish decrees established a synod system for French Jews similar to that created for Lutherans and Calvinists under the Organic Articles. Members of these synods, who were chosen by the government, exercised jurisdiction over ritual and dogmatic controversies and supervised certain aspects of secular life. For example, they ensured that Jews fulfilled their military obligations. In addition, prefects, rabbis, and synagogues controlled Jewish economic activity and mobility through their power to grant or deny permission to move within the Northeast or to establish new businesses. The synods also founded schools and collected the new religious tax imposed by the state.

The 1808 edicts, as well as the Organic Articles upon which they were modeled, partially restored France's prerevolutionary corporate structure. Napoleon's religious synods violated the concept of universal citizenship and uniform law. Designed to stifle conflict, because the synods exercised secular functions and could impose economic sanctions upon dissidents, they hindered creativity and prevented further development. The 1808 decrees bridged within France the traditional schism between Sephardim and Ashkenazim, but they intensified rather than resolved what until then had been a local division among traditionalists and progressives. After 1808 this distinction spread throughout France and led to bitter controversy in numerous congregations.

Grégoire ignored Napoleon's decision to reinstitute special regulations for the Jews and reinforce rabbinical authority. He helped congregations locate reform rabbis who would abide by the Sanhedrin's decisions. In addition, he found government positions for Jews, patronized their schools, and provided work for Jewish professionals and literary men. These services were similar to those which he performed for other minority groups.[36]

Grégoire, however, was more deeply concerned about Jews than about any other minority besides Negroes. The Sanhedrin represented for him an important stage in Jewish assimilation, and he delayed his departure from Paris until it terminated its sessions. He was anxious to defend it from anti-Semitic criticism and to encourage French Jews to adopt its innovations. He also tried to smooth the path for reform Jews by procuring government protection and giving them private advice. In his appeals to the government he pointed out how, during the Sanhedrin, conservative leaders and rabbis had infringed upon secular authority by preventing deputies from attending the sessions.[37] The French government, he insisted, should not permit such insubordination. In actuality, however, the Napoleonic and subsequent regimes refrained from interfering in the interminable quarrels which continued to embitter congregations long after the Empire collapsed.

Revolutionary changes in the status of the Jews proved more durable than the other egalitarian reforms for which Grégoire fought. In all likelihood, Napoleon's harsh measures did more to diminish anti-Semitic agitation in France between 1815 and 1870 than did Grégoire's pro-Jewish propaganda. For a time, at least, Napoleon succeeded where the idealists had failed; he provided the economic and religious foundations upon which Jew and gentile could coexist in the Northeast.[38]

Grégoire's contribution to Jewish enfranchisement was a unique one—one which only he could have made. Unsuccessful as a legislator, he served as a conscience for the nation, goading apathetic deputies into taking decisive action. Thus, the National Assembly rejected his proposals and the September 1791 law was written by others while the 1808 code embodying reforms which he had long advocated was devised by Jews under strict government supervision and was imposed by a Napoleonic synod. Nonetheless, even though he did not determine the form which these laws and reforms ultimately took, without his pre- and early revolutionary agitation, perhaps they would have taken much longer to accomplish.

Having seen the Jews adopt a way of life more compatible with modern European society, after 1808 Grégoire abstained from further involvement in their affairs. He thenceforth became a spectator and commentator, happily reporting certain aspects of the contemporary scene. He was particularly pleased with the progress of German and Dutch reform communities and with the educational experiments of others because he thought these developments showed the Jews' desire to live in harmony with Christians.

Although Grégoire continued to preach reconciliation, his later writings probably influenced more French Jews than Catholics. His unorthodox religious views antagonized his coreligionists, but the Jews never fully realized that his ultimate hope was to convert them. Until this day they have regarded him as a true friend and symbol of enlightened Catholicism.[39]

Grégoire's work for the Jews was limited by the influential anti-Semitic coalition in the National Assembly, by his inept political strategy, and by his fear of jeopardizing essential church reforms. During the Empire another problem implicit in Grégoire's pro-Jewish thought came to the surface, his underestimation of Ashkenazim conservatism.

When northeastern Jews persistently refused to assimilate, Grégoire asked the government to force recalcitrants to accept the reform program. In asking the government to hasten Jewish assimilation, he repeated a mistake which he had made once before. In 1789 he urged secular authorities to reduce episcopal tyranny over the lower clergy; under Napoleon he asked the government to assist reform Jews in their struggles against rabbinical control. Although he realized that religious change must reflect the desires of the faithful, he could not resist imposing either the Civil Constitution of the Clergy or reform Judaism upon reluctant congregations or parishes. He frequently reiterated that coercion could not alter men's beliefs, but he failed to see the incompatibility between democracy, religious tolerance, and a state supported schism. In addition, both Grégoire's Catholic and Jewish reforms unwittingly encouraged religious apathy among laymen and helped to create the environment in which the religious aspects of the Terror and the later defection of Jews from any and all religion became possible.[40]

Grégoire's pro-Jewish activities did not lead to the result that he had anticipated—the ultimate conversion of the Jews. Yet his philo-Semitic work played an important role in his political career and prepared him to engage in subsequent egalitarian campaigns. It intensified the differences between himself and men with whom he disagreed on other issues. It also divided him from others with whom he agreed on most points, such as the leading northeastern deputies in the National Assembly, Jean-François Rewbell and de Broglie of Alsace.

Grégoire's unsuccessful fight for Jewish rights during the early years of the Revolution made him more cautious about linking religious, republican, and egalitarian causes. Although he henceforth hesitated to adopt a campaign where his political convictions would prevent him from working with other interested deputies, he did become more flexible in his relations with other legislators. As the Revolution progressed, and particularly during the Terror and the Empire, he learned to compartmentalize his activities and to cooperate with men of all political and religious faiths in order to attain individual parts of his broad egalitarian program. He also learned to adopt a more diversified approach, to abandon a strategy when the obstacles proved insurmountable, to try alternative methods, and to work through private channels and associations when legislative action proved impossible to attain. Eventually he realized that he must consult with appropriate government officials, much as he might dislike them, instead of trying to coerce them by appealing over their heads to public opinion.

Grégoire did not learn all these lessons at once, but, as he advanced in age and experience, he avoided repeating some of his more painful mistakes. He therefore was able to exercise a more direct, albeit less lasting, influence over the solution of the Negro and mulatto problem than he had over the Jewish question.

NOTES

1. His powers as a deputy mandated him to work for the formation of a regularly held national assembly; see the powers written in his own hand in GS Nancy, MB 123. See *Nouvelle lettre d'un curé, à ses confreres* [sic] *députés aux Etats-généraux* (n.p., n.d.). He planned to submit his credentials to the Third Estate on 13 June along with the first group of clerics but decided to stay in his order one day longer, hoping to bring a majority along with him; Grégoire to Jean-Sylvain Bailly, 13 June 1789, AN, AE II 1077. Reviews of his *Essai sur la régénération: Affiches des évêchés*, 14 May 1789, p. 158; *Journal de Paris*, 6 July 1789, pp. 840–41, and *L'Esprit des Journaux*, July 1789, pp. 85–102 citing *Journal encyclopédique*.

2. *Lettre adressée à M. Grégoire*. Grégoire's recommendations for liberating all Jews in his *Motion en faveur des juifs*, pp. 46–47.

3. Grégoire turned against Louis XVI when the king refused to sanction the formation of the National Assembly. See "Notes sur les Etats Généraux et specialement sur ce qui s'est passé dans la chambre du clergé avant la réunion des ordres. par M. l'abbé Grégoire Député de nancy," (typed copy, anon. private collection in Paris), entries for 22 and 23 June 1789.

4. This statement does not take into consideration the anti-Semitism common among such intellectuals as Voltaire, which did not find nation-wide response in France until the time of the Dreyfus affair. Nineteenth-century French anti-Semitism followed the same pattern, according to Robert F. Byrnes, who asserts that between 1815 and 1866 anti-Masonic agitation served as a focus for those irrational fears which frequently center on Jews; see his *Antisemitism in Modern France*, 1:111.

5. The keeper of the seals, Champion de Cicé, gave Grégoire the *cahiers* drawn up by the various Jewish communities; see the introduction to Grégoire's *Motion en faveur des juifs* where he printed them. On 28 September 1789 Count Stanislas de Clermont-Tonnerre pointed out Grégoire's importance as a pro-Jewish spokesman; see his *Opinion*, pp. 1–2, and *Le Courrier de Versailles*, 2 Oct. 1789, pp. 18–19. Yet the moderates disapproved of Grégoire's radicalism; see the president's response to Grégoire's intemperate

speech on the ministry on 13 July in Brethé, *Journal inédit*, p. 129.

6. Grégoire raised the question of northeastern Jews on 3 and 14 Aug. and 2 Sept. 1789; *Point du jour*, 5 Aug. 1789, p. 19; *Affiches des évêchés*, 10 Sept. 1789, p. 293, and *Patriote françois*, 4 Sept. 1789.

7. First clause of the Declaration, see Stewart, ed., *A Documentary Survey*, p. 114.

8. See Miss Hyslop for the various elements which made up "nationalism" in the *cahiers: French Nationalism*, chaps. 2, 3, and Krieger, "Nationalism," pp. 103–13.

9. Hertzberg clearly shows the background of French nationalistic anti-Semitism. For examples during the Revolution, see Count Mirabeau's answer to northeastern radicals: *Moniteur*, réimpression, 25 Dec. 1789, p. 471, and Grégoire's *Motion en faveur des juifs*.

10. Several of Grégoire's correspondents in the Northeast wrote to him in German, for example. Alsace presented a somewhat different problem than Lorraine. It had been annexed sixty years earlier and had had quite a different history during the early modern period. Grégoire became a fervent linguistic nationalist in the sense that he tried to spread the use of French throughout regions where dialect or a foreign language was commonly employed; see Brunot, *Histoire de la langue française*, vol. 9, pt. 1, pp. 12–13 and passim.

11. *Motion en faveur des juifs*, pp. 45–47.

12. The question is a murky one. The Sephardim assumed that their royal letters patent of naturalization were equivalent to citizenship. The 24 Dec. 1789 law rejected this interpretation, as, indeed, did the 28 Jan. 1790 law which failed to grant citizenship to the few Ashkenazim, such as Cerf Berr, who had similar letters patent.

13. *Moniteur*, réimpression, 21, 23, 24, and 25 Dec. 1789, pp. 439–40, 455–56, 462–64, and 471.

14. *Point du jour*, 22 Dec. 1789, p. 197, and *Courrier de Provence*, 24 and 28 Dec. 1789, pp. 200 and 254–56.

15. *Courrier de Provence*, 29 and 30 Jan. 1790, pp. 330–36 and 349–50; *Patriote françois*, 30 Jan. 1790; *Point du jour*, 3 Feb. 1790, pp. 264–66.

16. For a general discussion of the destruction of the corporate state, see Lefebvre, *La Révolution française*, pp. 541–49.

17. Julien Raimond, a prominent mulatto who lived in France,

insisted that during the National Assembly Grégoire paid for some promulatto publications; see documents concerning Raimond's trial in AN, DXXV 56, no. 549.

18. Grégoire to Bing, 20 Aug. 1789 [*sic* for 1791], *Archives israélites*, 5:417.

19. *Patriote françois*, 19 [?] Jan. 1791, p. 77; *Moniteur*, réimpression, 20 Jan. 1791, p. 167.

20. *Gazette de Paris*, 6 and 20 Jan., 13 March, and 17 July 1791; *Courrier de Provence*, 7 Jan. and 2 Feb. 1791, pp. 102 and 31; see Kahn, *Les juifs*, pp. 61ff for additional quotes from newspapers. See also: *M. Grégoire, député à l'assemblée nationale, et évêque constitutionnel du département de Loir et Cher, Dénoncé à la Nation*, p. 7; [François], *Mon apologie*, p. 19; *La contre-révolution démontrée nécessaire*, pp. 40–41. Grégoire did not wholeheartedly approve of the Civil Constitution of the Clergy, but he thought it removed several outstanding abuses of the prerevolutionary church; see Introduction.

21. *M. Dumouchel; soi-disant évêque du département du Gard*, p. 8; *Histoire du serment à Paris*, p. 60n.

22. "Procès-verbaux des sociétés populaires," entry for 2 Feb. 1792, BM Blois.

23. I say this despite Parkes' denial that any sizeable number of Jews emigrated to France. Prefects and Christians alike feared an inundation, and their agitation encouraged revived anti-Semitism; see Parkes, A *History of the Jewish People*, pp. 134–35.

24. The North Italian reforms were noted in Scipione de' Ricci to Grégoire, 30 June 1796, BPR, EFGH, and the "Journal historique de la Société Libre et Littéraire de Philosophie Chrétienne," entries for 11 Aug., 22 Sept. 1796, and 12 Jan. 1797 (anon. private collection in Paris, typed copy). See Meyer, *The Origins of the Modern Jew*, for Moses Mendelssohn and his group.

25. "Prière" and Grégoire's manuscript note on a reform congregation in Holland, BPR, Rév. 168, no. 37; Grégoire, *Observations* (1806); Saladin, *Rapport*, p. 3.

26. Ensheim to Grégoire, 10 Nov., year 1 (1792), and Bing to Grégoire, 4 Thermidor year 3 (22 July 1795), BPR, MNO; Grégoire's article in *Correspondance sur les affaires du temps* 3 (1797): 88–91.

27. Grégoire to de Gerando, 3 March 1804, AD, L&C, F 592, fo. 84.

28. Berr, *Appel à la justice des nations et des rois*, pp. ix, 28, 59n, 60n, 62; Lamoureux, *Mémoire pour servir à histoire littéraire*, p. 76; Michel Berr to Grégoire, 5 Floréal year 10 (25 April 1802). BPR, MNO; Pastor Peterson to Grégoire, 3 Messidor year 10 (22 June 1802), BPR, AB.

29. Pietri, *Napoléon et les israélites*, p. 50.

30. De Bonald, "Sur les juifs," *Mercure de France*, 8 Feb. 1806, p. 253, italics in the original.

31. Grégoire, *Observations* (1806). This was completed in Dec. 1805; see "Journal historique," 5 Dec. 1805 (anon. private collection, Paris). For other replies to de Bonald see: Moyse P. . . de Bordeaux, *Réponse à un article sur les juifs*; *Journal agronomique, commercial, politique et littéraire des Deux-Sèvres*, 16 Aug. 1806, pp. 377–78; [Jean-Baptiste Justin Lamoureux], "De la régénération definitive des juifs," *Revue philosophique, littéraire et politique*, 11 July 1806, pp. 6–8; J. Rodrigues, "Observations sur un article de M. de Bonald, sur les juifs, inséré dans le Mercure de France du 8 Février 1806, *Revue philosophique*, 21 March 1806, pp. 3–4.

32. Pastor Saltzmann to Grégoire, 21 March 1806, BPR, AB; LeCoz to Grégoire, 30 Dec. 1806 and 28 Feb. 1807, Grégoire to LeCoz, 17 Feb. 1807, Pingaud, ed., *Correspondance de Lecoz et de Grégoire*, pp. 59–62; Grégoire to Dom Grappin, 9 Dec. 1807, BM Besançon, 622, fo. 324–25.

33. Between 1806 and 1810 Grégoire described millenarianism more fully; see his *Histoire des sectes*, 1:194–207 and his *Réflexions de M. Grégoire*, pp. 6–8. The Société de la Philosophie Chrétienne frequently discussed the Jews and the millennium, but Grégoire never participated in these debates; see "Journal historique," entries from 6 Dec. 1798 through 28 Aug. 1806 (anon. private collection, Paris).

34. Grégoire to Degola, 17 Aug. 1806, AS Vatican; also his letter to Joel Barlow, 1 Sept. 1806, Harvard Library, AM 1468 (603). For Napoleon's agenda see his memoranda to Champagny, 23 Aug. and 3 Sept. 1806, *Correspondance de Napoléon Ier*, 13:100–103, 130.

35. Anchel, *Napoléon*, pp. 217–18.

36. Grégoire to Count Daru, 12 Aug. 1811, AN, 138 AP 100, fonds Daru; Monin to Grégoire, 20 May and 18 Oct. 1809, BPR, MNO; [Schottlander], *Les premiers pas de la nation juive*; Posener, *Adolphe Crémieux*, pp. 58–59.

37. Grégoire to Ricci, 8 Aug. 1808, Florence, Carteggi Ricci; Grégoire, *Observations* (1807), pp. 5–9. Grégoire to Judge Eli, 28 Oct. 1807, BN, NAF 22737, fo. 68–69.

38. Howard Morley Sachar emphatically denies this; *The Course of Modern Jewish History* (New York: Dell Publishing, 1958), pp. 64–65.

39. Participants in one meeting of the Société des Amis de Grégoire in Paris attended by the author in 1961 included a few Jews, several Jewish converts to Catholicism, and one former Haitian diplomat. There were, as far as the author could tell, no Christian Frenchmen present. The president of the Alliance Israélite in 1967, moreover, was a great admirer of Grégoire. His father-in-law numbered among the organizers of a fund-raising campaign to erect a statue of Grégoire in Lunéville during the last decade of the nineteenth century.

40. Grégoire recognized that declining religious zeal among Jews was becoming a problem, and he compared it with similar phenomenon which he observed among Catholics, namely, the spread of atheism; see his letter to Ricci, 8 Aug. 1808, Florence, Carteggi Ricci.

PART ONE

The French Revolution and the Blacks

3

Grégoire's Commitment
to Mulattoes and Slaves

Grégoire's forty-year crusade for mulatto and Negro emancipation followed, but soon overshadowed, his sporadic campaign
for Jewish rights. Before the Revolution he knew little about
the colonies and, like many other Frenchmen, he considered the
status of colonial Africans a peripheral question. As a north-
easterner, he was primarily interested in Central European
economic and social problems and regarded the Caribbean as too
remote to merit his attention. As late as August 1789 he wrote:
"Too often one sees men of iron who profane the name of
goodness; they have the generosity to cherish men two thousand
years or two thousand leagues away, opening their hearts to
Helots and Negroes while the unfortunates whom they en-
counter [the Jews] scarcely receive a compassionate glance."[1]

Despite Grégoire's disinterest in Negroes, the theories which
he enunciated in his *Essai sur la régénération* applied as much
to them as to Jews. Both were foreigners whose culture
originated on the far side of the Mediterranean, and both were
generally regarded as ineligible for French citizenship. Be-
lieving all men were equal before God, Grégoire saw no reason

for denying civil rights to strangers, regardless of their current cultural or religious status. He certainly did not want to make naturalization contingent upon the acceptance of French customs. Assimilation, he thought, would follow rather than precede liberation.

Grégoire differed from his colleagues in his choice of methods rather than in his general goals. Regarding European Christian culture as superior to all others, he was just as anxious as were his contemporaries to make Frenchmen out of Jews and Africans, but he thought coercive means would have little success, at least initially. He believed Christians must first overlook deviant behavior among those people whom they had deliberately excluded from their society. Then, through education and personal example, Frenchmen would convince non-Europeans that their civilization and religion were superior.

Grégoire's prerevolutionary apathy toward colonial conditions was shared by many of his countrymen. Throughout France, concern over the empire was common only among those people who were directly involved in overseas trade or in the very small abolition movement. Although the nation had fought several colonial wars during the eighteenth century and although colonial products played an increasing role in everyday life, few Frenchmen expressed more than incidental curiosity about their overseas possessions.[2]

Even the *philosophes* paid little serious attention to the non-European world. A few French writers denounced slavery during the first part of the eighteenth century, but until the 1770s none devoted his full attention to the subject. Authors such as Montesquieu criticized the institution in passing, while Voltaire used it as a pretext for attacking the church. The latter compared Protestant involvement in the British abolition movement with Catholic apathy on the subject.[3]

Indeed, the Anglo-American example encouraged other humanitarians. In France, especially, abolitionist sentiment first spread among those who, for one reason or another, had had contact with the Quaker-led movement. In 1787 several of these men organized an abolitionist society modeled on the Slave Trade Committee which they called the Société des Amis des Noirs. Prerevolutionary regulations limited the activities of private associations and prevented the members from engaging in widespread publicity,[4] but they vowed to campaign against slave trading in whatever way they could.

The society's decision to concentrate on the trade was logical because this was the most dramatic and vulnerable part of the slavery system. Conditions aboard the vessels were atrocious and contradicted the colonists' portrayal of slavery as a paternalistic, benevolent institution. English and French abolitionists used lurid accounts of the means whereby Africans were kidnapped and transported to arouse an emotional response among readers who might otherwise accept the planters' argument that slaves were no worse off than European peasants.

The abolitionists believed that ending the slave trade would ultimately destroy the entire system of slavery. If fewer Africans were imported, high mortality rates in the West Indies soon would decimate the labor force, and landowners would be forced either to import free white workers or to improve laboring conditions on their plantations. In either case, slavery as it then existed would become uneconomical and would gradually disappear of its own accord.[5]

Despite their reasoning and the several pamphlets which they published in 1787 and 1788, the Amis des Noirs failed to elicit a significant response in France before the Revolution. The only public debate regarding the colonies which took place during the 1780s was provoked by whites who lived in the West Indies. They were very dissatisfied about existing regulations and demanded significant changes in France's imperial system. Above all, they objected to mercantilist policy and requested the right to control their own commercial and domestic affairs. Both the American Revolution and the periodic grain crises in France lent strength to the colonists' pleas for local autonomy and free trade. Influenced by both factors and protesting against what they called ministerial despotism, the white residents of Saint-Domingue rebelled against French rule in 1768 and 1772.

Frenchmen who owned colonial land and merchants who enjoyed monopolistic control over imperial trade opposed the colonists' demands. The landowners in France feared granting too much authority to the whites in the colonies, even though they saw the need to open West Indian ports to foreign vessels. The port merchants, for their part, insisted upon retaining their trade privileges. Distrusting the colonists' loyalty, they, too, opposed any measure which would decentralize imperial administration.

The monarchy sympathized more with the landowners (many of whom were nobles) than with the merchants and eased mercantile restrictions during periods of acute grain shortage. In 1784 the king's concessions provoked a pamphlet war between landowners and merchants. While the port merchants, organized in chambers of commerce, resisted all change, the landowners justified their laissez-faire trade policies by citing the doctrines of Adam Smith and the Physiocrats. Neither was a very good reference because the eighteenth-century French and English economic theoreticians had condemned slavery along with mercantilism.[6]

Landowners and merchants alike published pamphlets concerning imperial policy in 1784, but both groups feared to provoke a public debate until political developments forced them to do so. Both assumed they could accomplish their goals through private negotiations with the ministry. By the summer of 1788, however, new conditions convinced some landowners who lived in France that private, individual action would no longer adequately protect their interests.

Rumors of the formation of an abolitionist society and Louis' decision to convoke an Estates General led the landowners in Paris to organize in July 1788. All of them agreed that they must counter the Amis des Noirs' propaganda; yet they disagreed over their attitude towards this future assembly. Some regarded the king's decision to exclude the colonies from the impending Estates as a threat to their interests. Others feared the Estates might prove even less sympathetic than the ministry, and they hesitated to recognize the assembly's jurisdiction over the empire by demanding representation in it.[7]

While the planters in Paris argued over whether they should request admission to the Estates, Frenchmen in the Caribbean decided the question for them. Generally poorer than the landowners in France, the residents of the West Indies did not believe the planters in the metropolis could speak in their name. Consequently they illegally convoked electoral assemblies and selected deputies for the metropolitan legislature.[8]

Because the colonial whites were vying for representation in the Estates General, the landowners also would have to participate if they wished to protect their interests. Thus, shortly after the Estates opened, a delegation of Caribbean landowners appeared before the three orders and requested admission. During the subsequent debates three distinct parties emerged: landowners who lived in France, Frenchmen who lived in the colonies, and a few humanitarians who criticized both of the other parties because, according to them, whites could not represent either free mulattoes or slaves. Since most deputies wanted to forestall any independence movement, they agreed to admit West Indian delegations without distinguishing between residents and landowners. Few Frenchmen cared about how and by whom these deputies were chosen.

Grégoire sympathized with those who claimed to represent the French West Indies because the first letters of convocation had also denied Lorraine the right to be admitted to the Estates. Without questioning their ability to speak for the colonies, Grégoire voted to recognize the first delegation of Saint-Dominguean landowners that appeared before the Assembly.[9]

Shortly after the planters presented their case, the National Assembly appointed Grégoire to the Credentials Committee which judged between rival deputations. When the representatives elected in Saint-Domingue arrived in Paris, the committee was asked to determine the colony's legitimate spokesmen. Although throughout the Assembly's debates Mirabeau and a few other representatives questioned the right of any white delegation to speak for the entire colony, Grégoire ignored this controversy and showed no more interest in the West Indies than he had demonstrated several weeks before.

When Mirabeau challenged both the landowners in France and the deputies from the Caribbean, he was concerned primarily with slaves. Yet Mirabeau's ideas found little response among the metropolitan deputies, and the first serious attack on the whites' exclusive right to represent the islands came from mulattoes who lived in France.

The mulattoes' position was a peculiar one; they were not quite citizens, but they certainly were not slaves. Although King Louis XIV had tried to define their status in the Code Noir of 1685, whites in the West Indies had ignored the royal regulations. Generally they had treated their mulatto offspring as free and in some cases had willed them extensive property. A few mulattoes moved to France and were educated there. The mulattoes in the West Indies were not so fortunate. Many performed manual labor or were employed as artisans. During the eighteenth century the whites imposed new restrictions on their freedom. Fearing that they might arouse humanitarian sympathies in France, the colonists tried to keep the mulattoes in the Caribbean. The restrictions proved ineffective, but they stimulated hostility against the colonial whites.

As antagonism between whites and mulattoes mounted in the West Indies, the mulattoes who lived in France were placed in an ambivalent position. While they tried to attain increased rights for those who remained in the Caribbean, they identified with the whites rather than the blacks. Since most of their wealth came from plantations, they wished to retain slavery and slave trading, and they assumed that their mutual interest in the unfree labor system provided a common ground for negotiations with white landowners.

In August 1789 mulatto representatives met in Paris, drew up a *cahier*, and asked the planters to sponsor their petition to the National Assembly. Only after the planter spokesmen refused to help them gain a hearing before the National Assembly did the mulattoes appeal to the Amis des Noirs and to the nation at large.[10]

The Société des Amis des Noirs hesitated to assist the mulattoes. The members were very influenced by the English abolitionists who focused almost exclusively on terminating the slave trade. Hence they found the mulattoes' position selfish and unworthy. When, however, the mulattoes reluctantly agreed to support the abolition of slave trading, the society managed to arrange an audience for the white lawyer who served as their spokesman. After listening to the lawyer, the deputies referred the mulattoes' petition to the Credentials Committee.[11]

Grégoire was one of the members of the Credentials Committee when the mulattoes appeared before it in September 1789. For twelve sessions the committee listened to arguments presented by both mulattoes and landowners. After due consideration, Grégoire, along with a majority of the members who attended a rather sparse session, voted to recommend mulatto representation. The planters immediately protested that the committee's decision was illegal because they thought that the entire committee would have rejected the mulattoes' request. When the committee refused to reconsider its recommendation, the planters prevented it from presenting its report by creating disorders every time it was on the agenda.[12]

While the mulattoes were submitting their claims first to the planters, then to the Amis des Noirs, and finally to the Credentials Committee, the Amis des Noirs were concentrating on opposing the slave trade. As yet the French society had failed to arouse much sympathy for the slaves, and the Slave Trade Committee, convinced that French abolition might influence the British Parliament, decided to aid their continental colleagues by sending a deputy, Thomas Clarkson, to Paris. When Clarkson arrived in the summer of 1789, the Amis des Noirs translated his publications and introduced him to the king and the Council of State. Clarkson's appeals proved effective. His diagram and model of a slave trading ship revolted members of the National Assembly, and several called upon him for further information.[13]

Grégoire was one of the deputies who responded to Clarkson's propaganda.[14] The English abolitionist converted him to the anti-slave trade cause, and under Clarkson's influence Grégoire became interested in the broader aspects of the racial problem. Yet Grégoire naively believed that the mulatto question could be separated from the issues of slavery and the trade, and he thought that before the Assembly worried about the Africans, it must first fulfill its obligations to those children of French subjects who were being denied their birthright. The Amis des Noirs, however, regarded the slave trade as the prior problem, and they wished to solve it before dealing with the secondary consequences of slavery. Therefore they preferred to denounce the more dramatic injustices perpetrated upon Africans who had been kidnapped, enslaved, sent to a foreign country under intolerable conditions, and reduced to the legal status of moveable property.

For several weeks after Clarkson converted Grégoire to abolitionism, Grégoire found no opportunity to present his ideas before the Assembly. While he waited for the Credentials Committee to present its report on mulatto representation, he inserted in the introduction to his *Motion en faveur des juifs* a statement praising the deputies who supported the mulattoes' demands. This pamphlet provides the best testimony of how quickly Grégoire had adopted the mulatto cause. The body of the text, written probably in late August or early September, ranked Jewish rights over those of distant Africans, while the introduction, composed early in October, described mulatto rights as an equally important problem.[15]

Grégoire faced similar obstacles as a promulatto and as a philo-Semitic representative. Most deputies were apathetic toward both causes, and they resented anyone who raised such peripheral issues. In both cases the opposition encouraged this lack of interest by threatening to filibuster and by issuing dire warnings about the damage which any infringement upon existing colonial (or Jewish) race relations would inflict upon French prosperity. Colonial landowners were supported by port merchants as well as by political conservatives, and they could appeal to more honorable sentiments than could the anti-Semites, who relied almost exclusively upon religious prejudice.[16] Since the majority was anxious to write a constitution for France, it refused to permit ideological or humanitarian proposals to hinder its work by provoking acrimonious and lengthy debates.

Promulatto deputies had a few advantages over the philo-Semites. Although their opponents, the colonists and port merchants, wished to maintain the prerevolutionary social system, the planters also hoped to make fundamental revisions in the political and economic structure of the empire. The abolitionists cared very little about mercantile restrictions, but they could and did object to any proposal which would grant increased autonomy to the West Indian territories. As long as the empire was governed from Paris, the abolitionists had a chance of eventually achieving their goals. But if the whites were to attain self-government, they would probably refuse to modify the racial caste system. Abolitionists, therefore, had two advantages: the planters themselves would sooner or later raise · the colonial issue, and the promulatto deputies could play upon the Assembly's reluctance to relinquish any of its newly gained authority. If the abolitionists were to succeed in breaking the procolonial coalition, they might be able to propose social reforms for the West Indies.

Breaking the procolonial alliance was not a utopian goal. United only by the fear of abolitionism, the several groups who claimed to speak for imperial interests agreed on very little else.

The port merchants resisted all change in the colonial system. They not only wanted to maintain metropolitan authority over trade, but they also feared that alterations in the caste system might destroy the Caribbean economy. The landowners not only opposed the merchants' monopolistic rights, but they also were divided among themselves. The conservatives hoped to retain royal jurisdiction, while the radicals encouraged the Assembly to extend its control over the colonies.

To an extent the schism among landowners reflected ideological differences, but it also rested upon divergent theories as to strategy.[17] Both groups feared that the Assembly might interfere with the racial system in the colonies. Even those planters who thought the legislature should set policy for the empire realized how dangerous it might be to entrust their fate to an elected body. They hoped to circumvent this danger by establishing a colonial committee within the National Assembly which would have exclusive jurisdiction over the empire just as the Constitutional Committee had over Jewish naturalization. They expected the Assembly to appoint enough colonists to this committee to ensure their control. They also believed that the Assembly, unwilling to waste time on colonial debates, would readily adopt the committee's recommendations.

The conservative planters, for their part, distrusted their colleagues' tactics and feared that the Assembly would listen to the abolitionists rather than to the landowners. Much as they had criticized the Council of State during the previous decade, they believed they would have more influence with the ministry. Hence they thought it both wiser and safer to leave colonial jurisdiction in the king's hands.

As long as the issues clearly concerned race, differences within the procolonial alliance were masked by the members' fear of the Amis des Noirs. When the institution of slavery was not directly threatened, the two groups of planters and the merchants proved unable to follow a common strategy. Just such an occasion arose in November 1789 when one colonial deputy proposed the establishment of a colonial committee. Neither the conservative planters nor the merchants approved of such a step, and their hesitancy seemed justified when, on 3 December, Grégoire for the first time publicly spoke on behalf of the antislavery deputies.[18]

In his 3 December address on the question of a colonial committee, Grégoire insisted that the Assembly must first vote on admitting mulattoes before it decided whether to create a special committee. If the deputies admitted the mulattoes, then they would be entitled to join the committee.[19] The subject was not a dramatic one, but recognizing mulatto representation threatened the foundation of white supremacy over the colonies. He inserted enough of his egalitarian philosophy into his remarks to force the radical landowners to withdraw their proposal, at least temporarily. They hesitated to renew the motion because they feared giving the egalitarians another opportunity to spread their propaganda, and they certainly did not wish to form a colonial committee if mulattoes were to be represented on it.

Although Grégoire's speech on 3 December was moderate— indeed innocuous—his appearance on the side of the abolitionists greatly disturbed the planters because the militant ecclesiastic threatened to be a more formidable enemy than the Amis des Noirs had proven to be. The procolonists, having probably seen Grégoire's *Motion en faveur des juifs*, were not surprised by his shift in position. They did their best to prevent his speech from being heard, but his lungs were more powerful than theirs (a prerequisite for any legislative orator in premicrophone days), and he managed to present at least an outline of his ideas.

Grégoire was unable to elaborate his promulatto arguments on 3 December, and a short time later he published a *Mémoire en faveur des gens de couleur*. In this pamphlet he advanced several pragmatic reasons for enfranchising mulattoes and free Negroes. For example, he flatly denied that racial considerations outweighed social and economic ones. Free mulattoes, he asserted, would not unite with Negro slaves against whites, but, instead, would provide valuable aid in defending the French West Indies against both foreign invasions and domestic disorders.

But Grégoire permitted his chiliastic rhetoric to carry him beyond what was sensible at the moment. He characterized slavery as a temporary institution, one which did not fit into the natural order of human existence, and expressed his desire to see "a general universal insurrection" which would "stifle tyranny, resurrect liberty, and place it along side of religion and morals." Religion, he insisted, "by tempering enthusiasm, prevents [liberty] from degenerating into license."[20]

The white landowners were irritated rather than convinced by Grégoire's pamphlet. Having just learned about a slave rebellion in Saint-Domingue, they doubted whether religion would temper the savage instincts of unassimilated slaves, and they hesitated to experiment with their property or, perhaps, their lives. They not only found his apocalyptic remarks singularly inappropriate, but they also rejected his more moderate suggestions because they were fully committed to a rigid racial caste structure. Fearing that they would not be able to uphold Negro slavery unless they maintained strict racial lines, they could not, as Grégoire recommended, grant civil and political rights to either free Negroes or mulattoes. Indeed, they already had refused the alliance which mulattoes in Paris had offered them three months before.

Grégoire's *Mémoire en faveur des gens de couleur* clearly identified him as an abolitionist and showed his shortcomings as a promulatto spokesman. Substituting rational arguments for real information about the colonies, he permitted his enthusiasm to carry him beyond his original subject. Thus, although some of his reasoning made sense, the landowners could not accept his logic, and they used the pamphlet to justify their intransigence.

As the most persistent abolitionist deputy, Grégoire set the tone for the controversy over colonial race relations during the remainder of the National Assembly. Already disliked by conservatives for his radical stand on Jews, ecclesiastical reform, and constitutional provisions, he was a convenient focus for the landowners' attacks. Like the anti-Semites, the procolonists accused him of plotting to destroy France from within and without by overthrowing throne, altar, and empire. Grégoire, they asserted, was cooperating with France's English and Free Masonic enemies.[21] His participation in abolitionist affairs encouraged the procolonists to ally with conservatives, although individual landowners retained their ties with radicals and tried to win Jacobin support for their interests.

The Amis des Noirs were also influenced by Grégoire's public adherence to their cause. From the first his evaluation of the colonial problem differed from theirs. He saw no reason to make mulatto enfranchisement conditional upon the abolition of either slavery or the slave trade, no matter how desirable the latter goals might be. He was able to impose his ideas on the society because very few Amis des Noirs had been elected to the Estates. Of the organization's prerevolutionary members, only Jérôme Pétion and the Marquis de Lafayette played an important role in the Assembly. In 1789, such other leading figures as Jacques Necker, Count Mirabeau, and the Abbé Sieyès had briefly belonged to and still sympathized with the club's goals, but, completely involved in other matters, they had ceased attending the society's meetings even before the Estates General opened.

The Amis des Noirs needed a spokesman in the legislature, a delegate with some influence who was not too absorbed by major issues, who had an unsullied reputation, and who could devote time to the Africans in the colonies. Grégoire met these qualifications, and as the abolitionists' major representative, he increasingly focused their energies upon the mulatto cause until it overshadowed all other aspects of the colonial race problem.[22]

Immediately after Grégoire addressed the National Assembly,

the Société des Amis des Noirs elected him to honorary membership. His subsequent relations with this society are unclear. Honorary membership apparently gave him full rights, and in 1791 he briefly served as president. In cooperation with Pétion, he presented the club's addresses to the Assembly; in return, the society answered the planters' charges against him. It also paid for some of his promulatto publications and provided him with favorable publicity in the pages of its unofficial journal, the *Patriote françois*. Yet the society continued to be controlled by its founders, Jacques-Pierre Brissot, the Marquis de Condorcet, Pétion, and Etienne Clavière, until it faded out of existence in 1792.[23]

As long as the society survived, Grégoire's actions on behalf of mulattoes and Negroes were not always well coordinated with its strategy. Much as he agreed in theory with the need for concerted action, he was too much of a dogmatist to be limited by his friends' opinions, and he never became a good party man. In a way, the Société des Amis des Noirs needed him more than he needed it, and he was not afraid to act alone. If the club did not wish to follow his advice, he could get along without it, and he pursued egalitarian principles long after it passed out of existence.

NOTES

1. *Essai sur la régénération*, p. 128 and *Motion en faveur des juifs*, pp. 43–44. Compare with Roederer to the editor of the *Journal de Paris*, April 1788, AN, 29 AP 101, p. 278 verso. One of Grégoire's distant relatives owned land in Saint-Domingue. Quite probably Grégoire knew nothing about this individual or his land claims before he became a national figure; see Grégoire to Cher citoyen et cousin, 29 Pluviôse year 5 [*sic* for 7] (17 Feb. 1799), BM Lunéville, 52, and St. Hillaire to Grégoire, 17 Ventôse year 7 (7 March 1799), BPR, MNO.

2. Hyslop, *French Nationalism*, pp. 142, 276–77. The works of Guillaume-Thomas Raynal and Jacques-Henri Bernadin de Saint-Pierre were best sellers for their time; still they circulated among a very limited audience.

3. Seeber, *Antislavery Opinion in France*, pp. 42, 84.

4. Cahen, "La Société des Amis des Noirs et Condorcet"; Perroud, "La Société française des Amis des Noirs"; Gottschalk, *Lafayette Between the American and the French Revolution*, p. 370. See Martin, "La Doctrine coloniale de la France en 1789," pp. 38–39 for English motives in encouraging the French abolitionists.

5. For antislavery opinion in general, see Seeber, *Antislavery Opinion*, and Hardy, *The Negro Question in the French Revolution*.

6. Davis, *Problem of Slavery*, pp. 428–34 and Seeber, *Antislavery Opinion*, p. 91. Dobson points out how the 1784 decree led the port merchants to defend slavery as part of the status quo which had been so profitable for them; see "The Philosophe and the Negro Question," pp. 9–10. For aristocratic interests in the colonies, see Soboul, *La France*, p. 75.

7. Debien, *Les colons de Saint-Domingue et la Révolution*, pp. 58–59, 65–66; Boissonnade, *St. Domingue à la veille de la Révolution*, p. 70.

8. The problem of absentee ownership was more acute in Saint-Domingue than in the rest of the French West Indies, but whites in all of the French Caribbean territories were divided between wealthy landowners and the poorer class who served as superintendents, commercial agents, and the like; Roberts, *The French in the West Indies*, pp. 69, 127.

9. The first royal letters of convocation were sent only to those provinces which had participated in the last Estates General. This excluded Lorraine and Corsica as well as the West Indian territories. Protests from the Northeast forced the ministry to reverse its stand, but Louis had not acceded to the planters' request by the time that the Estates opened. For Grégoire's nonchalant acceptance of the landowners' request for representation; "Notes sur les Etats Généraux," entry for 8 June 1789, anon. collection in Paris, and letter to Guilbert, 6 July 1789, GS Nancy, MB 17, p. 5.

10. Brette, "Les Gens de couleur libres et leurs députés en 1789," pp. 329–31; minutes of the Massiac Club, 7 Sept. 1789, AN, W 15, no. 3; *Extrait du procès-verbal de l'assemblée des*

citoyens libres et propriétaires de couleur des isles et colonies Françoises, constituée sous le titre de Colons Américains (n.p., 1789), p. 3. The Massiac Club, to which the mulattoes first appealed, disapproved of all colonial representation in the legislature, white, mulatto, or Negro.

11. Adresse à l'Assemblée Nationale, pour les citoyens-Libres de Couleur, des Isles & Colonies Françoises (n.p., 1789); Patriote françois, 23 Oct. 1789.

12. Labourie to the Massiac Club, 1 Dec. 1789, AN, W 15, no. 3; Courrier de Provence, 24 Oct. 1789, pp. 72, 74; Lettre des citoyens de couleur; Dernieres observations des citoyens du couleur des isles et colonies françoises; Observations très-essentielles; Cocherel, Observations; Cournand, Réponse aux observations, pp. 18–19; Bradby, Life of Barnave, 2:334.

13. The question of why the English encouraged French abolitionists will continue to provoke controversy as long as anyone is interested in the antislavery movement. English authors argue that the British supported French abolition because they feared that unilateral renunciation of the trade would be both ineffective and disastrous for British planters. Frenchmen, however, believed that Pitt cynically used humanitarian sentiment as a way to destroy the French empire, and they doubted that the English intended to outlaw the trade. Hence any French abolitionist was a witting or naive tool of the old commercial rival; see: the controversy over Clarkson in the Patriote françois throughout September 1789; [Moreau de Saint-Méry], Observations, pp. 51–54; Découverte d'une conspiration contre les intérêts de la France, pp. 3–4; Clarkson, History of the Rise, pp. 123–63.

14. Clarkson, History of the Rise, p. 152.

15. See his Motion en faveur des juifs, pp. xvi, 43–44. Contrary to the planters' later assertion, Grégoire was not responsible for reporting on mulatto representation; ibid., pp. xv–xvi.

16. Cobban includes, among other reasons for retaining the colonial caste system, the nobles' desire to retain in the colonies economic opportunities which were closed to them in France; see Aspects of the French Revolution, p. 146.

17. Debien (Les colons, pp. 58–59) indicates that one of the incentives for the planters' organization was the news of the forma-

tion of the Société des Amis des Noirs. In July 1789, however, the Massiac Club split over the issue of participation in French political affairs, and the radical landowners, led by the Marquis Louis-Marthe Gouy d'Arsy, formed a separate society; Debien, *Les colons,* pp. 65–66.

18. De Curt, *Motion; Point du jour,* 28 Nov. 1789, p. 297. The Massiac Club protested against the presentation of such a petition; see Labourie to the Massiac Club, 1 Dec. 1789, AN, W 15, no. 3; Massiac Club to Bordeaux colons, 15 Dec. 1789, AN, DXXV 90, vol. 2, pp. 7–7 verso, and different version in AN, W 15, no. 3.

19. Somewhat different versions of Grégoire's speech are given in AP 10:362; *Patriote françois,* 5 Dec. 1789; *Journal des Etats-Généraux* 6:277; *Courrier de Provence,* 5 Dec. 1789, pp. 340–42.

20. Grégoire, *Mémoire en faveur des gens de couleur,* p. 35.

21. "La conviction des faux principes de la Société des Amis des Noirs et des defenseurs des gens de couleurs," minutes of the Massiac Club, Dec. 1789, AN, DXXV 88, no. 840, p. 11; [Moreau de Saint-Méry], *Observations;* Debien, *Les colons,* pp. 58–59.

22. Pétion was involved in financial questions and Lafayette in military affairs. Grégoire had not been appointed to any committee which discussed his major interests—religion, agriculture, and education—and although he spoke on widely diverse topics, his activities lacked focus. Some members of the society, moreover, hesitated to rely too heavily upon Mirabeau because of his personal reputation; see Ellery, *Brissot de Warville,* pp. 189–94. The *Patriote françois,* between December 1789 and March 1790, shows how the mulatto question displaced the slave trade issue.

23. Grégoire probably could not have joined as a regular member because its dues were one louis or one hundred livres, equivalent, in 1947, to $100 in American currency; see R. R. Palmer's note in Georges Lefebvre, *The Coming of the French Revolution,* trans. R. R. Palmer (New York: Vintage Books, 1958), p. 11n. For Grégoire's admission as an honorary member: extract from minutes of the Société des Amis des Noirs, 4 Dec. 1789, BPR, TUVWXYZ; *Patriote françois,* 7 Dec. 1789. All of the society's publications were signed by Brissot, Condorcet, Clavière, or Pétion as president or secretary.

4

The National Assembly
and the Mulattoes

The National Assembly's regulations circumscribed Grégoire's ability to assist the mulattoes. Since he did not belong to any of the committees which had jurisdiction over imperial or constitutional questions, he could only try to prevent the planters from achieving a dominant voice in colonial affairs. His 3 December speech, for example, temporarily blocked their motion to establish a colonial committee; yet his intervention brought mulattoes no closer to citizenship or to social equality than they had been before.

The possibility of promoting egalitarian legislation increased for Grégoire when he became president of the Committee for Reports in January 1790. This committee was responsible for studying and making recommendations on petitions and addresses submitted to the Assembly, but it could act only on matters that were referred to it. Grégoire, however, did not have to wait for very long after his appointment because in February the Bordeaux patriotic society asked the Assembly to guarantee both the metropolitan monopoly over colonial trade and the maintenance of slavery.

The Bordeaux petition naturally antagonized the abolitionists; it also divided the procolonial alliance. Rather than ignore
the petition, the planters, anxious to open Caribbean ports to
foreign vessels, wanted the Assembly to reject it formally. The
Assembly, therefore, referred the address to its Committee for
Reports and scheduled a debate.[1]

Grégoire assumed personal responsibility for recommending
to the Assembly what action it should take on the Bordeaux
petition. He was not interested in the commercial question, but
he hoped to use the address as a pretext for proposing mulatto
enfranchisement. However, when he canvassed the deputies, he
found that even the Jacobins were reluctant to interfere with
the colonial caste system. Several of the club's more prominent
members owned colonial land, and, although these members
previously had refrained from mentioning the colonies in the
society, they now prevented the club from adopting a uniform
imperial policy.

Realizing that the Assembly would refuse to enfranchise
mulattoes, Grégoire limited his report on the Bordeaux petition
to a description of the disorderly conditions in the French West
Indies. But his speech had a different effect from what was intended. His analysis was rambling and confused, and, by ob-
scuring rather than clarifying the issues, he clearly demonstrated
his inability to propose a coherent colonial policy. His speech
convinced the Assembly that imperial regulations should be left
to deputies who knew something about the colonies.

On 2 March the Assembly appointed a colonial committee
composed of planter and mercantile representatives and led by
Antoine-Pierre Barnave, a deputy who had helped organize
the Jacobin Club a year before. Although he had no personal
interest in the Caribbean, he lived with Alexandre Lameth, a
radical noble who owned extensive property in the West Indies.
Under Barnave's leadership, this committee could scarcely be
expected to sympathize with the mulattoes' demands. Yet it
took from Grégoire and the Committee for Reports the right

to make recommendations on both slave trading and mulatto enfranchisement.[2]

The Assembly asked the Colonial Committee to propose solutions for such urgent West Indian problems as providing adequate food supplies and preventing slave revolts. Because these questions went far beyond the racial and commercial issues which appeared on the surface, the Assembly also authorized the committee to prepare a general outline for an imperial constitution. This latter task absorbed most of the committee's energy, but it was an impossible assignment.

Until the Assembly clearly defined the nature of the metropolitan constitution, the Colonial Committee could hardly write one for the colonies. For example, the problem of dividing authority between central and local governments depended ultimately upon whether France was to be a federated or a centralized nation. Such a decision by the Assembly would have established which body should specify electoral qualifications and trade regulations. Yet the National Assembly waited until its final sessions before it agreed to decentralize the empire. In the meantime, the Colonial Committee could only propose contradictory measures that went from one extreme to the other.

The Colonial Committee was also caught in the midst of a jurisdictional dispute between the ministry and the legislature. Traditionally, the minister of the navy determined and administered policy for the empire. Although conservative landowners urged the minister to resist legislative encroachment, he usually failed to defend his authority. Still, the Assembly expected the minister to enforce decisions which he had not made and of which he frequently disapproved. This situation not only created friction between the two branches of government, but it encouraged the colonists to ignore metropolitan regulations.

Even if it could not decide the constitutional issues, the Colonial Committee had to present a preliminary report before the situation in the colonies worsened. Current West Indian disorders had arisen out of a conflict between royal officials and the colonial assemblies that had sprung up illegally during 1788 and 1789. The National Assembly had to determine the status and jurisdiction of these local bodies.

Early in 1790 most metropolitan deputies thought the colonies should have their own legislatures. The members, however, disagreed about the legality of the existing assemblies and how much authority should be allotted to them. Some deputies objected to recognizing the assemblies because they lacked mulatto members. Others were willing to legitimize the existing bodies but insisted upon limiting their jurisdiction to purely domestic matters. The colonial deputies, for their part, wanted the all-white legislatures to be virtually autonomous. Somehow the Colonial Committee had to propose regulations which a majority of the deputies would accept and which the ministry would be willing to enforce.

On 8 March, Barnave, speaking for the Colonial Committee, proposed granting a broad series of powers to the existing legislatures. He suggested that these bodies be authorized to write their own constitutions within a general framework designed to safeguard metropolitan interests. Anxious to avoid the most emotional issue, he recommended leaving each colony free to decide upon mulatto enfranchisement.[3]

Both colonists and promulatto deputies objected to the last provision in Barnave's report. They believed indecisiveness in this matter would encourage uprisings in those colonies where the local assemblies denied civil rights to mulattoes. On the whole, Barnave's bill assigned far more authority to the colonies than either the promulatto or the port deputies were willing to relinquish. The Assembly, therefore, refused to adopt the guidelines without a thorough discussion.

In the debates on Barnave's guidelines held on 28 March 1790, the mulatto question provoked considerable controversy and overshadowed all other issues. Grégoire, speaking for the abolitionists, demanded clarification of the article (number 4) which enfranchised "all persons" who had lived in a district for two years and had paid the requisite amount of taxes. Were mulattoes persons or not? One planter, Grégoire asserted, had conceded mulatto eligibility under the phrasing of this clause.

Although Grégoire avoided philosophical or theoretical arguments, his statements enraged the planters. They asked the Assembly either to suppress article four or to reword it so as to exclude mulattoes explicitly. Contrary to advice from pro-mulatto and colonial deputies, the majority of the Assembly decided to retain the original vague phrasing and thereby to leave local assemblies free to establish their own electoral requirements. Since these bodies had been elected without mulatto participation, the Assembly's decision effectively excluded free men who fulfilled residence and property requirements.[4]

The colonial deputies had to be satisfied with the 28 March law's implicit disenfranchisement of mulattoes. Anxious to prevent the mulattoes from interpreting the law in their own favor, the planters insisted upon deleting all references to mulatto eligibility from the Assembly's minutes. The official records of the 28 March session condensed Grégoire's proposal and the subsequent debate into two laconic statements: "A member made a proposal regarding article IV relating to mulattoes" and "several [members] demanded that there be no discussion of this proposition." Grégoire, according to the revised minutes, was the only deputy interested in mulattoes, and in the future, the colonists would vent most of their venom on him.[5]

The majority of the Assembly assumed that it had settled the colonial problem by authorizing a committee to determine policy and by granting colonial legislatures jurisdiction over mulatto rights. Yet the March 1790 legislation exacerbated rather than resolved racial tensions in the French West Indies. These laws dissatisfied everyone, and they provided no peaceful means for judging between conflicting interpretations.[6]

While both sides were deciding for themselves what the March laws meant, civil war between whites, mulattoes, and royal officials erupted again in Saint-Domingue. In the midst of this chaos, shortly after the 28 March instructions were adopted a young mulatto named Vincent Ogé secretly left France for Saint-Domingue. He had played an active role in mulatto affairs in Paris and had consulted with Grégoire and others concerning the interpretation of the March guidelines. After leaving France he reportedly received money from a member of the English Slave Trade Committee, purchased weapons in the United States, and then sailed to the Caribbean.[7] His departure bode ill for the already troubled colony.

In mid-October, reports of renewed disorders in the Caribbean forced the white colonists to bring the imperial question before the Assembly. In desperation they requested military reinforcements, and the Assembly agreed to send more soldiers. But on 12 October, without debate, the Assembly added two controversial and contradictory provisions to the legislation which authorized the minister to send troops. Angered by the Saint-Domingue General Assembly's inability to maintain order, the metropolitan legislature ordered its dissolution. Even while the deputies abolished the colony's constitutional assembly, they pledged not to enact any laws "on the status of persons" save by request of the colonists themselves. The October law did not explain precisely how the people of Saint-Domingue were to make their desires known.[8]

The October law was enacted without debate. Grégoire and his promulatto colleagues objected to its provisions and protested their inability to speak against it. They thought that the metropolitan assembly should not renounce its power to determine citizenship. They also criticized the representatives for repudiating an assembly which they had already recognized.

Grégoire's objections to the 12 October law went even further than did those of his colleagues. He thought it contradicted the promises and principles embodied in the March law. In addition, it violated the abstract standards of justice proclaimed in the Declaration of the Rights of Man. Liberty and equality, he asserted, were natural laws "outside and prior to the constitution"—an argument which he previously had used to justify Jewish requests for civil rights—and the only way to achieve stability was to incorporate the principles of natural law into the constitution. Because mulattoes inevitably would be influenced by the "volcano of liberty set alight in France," they would revolt unless they were granted their natural rights. Without the "grand principles of equality, of justice, which nature inspires, which religion consecrates," he asserted, "men will be degraded and empires will collapse."[9]

Grégoire objected to the 12 October law on constitutional as well as egalitarian grounds. He was a rigid centralist, and he thought colonial assemblies should control only those day-to-day questions which the metropolitan legislature, located at least three weeks' sailing time away, could not supervise. He certainly did not wish to give colonial legislatures jurisdiction over citizenship. Yet, along with his abolitionist colleagues, he saw no reason to dissolve an assembly which had received official sanction. To do so would be inconsistent and, he feared, would lead to further confusion and disorder in the colonies.[10]

Unable to voice his opinions before the Assembly, Grégoire published the speech which he had planned to present on 12 October. His fellow deputies found the arguments in his *Lettre aux philanthropes* unconvincing. They were certain the empire would collapse if the Assembly tried to impose the Declaration of Rights upon unwilling colonists.

Since appeals to self-interest contradicted Grégoire's moralistic outlook, he tried to deemphasize them. Yet he might have persuaded more of his uncommitted colleagues if he had tempered his rhetoric and concentrated upon his psychologically sound arguments concerning the mulattoes' desire to maintain colonial stability (including slavery). Although he tried to present practical reasons for enfranchising mulattoes, he knew far too little about the colonies, and this part of his pamphlet was either ignored or easily refuted by planters who had actually lived in the West Indies.

The planters disregarded Grégoire's common sense arguments and cited his appeals to natural law as grounds for accusations of incendiarism. Their charges seemed to be substantiated when, at almost the same time as he warned that a mulatto uprising would occur, his young friend Ogé arrived in LeCap and led a revolt against the whites.

French colonial officials captured Ogé a few weeks after he landed and tried to discover who in France had helped and advised his expedition. Ogé probably had not confided his plans to his friends in Paris, and he refused to implicate any of the promulatto deputies. Instead he attributed his interpretation of the March laws to "the reporter [Barnave] and to all the members of the National Assembly" who had advised him "that the words *all persons* include all free men without distinction of color." He quoted the Assembly as having refused to make "any color distinctions among men."[11] Even though Ogé's testimony could not be used against the promulatto deputies in general or Grégoire in particular, planters in Saint-Domingue and France remained convinced of the philanthropists' complicity in the mulatto uprising.

Ogé's rebellion led the National Assembly to usurp what remained of the ministry's authority over the colonies. The deputies were willing to send more troops only if French civil authority were strengthened. Because royal officials under the Council of State no longer governed the colonies, and because the deputies refused to place French soldiers under the jurisdiction of local assemblies, the National Assembly had to send its own officials. Consequently, at the end of November the Assembly suspended those colonial legislatures which had led rebellions against the metropolis and instructed the minister of the navy to send civil commissioners to all the Caribbean territories.

A number of deputies criticized the plan to send civil officials to the colonies. Grégoire tried to point out the contradiction between this law and the Assembly's two previous colonial laws. But the members were in no mood to listen to a delegate whom they held responsible for Ogé's expedition, and they shouted him down when he tried to speak.[12] Although the planters were pleased with the Assembly's decision to dispatch additional soldiers to the embattled colony, they were no more in favor of appointing civil commissioners than was Grégoire.

Both procolonial and promulatto deputies persisted in their objections, and the commissioners did not leave France for another year. The troops they were supposed to accompany also remained in France. Thus the Assembly destroyed the vestiges of royal authority in the colonies and antagonized the whites there, but it failed to reassert its own control. It aggravated tensions and was unable to restore tranquility to the French West Indies.

The colonial deputies were now faced with a dilemma. Unsettled conditions in the Caribbean demonstrated to the landowners how greatly they depended upon the metropolis and how impractical were their demands for colonial autonomy.[13] Since they needed French troops, they could not refuse to discuss the colonies in the Assembly. Yet they saw no reason for defending the islands or, indeed, for even remaining within the French empire if the institution of slavery were to be challenged.

The colonial deputies, hoping to escape the dangers posed by their reliance upon the metropolis even while they benefited from their ties with France, asked the Assembly to grant to the Colonial Committee the exclusive right to initiate all imperial legislation. This measure would prevent other committees, such as the Commercial Committee, from proposing the abolition of slave trading. The procolonialists suffered a significant defeat when, in mid-January 1791, the Assembly refused to remove subjects related to the empire from the jurisdiction of the Agricultural, Commercial, and Naval Committees.[14]

While the planters pondered their next move, the promulatto deputies maintained their silence in the Assembly. The abolitionists assumed that additional time would work to their advantage. Certain they could gain new adherents in the Assembly by arousing public opinion, the Amis des Noirs increased their propaganda in the spring of 1791. Most of their pamphlets were addressed to the rapidly proliferating popular societies affiliated with the Jacobin Club in Paris. These provincial associations proved increasingly receptive to egalitarian propaganda, but until 1791 they did not have sufficient influence to sway either the Paris club, which still was dominated by Barnave and his friends, or the National Assembly.

The abolitionists' patience was eventually rewarded. After Grégoire became president of the Assembly on 18 January 1791, the planters dared not renew their attempt to establish the Colonial Committee's exclusive jurisdiction over all aspects of imperial policy. By the time Grégoire's term ended, reports of a new uprising in Martinique forced the planters to request military reinforcements, even though in doing so they risked an open debate on the colonies.

In February the Assembly quietly voted to send more troops. But, according to the November 1790 law, these soldiers could not depart until the Assembly adopted instructions for the civil commissioners who were supposed to accompany them. The promulatto deputies, supported by the port merchants, who by this time had lost their exclusive trading rights, prevented automatic passage of the Colonial Committee's instructions. Reluctantly, the planters agreed to an unlimited debate.[15] Thus desperation over the military situation in the Caribbean proved a useful tool for the promulatto deputies.

Planter and promulatto deputies alike prepared for the first open debate on colonial affairs to be held in almost a year. Although both sides appealed to public opinion, they also maneuvered behind the scenes, hoping to convince additional deputies. The planters, for example, launched a bitter attack on what they called incendiary writings by Grégoire, Pétion, and Brissot in order to undermine the abolitionists' influence among the uncommitted representatives.[16]

The planters tried to lure Grégoire away from his abolitionist allies. As unofficial spokesman for the Amis des Noirs in the Assembly and as a prominent supporter of the Civil Constitution of the Clergy—a very popular reform among radicals—Grégoire's desertion would have seriously injured the mulatto cause.[17] Even while some landowners vehemently attacked his writings, others asked him to temper his humanitarianism in the interest of reason and tranquility. Grégoire's sensitivity to human suffering, they asserted, was making him an "instrument of private interests." Grégoire tried to be reasonable. In private conversations he spoke in favor of gradual emancipation and reportedly said that immediate abolition would have the same effect as "kicking a pregnant woman to make her give birth sooner."[18]

Grégoire's unfortunate language revived the landowners' suspicions concerning his motives. When they tried to show him how any change in the imperial caste system would lead first to colonial independence and then to an alliance between the colonies and England, Grégoire, according to later testimony, interrupted the speaker "with the impatience of a man whose secret had been discovered."[19] He was, the landowners decided, committed to the destruction of the empire, and they were convinced that his egalitarian stand merely masked his subversive activities.

The planters could not persuade Grégoire because they misunderstood his reasons for advocating racial equality. They erroneously attributed his concern about mulattoes to either humanitarian or treasonable motives. The later charge had no foundation in reality, and humanitarianism played only a secondary role in Grégoire's thought.

Much as Grégoire sympathized with human suffering, he was

above all a Catholic priest. Because his interest in social questions was rooted in his religious ideology, he could not compromise as the planters expected him to do. For him the eternal
principles embodied in the Declaration of Rights were secular
versions of God's commandments which could not be modified,
but he tried to be practical. Even though he admitted that
slavery could not be abolished, he rejected as anti-Christian the
racial system upon which it was based and could see no justification, either pragmatic or ideological, for discriminating against
mulattoes.[20] He had felt the same way about enfranchising
Ashkenazim, and, because mulattoes were descendants of
Frenchmen, he saw even less reason for excluding them from
citizenship.

Finding Grégoire adamant in his defense of mulatto rights,
the planters tried a new tactic. They asked Barnave to institute
legal procedings against him under a provision of the 8 March
1790 law that made responsibility for colonial disorders a crime
against the nation. In so doing they established a dangerous
precedent of demanding judicial revenge against their opponents, the full implications of which would not be evident for
another year.

Barnave refused to comply with the colonists' plans. Although
Grégoire had launched a bitter personal attack on him one
year before, and although he thought Grégoire's pamphlets had
encouraged mulatto insubordination, he did not share the
planters' hatred. In any case, Grégoire's recent election as
Constitutional bishop of Blois probably would have made such
a step ill advised.[21]

For a short period in the spring of 1791 both Grégoire and
Barnave tried to avoid personal vituperation. Early in March,
when new and acrimonious arguments erupted between promulatto and procolonial deputies, Grégoire attempted to live
up to his new episcopal dignity and unsuccessfully tried to serve
as a moderator. Barnave, for his part, recognized the personal
animosity his name aroused among both planters and aboli-

tionists.[22] When the long-awaited instructions for the civil commissioners were completed, he assigned the task of reporting them to another member of the Colonial Committee, the merchant deputy, François-Pascal Delâtre. This move also proved unsuccessful, and Barnave was forced to take an active part in the subsequent debates.

Delâtre presented the Colonial Committee's proposed instructions on 9 May 1791. Grégoire rapidly forgot his role as prelate and entered the debates with his customary vigor. Throughout the week-long discussion which preceded the Assembly's decision to enfranchise a very limited number of mulattoes, he played an active, sometimes violent, and definitely unepiscopal role. He placed responsibility for colonial disorders at the planters' feet and reproached the Colonial Committee for having listened to the landowners rather than to the Amis des Noirs. Instead of discussing Delâtre's proposals, he read a long speech explaining why mulattoes should be given political rights. In it he repeated the arguments he had used during the preceding eighteen months. His speech probably did not persuade many deputies.

Grégoire's most important function during the May 1791 debates was to act as an irritant, deliberately goading the planters into taking an extreme position which discredited them before the rest of the Assembly. He argued that the abolitionists were being reasonable and moderate because they were asking only for mulatto enfranchisement rather than immediate freedom for slaves. Turning to Barnave, he forced the deputy to concede that the controversial article four of the 28 March 1790 instruction "obviously [did] not contain any exclusions." But Barnave added in the defense of its vague phraseology (and in the interest of sanity and pragmatism), "if you demand more you will bring trouble to the colonies."[23] He, at least, did not regard Grégoire's request for mulatto enfranchisement as moderate.

Grégoire figured conspicuously in the debates on Delâtre's

report, but for once his oratory paled in comparison with that of another colleague, Maximilien Robespierre. This deputy had only recently begun to take a prominent part in the Assembly's debates. Now he pleaded with the representatives not to destroy the foundation upon which French liberty rested, the Declaration of Rights.

> Let the colonies perish! [he declaimed] if they cost you your happiness, your glory, your liberty. I repeat, let the colonies perish if the planters, with their threats, try to force us to legislate in their private interests! I declare in the name of the Assembly, in the name of those members of the Assembly who do not want to destroy the Constitution, I declare in the name of the entire nation which wishes to be free, that we will not sacrifice to the colonial deputies . . . neither the nation, nor the colonies, nor the whole of humanity. I conclude, and I say that any other course, whatever it might be, is preferable.[24]

This heated dispute over mulatto rights overshadowed the supposed topic of debate, the instructions for the civil commissioners. The issue was fought in the press, in the Assembly and its galleries, and, most important of all, in the Jacobin Club. Focusing on Grégoire, the planters accused him of voting for England by supporting mulatto enfranchisement. He ignored their charges, and Julien Raimond, the leading mulatto pamphleteer, answered in his stead.[25]

By this time the crucial struggle within the Jacobin Club had been in progress for several weeks. Throughout April, Brissot had steadily undermined the landowners' influence in the society, both through his own membership and through his attacks on individuals in the pages of the *Patriote françois*. Quite unexpectedly, his efforts bore fruit on 12 May when the society chose Robespierre as its president. Under Robespierre's leadership, the Jacobins admitted a mulatto delegate and expelled a leading planter. Confident of the society's support in the Assembly, the promulatto deputies decided to risk a vote on the question of enfranchising mulattoes.[26]

When the debates resumed on 13 May Grégoire again served as spokesman for the mulatto cause. In another lengthy speech he repeated his usual appeals to the eternal principles of justice, rephrasing the arguments which he had used in his *Lettre aux philanthropes*. By this time he apparently had forgotten about the Jews because he ignored several attempts to compare Jewish and mulatto disenfranchisement. French voting requirements, he insisted, were based on financial qualifications rather than hereditary distinctions. He disapproved of excluding people on racial grounds, especially if racial heritage also served as the basis for social and economic discrimination. This type of racially founded civil discrimination characterized Jews as well as mulattoes, but Grégoire refused to be distracted and did not mention his former protégés.[27]

The motion discussed on 13 and 15 May dissatisfied the abolitionists because it proposed to enfranchise only a very small number of mulattoes. The bill limited civil rights to those whose parents had been legally married and who met the financial qualifications established in the still uncompleted French constitution. By recognizing existing colonial legislatures—all of which disqualified mulattoes and which supposedly had been disbanded by the November 1790 law—the Assembly further reduced the number of enfranchised mulattoes. Incidentally, the law also added to existing confusion about the status of the colonial legislatures.

During the closing debates on the 15 May law, Grégoire displayed an unusual degree of realism by concentrating on the mulatto question and agreeing to postpone the entire problem of Negro emancipation. Yet he disliked the bill. When he tried to protest against the small number of mulattoes that it enfranchised, however, the majority, disgruntled over the amount of time consumed by what it considered to be a peripheral question, denied him the floor and closed the debate.

*"All men are equal; it is not birth but virtue alone that
makes the difference."*
*"Reason, portrayed by a woman crowned with the sacred fire of
patriotism, places a level over the white man and the man of
color. Behind [the latter] are a cornucopia, a banana tree,
and fertile lands. He leans on the Rights of Man and holds in
his other hand the Decree of 15 May concerning men of color.
Reason is impelled by Nature who is crowned with fruits and has
fourteen breasts. She is seated on a leather sack out of
which fly the demons of aristocracy, egoism—who by its avarice
wishes to have all, injustice, [and] discord or insurrection,
[all of whom are] about to cross the sea in the background."*

The law passed even though Grégoire, along with Pétion and
Robespierre, voted against it.[28] Once again the majority believed that it had permanently solved the racial problem in the
colonies.

NOTES

1. The Société des Amis des Noirs had submitted a petition on 5 Feb. 1790, and the Bordeaux petition was, in part, a response; see AN, DXXV, C 115, no. 3, p. 3; *Courrier de Provence*, 27 Feb. 1790, pp. 397, 398; *Patriote françois*, 23 and 27 Feb. 1790; *Gazette de Paris*, 28 Feb. 1790; AN, C 37, dos. 319, p. 1; AP 11:760; *Journal des Etats-Généraux* 9:81–85. The conservative planters cautioned against all petitions to the Assembly, but their advice was ignored; Massiac Club to Colons réunis à Bordeaux, 20 Feb. 1790, AN, DXXV 86, no. 827, p. 31.

2. Minutes of the National Assembly, 1 and 2 March 1790, AN, C 37, dos. 319, pp. 1, 3; *Patriote françois*, 2 and 3 March 1790; *Affiches des évêchés*, supplement, 7 March 1790, p. 103; *Courrier de Provence*, 2–5 March 1790, pp. 445, 463–66, 472–82, 490–93; *Journal des Etats-Généraux* 9:106–8; *Moniteur*, réimpression, 3 and 4 March 1790, pp. 505–7 and 512–13; AP 11:760–63; Pellerin, *Réflexions sur la traite des noirs*, submitted to the Assembly on 1 March 1790. This committee's jurisdiction, however, overlapped with the various committees which discussed commercial, agricultural, and constitutional questions.

3. Barnave, *Rapport fait a l'Assemblée nationale*; Deschamps, *La Constituante et les colonies*, pp. 81, 89.

4. AP 12:383; *Gazette de Paris*, 30 March 1790; *Point du jour*, 30 March 1790, pp. 221–24; *Journal de Paris*, 29 March 1790, p. 349; *Moniteur*, réimpression, 30 March 1790, pp. 732–33.

5. Minutes of the National Assembly, 28 March 1790, AN, C 37, dos. 324, p. 28; *Affiches américaines du Port-au-Prince*, 26 June and 10 July 1790, pp. 360 and 387; AP 31:304; *Journal de Paris*, 4 April 1790, p. 375.

6. Michel Colon to Labuissonière, 17 May 1790, copy in AN, F³ 195, colonies; Raimond letter of March 1790 in *Correspondance de Julien Raimond avec ses frères, de Saint-Domingue*, pp. 12–14; Clavière, *Adresse de la Société des Amis des Noirs, a l'Assemblée nationale*, pp. 19, 31; AP 31:304.

7. Various letters of the Massiac Club to port cities and to Saint-Domingue warning them of Ogé's plans, dated April and May 1790

in AN, DXXV 89, IX, pp. 52, 64 verso; AN, DXXV 86, no. 828, p. 34. Letters from the various port cities in May and June 1790, AN, DXXV 86, no. 828, pp. 38–47; Massiac Club minutes, 4 June 1790, AN, DXXV 89, IX, 72 verso; Cole, *Christophe*, p. 32.

8. *Procès-verbal de l'Assemblée nationale* 51 (9 and 11 Oct. 1790): 22–23 and 9; *Moniteur*, réimpression, 12 and 13 Oct. 1790, pp. 97–100 and 102–7; *Courrier de Provence*, 14 Oct. 1790, pp. 201–2; *Point du jour*, 13 Oct. 1790, p. 141.

9. Grégoire, *Lettre aux philanthropes*, pp. 5n, 12, 21; *Motion en faveur des juifs*, p. 27.

10. *Journal des Etats-Généraux* 25:386; *Moniteur*, réimpression, 12 May 1791, p. 367.

11. Interrogation of Ogé, 20 and 21 Jan. 1791, italics in the original, AN, DXXV 58, dos. 574, p. 8ff; *Journal général de Saint-Domingue* (Cap Français), 1 Dec. 1790 and 26 Feb. 1791, pp. 76–77 and 255; *Courrier politique et littéraire du Cap-Français*, 3 March 1791, pp. 6–7; *Gazette du jour* (Cap Français), 6 Nov. 1790, p. 22; *Moniteur coloniale*, 28 and 30 Nov. 1790, pp. 103 and 111; *Adresse de l'Assemblée Provinciale de la Partie du Nord de Saint-Domingue, à l'Assemblée Nationale. Notes des Membres du Comité de Rédaction de l'Assemblée générale sur cette Adresse; Adresse de l'Assemblée provinciale de la partie du Nord de Saint domingue* [sic], *à l'Assemblée nationale.*

12. *Moniteur*, réimpression, 30 Nov. 1790, pp. 503–4, and 12 May 1791, p. 367; AP 21:126–27.

13. The planters already had requested military assistance from Governor Effingham in Jamaica. Since the British could only provide token forces, the planters had to renew their appeal to the National Assembly; Cole, *Christophe*, p. 38.

14. *Moniteur*, réimpression, 13 Jan. 1791, p. 99.

15. The law of 29 Nov. 1790 opened several additional Caribbean ports to foreign vessels; see *Moniteur*, réimpression, 30 Nov. 1790, pp. 502–4 and 13 Jan., 3 Feb., and 12 May 1791, pp. 99, 281–83, and 367; *Patriote françois*, 15 Jan. and 4 Feb. 1791; *Courrier de Provence* 12:343 and 14:38–39; Massiac Club to MM. & Chers Compatriotes, undated draft, AN, DXXV 88, no. 841, p. 58.

16. *Journal des Etats-Généraux* 22:222–23; *Procès-verbal de*

l'Assemblée nationale, vol. 73, annex 580, pp. 1–3; Dunkirk Chamber of Commerce to the National Assembly, 17 March 1791, copy in AN, F³ 126, colonies, pp. 425–27. For the abolitionists' influence in the provinces see: *Courrier de Provence*, 6 March 1791, p. 84; Angers patriotic society to the National Assembly, 21 March 1791, copy in AN, F³ 126, colonies, pp. 433–34; *Patriote françois*, 2 April 1791, p. 352.

17. The mulattoes had realized this one year before; see their letter to Grégoire, 27 July 1790 in Brissot, *Lettre à M. Barnave*, . . . *etc*. p. 32n; Saint-Domingue mulattoes to Raimond, 27 July 1790, *Correspondance*, p. 28.

18. Thomas Millet to Grégoire, open letter in *Annales politiques et littéraires*, 13 May 1791, p. 399; hearings of the Colonial Commission, 28 Pluviôse year 3 (16 Feb. 1795), AN, DXXV 91, no. 1045, p. 43; *Moniteur*, réimpression, 7 March 1791, pp. 556–57.

19. Hearings of the Colonial Commission, 21 Pluviôse year 3 (9 Feb. 1795), AN, DXXV 91, no. 1038, pp. 34 verso-35; statements by Pierre-François Page and Thomas Millet in [Garran de Coulon], *Débats entre les accusateurs et les accusés*, 2:225; Brissot, *Réplique*, pp. 53–54; *Patriote françois*, 21 and supplement, 28 Feb. 1791, pp. 188 and 217–18; ibid., supplement, January to June 1791, p. 7; Aulard, ed., *La Société des Jacobins*, 2:263; Mme Roland to Bancal-des-Issarts, 15 March 1791, BN, NAF 9534, p. 95, reprinted in Bancal-des-Issarts, ed., *Lettres autographes de Madame Roland*, p. 200; Moreau de Saint-Méry, *Considérations présentées*.

20. This attitude was shared by other abolitionists; Jordan, *White Over Black*, p. 294.

21. Massiac Club minutes, 28 April 1791, AN DXXV 89, X, 52–56. The planters' request was not unique. For a similar attempt to silence Marat; Louis R. Gottschalk, *Jean-Paul Marat: A Study in Radicalism* (1927: reprint ed., Chicago: University of Chicago Press, 1967), p. 67. See also Bradby, 2:211 and 1:288; Grégoire, *Réflexions générales sur le duel*.

22. Debien, *Les colons*, p. 189. For the planters' attacks on Barnave: *Journal de M. Suleau* 2:71.

23. AP 26:43; *Journal des Etats-Généraux* 25:381–94, 395–411; *Patriote françois*, 13 May 1791; *Moniteur*, réimpression, 12 May 1791, pp. 366–67. For alteration of the minutes, see n. 4 and

n. 5; AP 25:737; *Journal des Etats-Généraux* 25:382–84.

24. Ellipsis in the original; *Moniteur* réimpression, 15 May 1791, p. 395.

25. "Liste des députes qui ont voté pour l'Angleterre contre la France . . ." reprinted in AP 26:25; Raimond, *Reponse aux considerations de M. Moreau, dit Saint-Méry*, p. 31.

26. Aulard, *Jacobins*, 2:413–15; Mme Roland to Bancal, 12 May 1790, BN, NAF 9534 p. 107, reprinted in Bancal-des-Issarts, *Lettres*, pp. 241, 245. Robespierre had only begun to play a significant role in the National Assembly during the previous month. Cobban (p. 145) attributed Robespierre's subsequent popularity among radicals to the speech on universal suffrage which he presented in April 1791.

27. AP 26:25–26. See Grégoire's *Lettre aux philanthropes*, p. 11. There are numerous reasons for Grégoire's different attitude. Some antimulatto deputies, like Goupil de Prefeln and Moreau de Saint-Méry, deliberately brought up the Jewish question to distract attention and to prove their point. If Grégoire fell into their trap he risked antagonizing such anti-Semitic promulatto deputies as Rewbell. Hence he followed the same strategy as did the moderate philo-Semites in December 1789 and January 1790 when they refused to link Jewish and Protestant emancipation. Moreover, the mulatto question in no way jeopardized religious reform, and it did not evoke the same emotional response which was used by conservative agitators in the Northeast to provoke antirevolutionary sentiment; *Moniteur*, réimpression, 14 May 1789, p. 381; Necheles, "The Abbé Grégoire's Work in Behalf of Jews, 1788–1791," *French Historical Studies* 6 (1969): 180–83.

28. AP 26:70–75; *Patriote françois*, 15 and 16 May 1791, pp. 534 and 537–38; *Procès-verbal de l'Assemblée nationale* 84 (15 May 1791): 5–8; *Ami des patriotes*, 21 May 1791, p. 179.

5

The Victory of the Planters and the End of the National Assembly

The May 15 law could have fulfilled its dual purpose of resolving racial conflict in the Caribbean and ending controversy in the metropolis only if it had been promulgated immediately. Several factors prevented this from happening, however. Among other considerations, the Assembly had to adopt precise instructions for any law which it sent to the colonies. But events intervened. First of all, before the members could discuss the necessary guidelines, the planters' reaction led some deputies to question the wisdom of this law.

As soon as the law was enacted, conservative and radical planters withdrew from the Assembly. Anxious to provide the metropolis with dramatic proof of colonial opposition to racial equality, the West Indian representatives deliberately fermented renewed civil strife in the Caribbean by sending to the islands copies of all recent speeches in favor of mulatto enfranchisement.[1]

The planters were more dismayed by the law's potential than by its immediate threat. It had been adopted over stifled opposition from egalitarians but with the support of French mercantile interests. Its passage marked the complete collapse of the procolonial alliance that, in the past, had usually prevented the Assembly from regulating Caribbean race relations. The breakdown of this coalition justified the conservative planters' earlier refusal to recognize legislative jurisdiction over the empire. Now, anticipating the worst, they planned to return (or to make their first visit) to their colonial properties.

The radical landowners, for their part, had suffered a rude shock. Confident that they could restrain humanitarian or egalitarian impulses, they had expected to use the revolutionary movement to achieve control over the colonies. Now only one course of action appeared open to them; they could withdraw from the Assembly because they reasoned that this might prevent further metropolitan interference since, according to them, the legislature had no jurisdiction over unrepresented territories. They consciously adopted many of the arguments employed by the British-American revolutionaries two decades before. Although their logic no more convinced the National Assembly to grant colonial autonomy than the American colonists' reasoning had persuaded the British Parliament in the 1770s, most deputies hesitated to aggravate colonial disturbances by promulgating the 15 May law.

The colonists' dismay over the 15 May law convinced the leading promulatto representatives, Grégoire, Robespierre, and Pétion, that its passage had been a significant victory. Upon reflection, they realized how far they had come since the days when the Assembly had stricken references to promulatto speeches from its records. The planters' withdrawal served the promulatto deputies' purposes even more than the law itself did.

The Jacobin Club suspended the colonists for "treason against the nation" when they refused to attend the Assembly. This gave Brissot an opportunity to wrest control over the Jacobins from Barnave and his friends, and for a brief time the Paris members could be expected to support the proposals of the Amis des Noirs in the Assembly.[2] Still, the Assembly failed to adopt the necessary guidelines, and controversy over imperial policy continued throughout the summer.

In the public debate over mulatto enfranchisement, Grégoire used his new dignity as bishop to justify his egalitarian activities. He insisted that as a priest he must defend those who were persecuted and underprivileged, such as Jews and mulattoes. He stressed Christian charity and mentioned neither his desire to achieve the same rights for all French subjects nor his intention to use egalitarian reforms as a vehicle for spreading Catholicism.

Grégoire's emphasis was politic because the leading figures in the colonial controversy—Brissot, Barnave, and Robespierre —were anti-Catholic, and many other influential deputies retained only a nominal allegiance to the church. Grégoire's devout Catholic colleagues, for their part, had constantly rejected his egalitarian ideas. Now they renewed their attacks on his philo-Semitism and again accused him of treason and subversion. On the whole, Grégoire rested upon his episcopal title and ignored his critics. While the Société des Amis des Noirs and the *Patriote françois* defended his activities, he concentrated on furthering the mulatto cause.[3]

Grégoire signaled his acceptance of the 15 May law in a jubilant *Lettre aux citoyens de couleur*. This pamphlet, rather than the law itself, became the center around which future controversy would rage because in it Grégoire not only bitterly attacked the planters but he also expressed dissatisfaction with the limitations incorporated into the recent law. Complete mulatto enfranchisement, according to him, was a practical necessity as well as an inevitable fulfillment of revolutionary promises. Only the mulattoes, he warned, would be able to counter the planters' schemes. He insisted that the white colonists wanted independence in order to escape their debts to French merchants, and he predicted that they would use the recent law as a pretext for severing all ties with France.

Grégoire expected the mulattoes to follow their economic

rather than their social interests. Thus he assumed that they would unite with white landowners because they also depended on slavery. Rather illogically, even while he pointed out how mulattoes would defend the West Indies, he threatened whatever status and wealth they presently had by pleading for the Negroes. "One day," he informed the mulattoes, "the sun will rise only on free men among you, and the beams of the stars which reflect this light will no longer shine on chains and slaves." Negroes, he added, "like you, are born and remain free and equal." Slavery was a temporary institution, created by "ridiculous prejudices," which would wither away when the time was ripe.[4]

Grégoire's *Lettre aux citoyens de couleur* received a mixed reception in France. In it he did not propose a practical program for abolishing slavery. Yet his prophetic statements sufficed to condemn the pamphlet in the eyes of both the conservatives, who rejected the principle of universal enfranchisement and the colonists, who demanded the retention of a racial caste system. The procolonial deputies violently attacked this pamphlet in the Assembly. One former colonial official criticized Grégoire's "apostolic zeal" as dangerous for the empire. But the delegates' mood had changed since October, and they now refused to silence Grégoire. Instead they shouted down his accusors and applauded when, in reply to charges of incendiarism, he read aloud passages purportedly showing his moderation.[5]

Despite this personal success, Grégoire and his promulatto friends again failed in their ultimate purpose. One of his colleagues hastily drew up instructions for the 15 May law, but the Assembly failed to adopt them, and the ministry refused to promulgate the law.

Disturbing as the planters' reaction to both the 15 May law and Grégoire's pamphlet were, still the most important reason why the Assembly failed to approve instructions for this law could be traced to the political crisis of June 1791, which overshadowed all other issues. Louis XVI's attempt to flee France on 21 June threatened to destroy the unfinished constitution and led to significant changes in the political balance in France.

Louis' defection permanently divided the deputies who two years before had advocated radical reforms for ailing French institutions. Although most of the 1789 conservatives had already abandoned politics and many of them had left France, the radicals' victory was still incomplete because a new conservative coalition was beginning to form. Deserters from the original Jacobin Club formed an alliance called the Feuillants. These deputies had once criticized the king's reluctance to accept such innovations as the religious reforms of 1790; now they regretted their harsh words and hoped to work out a compromise under which the king would resume his functions. Barnave acted as spokesman for the new conservatives and led the secession from the Jacobins.

Although a few of the remaining Jacobins advocated republicanism and Grégoire (who did not go quite so far) loudly denounced royal treason, he and many other radicals attended the meetings of both societies. Attempts at reunion failed, and a bitter fight developed between the two clubs over the loyalty of the members in Paris and in the affiliated provincial societies. Early in August the Feuillants instructed their followers to choose between them and the Jacobins. Grégoire, of course, remained with the more radical group. By 17 August the Jacobins claimed a majority of the original members because they continued to carry the Feuillants on their rolls. But the conservatives probably reflected the wishes of a greater part of the French population.[6]

The Feuillant secession from the Jacobins for a time completely destroyed the colonists' influence in that club. Even before Barnave and his followers withdrew, Brissot, who had joined only in January 1791, became a member of its committee of correspondence and on 17 October was elected president.

But the radical planters soon returned to the National Assembly and to the Jacobins. Their absence had not prevented the Assembly from discussing imperial problems as they had hoped, and they seized the opportunity presented by the June crisis to prove their loyalty to France by returning to the legislature. Without Barnave's prestige, they could not regain their controlling position in the Jacobins, but they persistently tried to reduce Grégoire's and Brissot's influence in the society. They were usually able to persuade the members not to adopt a uniform policy concerning imperial problems.

Shortly after returning to the National Assembly, the radical planters were rejoined by the conservative landowners. The conservatives still distrusted the legislature, but they hoped to use the wave of moderate or counterrevolutionary sentiment which followed Louis XVI's flight to overthrow the 15 May law. Both groups refrained from proposing any modifications, however.

Deliberate sabotage and unanticipated developments rendered the 15 May law unenforceable. Although it enfranchised only a few mulattoes, it undermined the rigid caste system upon which slavery was based. It would have had to be imposed with at least a show of military strength. By immediately dispatching promulatto publications, the planters in France had guaranteed that the whites would rebel before additional troops could be sent. They took advantage of the political crisis that prevented the Assembly from promulgating the law and sending the necessary reinforcements. By August 1791 all of the planters were satisfied to wait until news from the Caribbean arrived in France.

Sailing conditions were favorable during the summer of 1791, and unofficial reports of the 15 May law rapidly reached the West Indies. The news provoked such serious disturbances among the inhabitants of Saint-Domingue that French officials in the colony forecasted civil war if the Assembly tried to impose even such limited racial equality. One official predicted that the whites would declare their independence because the legislature had violated its promise of 12 October 1790 to respect the racial caste system upon which slavery rested.[7]

By 5 July rumors reached Saint-Domingue of a new publication by the "fanatic Grégoire," his *Lettre aux citoyens de couleur*. At the same time, the General Assembly, regarding independence as inevitable, published long excerpts of the May debates. Local officials imposed even stricter censorship than before on unauthorized publications by or about mulattoes. They also confiscated mulatto correspondence with France, hoping to find evidence of a general conspiracy against the whites.[8]

Despite the colonists' vigilance, Grégoire's *Lettre aux citoyens de couleur* reportedly circulated throughout all of Saint-Domingue, and on 22 August a slave rebellion erupted in the West. The whites burned Grégoire in effigy while, simultaneously, they successfully appealed to the mulattoes for support against the Negroes by promising civil rights to more of them than would have been eligible under the 15 May law. The colonial assembly also solicited military assistance from the English in Jamaica and urged the National Assembly to silence the Amis des Noirs, especially Grégoire and Brissot.[9]

Grégoire's enemies, now joined by Louis XVI, blamed the August rebellion on him. Barnave again refused to promulgate the 15 May law because, he insisted, Grégoire's overenthusiastic pamphlet made it impossible to do so. Conservatives and colonists charged Grégoire with scheming to overthrow the monarchy, the church, and the colonies.[10]

In blaming Grégoire for the latest uprising in Saint-Domingue, his enemies ignored the role played by metropolitan political developments. Even more important, the procolonial deputies failed to realize how the Assembly's inconsistent policies had permitted existing social conflicts in the West Indies to grow out of control. At first the Assembly had encouraged local self-government; then it belatedly attempted to impose uniform requirements on colonial assemblies without providing the soldiers necessary to enforce its decisions. Contrary to the evidence, the planters attributed West Indian disturbances to subversive propaganda alone, and, according to them, Grégoire was the leading provocateur.

Grégoire's enemies found adequate justification for their charges in his several promulatto pamphlets. They maintained that his remarks on universal freedom, his call for a general insurrection "to smother tyranny, to revive liberty, and to place it at the side of religion and morality," his conviction that mulattoes would react to the "volcano of liberty set alight in France" if they did not receive their rights, and his prediction that "one day the sun will rise only on free men" in the colonies[11] did not encourage Africans to wait patiently until their white oppressors granted them freedom.

As a statesman, as a man with significant moral influence among radicals, Grégoire undoubtedly should have refrained from rhetorical, impassioned phrasemaking whether he expected people to interpret his statements literally or not. While these remarks reflected the latent violence implicit in his chiliastic beliefs and foreshadowed the hyperbole of the Terror, they contradicted the impartial, dispassionate image of himself which he unsuccessfully attempted to create. Moreover, he realized that he was addressing men who, for the duration of their contact with whites, had been denied the moderating influences provided by religious guidance and civic responsibility. He could not expect these men to wait with patience and restraint while they were being denied rights which he insisted were legally theirs.

In discussing the Jewish problem, Grégoire never had used the "rabble rousing" type of rhetoric that occurred in his pro-Negro publications.[12] Jews, moreover, were victims rather than potential perpetrators of mob violence. They were not in a position to endanger public tranquility. Mulattoes and Negroes, in contrast, numbered more than half the population in the French West Indies. Although they presently were unarmed, their sheer numbers and physical strength made them a potential danger. As a politician and as an ecclesiastic, Grégoire should have considered more carefully how others might use his words.

Grégoire's writings, by themselves, probably exerted very little direct influence on the Africans in the French West Indies. It is debatable whether many Africans even knew of their existence. Grégoire's pamphlets reached the colonies through the efforts of provincial patriotic societies who, late in 1791, gave copies to the soldiers sent to quell disorders in the Caribbean.[13] According to the planters, the pamphlets circulated widely in the islands, but this assertion is impossible to substantiate or refute. In any case, who read them? Most slaves were illiterate, and although whites accused metropolitan agitators of reading Grégoire's writings aloud in the Negroes' workshops, the length and pedantic style of his works, save the few slogans cited earlier, hardly suited them for oral recitation. More mulattoes could read and write, but they needed no outside encouragement to protest when the occasion arose. In all probability, Grégoire's writings did not serve as a call to revolution, although they were used to justify it among the limited number of Africans who knew of their existence.

Grégoire's pamphlets had more influence on colonial whites than on mulattoes and Negroes. A Constitutional bishop and spokesman for Jews, Grégoire represented to most planters, as he did to orthodox Catholics and convinced anti-Semites, the undesirable direction that the Revolution was taking in France. He stiffened the planters' determination not to compromise with the mulattoes by clearly stating in his writings what whites had suspected all along: mulatto enfranchisement was merely a preliminary step toward black emancipation. Thus he gave them a convenient rationale for their intransigence towards mulatto demands.

Because they feared destroying their racial system, the colonists hesitated to ally with mulattoes against Negro rebels.

Their delay proved fatal to white rule, at least in Saint-Domingue, since the whites lacked adequate military support from France and could not suppress slave rebellions by themselves. Grégoire had pointed out this possibility as early as December 1789, but by that time the planters had already refused to unite with the mulattoes. He, therefore, cannot be accused of creating planter shortsightedness but merely of unintentionally encouraging it.

Grégoire's most important achievement was to stimulate abolitionist sentiment among provincial patriotic societies. Here he succeeded where the Amis des Noirs had failed in 1788 and 1789. In part his success was only possible because the societies had proliferated rapidly in 1790, and they now served as important channels for the diffusion of revolutionary ideology among literate bourgeois.

By early 1791 members of provincial patriotic societies were more anxious to see drastic changes, especially in such matters as colonial affairs which did not directly affect them, than were the Jacobins in Paris or the representatives in the National Assembly.[14] The enthusiasm of both the club and the legislature was tempered by the need to find practical rather than ideological solutions to national problems. They had to consider how much opposition proposed changes would arouse among Alsatian anti-Semites or colonial whites, and they had to measure this potential resistance against the amount of force available to them. Such considerations were less important to the people of the small towns who eagerly accepted the slogans of liberty, equality, and fraternity, as well as the promises embodied in the Declaration of Rights.

The provincial bourgeoisie became Grégoire's most enthusiastic audience. Knowing even less about colonial conditions than he, they responded to his logical deductions from abstract principles. They used his slogans as standards and criticized the legislature's failure to apply the Declaration of Rights to all men. Eventually, their increasing concern helped persuade

"This useful priest, this model pastor
Who to religion joins philosophy;
Frivolous bishops, respect such rare modesty,
His virtue puts to shame your proud grandeur."

apathetic members of the legislature to enfranchise at least a limited number of mulattoes.

Grégoire's enemies tried to undermine his influence among patriotic Frenchmen by questioning his reasons for advocating egalitarian reforms. Colonists and conservatives charged him with furthering philo-Semitic and pro-Negro measures in order to destroy the foundations of French society and prosperity. The more vituperative and less reflective of his accusors attributed his motives to a Free Masonic plot, but more sophisticated ones linked his activities with an English conspiracy.

Rumors of a foreign plot would play a more prominent role in politics after France declared war on England in March 1793. Yet resentment of British commercial and colonial rivalry predated the formal outbreak of hostilities. According to mercantilist writers, Grégoire was the willing or unwitting dupe of English politicians who hoped to destroy French prosperity and were particularly anxious to incite upheavals in the profitable French West Indies. They claimed that the Slave Trade Committee had deliberately encouraged the founders of the Société des Amis des Noirs and that the English had even sent Clarkson to Paris to further their subversive schemes.

The colonists could never substantiate their charges of bribery, but individual English abolitionists did provide some Girondins who were also members of the Amis des Noirs with funds for an unspecified project.[15] The public support given to the English abolitionist movement by such British officials as the wartime prime minister William Pitt also seemed to justify the planters' accusations.

Grégoire's loyalty to France was not affected either by English propaganda or by their money. Despite Clarkson's efforts, he only became an advocate for black rights after he listened to mulatto testimony before the Credentials Committee. For two years thereafter he regarded mulatto enfranchisement as more important than the emancipation of the slaves or the abolition of slave trading. Rather than profit from his ties with the Slave Trade Committee, he evidently used his own money to subsidize mulatto publications[16] because he firmly believed that egalitarianism would serve French interests.

Grégoire tempered his patriotism with a transcendent concern for mankind and did not share the intolerant nationalism which disfigured late revolutionary history. For him the nation was only important as a vehicle for reform, and, much as he hoped the Revolution would succeed, he thought it would lose its validity if it did so at the expense of innocent people in Africa, in the colonies or, later, in the conquered territories. Nor would he let patriotic considerations blind him to the virtues of the English abolitionists who were, in his opinion, entirely sincere and disinterested.[17]

Other questions arise concerning Grégoire's role in the National Assembly. Could his egalitarian reforms have been accomplished peacefully? Was he responsible for contributing to the violence which erupted in the French West Indies by prematurely demanding changes which could not be enforced? Should the promulatto deputies have waited for slavery to become uneconomic—a development which late eighteenth-century legislators could not anticipate? The lingering suspicion remains that France might have avoided considerable bloodshed if the mulatto question had not been raised during the decade of revolution.

But the white colonial residents did more to foment mulatto discontent than did the abolitionists in Paris. From 1788, whites subverted royal authority in the colonies, and once the Estates opened they asked the deputies to usurp the minister's jurisdiction. But at the same time as they destroyed the traditional basis of government, they began to quarrel among themselves. These disputes arose out of social and economic conflicts which the metropolitan legislature could not resolve. Division among the whites proved fatal because, unlike the British colonies in 1776, the French Caribbean territories had a sizeable class of educated free blacks ready to use dissent within the dominant class to further their own cause.

Thus the French West Indies could not have achieved autonomy or independence with as little internal bloodshed as did the North American colonies. Indeed, the colonists would have had to remain isolated from French events in order to have remained tranquil. The responsibility for West Indian strife rests not with Grégoire and a few other determined egalitarians but with the rapidity of the revolutionary movement itself, the "volcano of liberty" as Grégoire described it, and the effect of radical slogans on the peculiar racial, social, and political tensions in the Caribbean.

Grégoire was the product of a society which had created different and incompatible groups of articulate, dissatisfied people. He took advantage of revolutionary developments to work for more than his own personal ambitions, or even for those of his own class because he was anxious to build the secular utopia which he believed must precede the heavenly one. Before 1792 he had not convinced many Jews or Negroes to accept Catholicism. Yet in his own mind, by agitating for the enfranchisement of the former and by laying the foundation for emancipating the latter, as well as by helping to democratize the church and thereby making it more acceptable to non-Catholics, Grégoire took the first steps towards achieving his goals.[18] That these goals led to bloodshed and misery arose out of circumstances which he did not understand and could not control.

The bloodshed and misery which threatened to decimate the French West Indies during the summer of 1791 frightened many members of the National Assembly. Towards the end of August reports of new colonial disorders reached France. At that moment the representatives were attempting to complete the constitution, and they refused to discuss colonial problems until September.

Realizing that the 15 May law would serve as the focus for

the planters' attack, Grégoire read a long speech in its defense before the Jacobin Club. The society did not regard his address as important and did not publish it. Grégoire met with no greater success when he asked the Assembly to postpone considering repeal until the next legislature. When he and Barnave engaged in their final acrimonious argument, the Assembly, tired of such fruitless discussions, refused to listen to Grégoire's prepared speech and rescinded the 15 May law without further debate.[19]

The egalitarian deputies achieved two minor victories during the last days of the Assembly. On 28 September 1791 the deputies theoretically enfranchised Jews. In addition, they voted to consider as free all Negroes who resided in France and, indeed, all men of "whatever color, or whatever origin, of whatever country they might be."[20] Thus in its last session the Assembly enacted into law the implications of the Declaration of Rights.

Yet the egalitarians' victory was incomplete. The decree enfranchising metropolitan Negroes confirmed what planters had insisted all along: the Declaration applied only to France and not to the empire. The Assembly finally stated what it should have clarified two years earlier; France's empire was a federation rather than a unified state. Even within continental France, the 28 September law did not automatically create a homogeneous body of French citizens. Inequality, now based on wealth and voluntary choice rather than on hereditary status, was recognized in the constitutional distinction between active and inactive citizens—a distinction which Grégoire had unsuccessfully fought to eliminate—and in the provisions of the 28 September law which required Jews to renounce their corporations before receiving naturalization.

Grégoire ignored the 28 September resolution liberating all French residents. It was a meaningless statement because Frenchmen technically had been free throughout the eighteenth century. Completely disillusioned by the events which followed

Louis' flight in June, and particularly by the repeal of the 15 May law, he was relieved that the National Assembly finally had terminated its work. As one of his last gestures, he warned the newly elected representatives to the Legislative Assembly against the planters who, he insisted, were still plotting their independence.[21]

Both the galleries and—belatedly—the Jacobins supported Grégoire and the mulatto cause. The former expressed its indignation during the Assembly's debates. As Grégoire and the other deputies filed out of the National Assembly's final session, a large crowd of spectators hissed and spat on Barnave and Alexandre Lameth and applauded Grégoire and Pétion. At the same time, the Jacobin Club expelled all members who were not "true friends of the constitution and humanity," specifically the Feuillant leaders, Lameth, Barnave, and Adrien Duport.[22]

For Grégoire, public applause and Barnave's expulsion from the Jacobins appeared unimportant. He did not expect ever again to play a political role, nor did he anticipate having to deal with the problems which would arise out of his egalitarian activities during the National Assembly. He prepared instead to embark on his new career as bishop of Blois, far from the scene of legislative activity.

NOTES

1. *Feuille du jour*, supplement for 15 June 1791, pp. 1–8; Jean-Baptiste Larchévêque-Thibaud to wife, 5 July 1791, AN, DXXV 38, dos. 385; Massiac Club minutes, 14–16 May 1791, AN, DXXV 89, X, 63–65.

2. Aulard, *Jacobins*, 2:493–96; *Journal de la Révolution*, 19 and 20 June 1791, pp. 844–45; *Patriote françois*, 26 and 31 May, 10 and 13 June, and 9 Aug. 1791, pp. 381–82, 603–4, 658, and 165;

Courrier des 83 départemens, 23 and 25 May, 14 June 1791, pp. 359, 393, and 220; Mme Roland to Bancal-des-Issarts, 22 May 1791, BN, NAF 9534, p. 119 verso.

3. Grégoire to the editor of *L'Ami des patriotes,* 28 May 1791, p. 328; *L'Ami du peuple,* 18 May 1791, pp. 2–7; *Gazette de Paris,* 15 May 1791, p. 1.

4. Grégoire, *Lettre aux citoyens de couleur et Nègres libres,* pp. 4, 12, 9.

5. The former colonial official was Médéric-Louis-Elie Moreau de Saint-Méry. See: AP 27:231–32; *Courrier des 83 départemens,* 15 and 16 June 1791, pp. 240 and 251–52; *Patriote françois,* 15 June 1791, p. 665.

6. Lepage to Grégoire, 16 July 1791, BM Nancy, 532; Millet to Grégoire, 10 Aug. 1791, BPR, MNO. For the Feuillants see: *Gazette universelle,* 18, 20, and 21 July 1791, pp. 795, 802–3, and 811; *Spectateur national,* 25 Aug. 1791, pp. 1112 and 1116. For the Jacobins: *Courrier des 83 départemens,* 19 and 30 July, 5 and 17 Aug. 1791, pp. 311, 481, 72–73, and 264.

7. Governor Philbert-François Blanchelande to Minister Antoine-François Bertrand de Moleville, 3 July, 2 and 14 Sept. 1791, AN, DXXV 46, no. 431, pp. 5, 13, and 14.

8. Unsigned note, 5 July 1791, copy in AN, F³ 196, colonies, p. 859. This either is misdated or a forgery since news of Grégoire's *Lettre aux citoyens de couleur* (published 8 June) could hardly have spread through the colony by that date.

9. Brissot, of course, was not a deputy. Stanislas de Longuemare de La Salle to Magnon la Forest et Cie., 16 July 1791, AN, AA 54, 1509, p. 5; Nicoulas to Moreau de Saint-Méry, 10 Sept. 1791 and Arthand to Moreau, 14 Sept. 1791, AN, F³ 197, colonies; "Mémoire concernant la colonie de Saint-Domingue," AN, DXXV 88, no. 840, p. 36: *Feuille du jour,* 23 and 25 Aug. 1791, pp. 427 and 450; *Spectateur national,* 23 Aug. 1791, p. 1103; *Courrier politique et littéraire* (Cap-Français), 7 and 14 July 1791; *Gazette de Saint-Domingue,* 5 Sept. 1791; *Journal du Port-au-Prince,* 8 Sept. 1791, pp. 22–23.

10. [Chabanon], *Le dénonciation de M. l'abbé Grégoire,* pp. 46–47; *Le Mot du vrai législateur,* pp. 13–14; *Journal de M. Suleau* 5:14; Ellery, *Brissot de Warville,* pp. 140–41; Champaze to

Barnave, 28 Aug. 1791, AN, W 12, dos. 850; Massiac Club minutes
for 23 and 31 Aug. 1791 and letter to provincial assembly, 9 Sept.
1791, AN, DXXV 89, XI, pp. 19–20 verso, 22, 28 verso; Larchévêque-Thibaud to wife, 14 Sept. 1791, AN, DXXV 38, dos. 385;
Bérenger de la Drôme, ed., *Oeuvres de Barnave* 2:239–52.

11. *Mémoire en faveur des gens de couleur*, p. 35; *Lettre aux
philanthropes*, p. 12; *Lettre aux citoyens de couleur*, p. 12.

12. The one possible exception is August 1791 when he urged
the Jews in the Northeast to participate in electoral assemblies even
though the National Assembly had not yet recognized their citizenship. This might have led to disorders, but the Ashkenazim refrained from following his advice; Grégoire to Bing, 20 Aug. 1789
[*sic* for 1791], *Archives israélites* 5; 417.

13. "Procès-verbaux des sociétés populaires," between 21 and 25
Nov. 1791, BM Blois.

14. Macinnes gives virtually the same explanation for the spread
of abolitionist sentiment in England after 1815, but, as will be seen
in Part Three, British abolitionist sentiment proved more lasting
and politically effective than mass French interest in antislavery;
Macinnes, *England and Slavery*, p. 168. For petitions from the
provincial societies to the Paris Jacobin Club see *Patriote françois*,
spring 1791.

15. In 1790 members of the Société des Amis des Noirs received
funds from England for unspecified purposes; Francis Lanthénas to
Bancal-des-Issarts, 17 May 1790, BN, NAF 9533, p. 233. Subsequent historians, such as Gaston Martin in his *Histoire de l'esclavage dans les colonies françaises*, p. 190, and in his "La Doctrine
coloniale," pp. 38–40, repeat the eighteenth-century accusations.
This will be discussed more fully in Chapter 6 in connection with
the Girondin trials.

16. Raimond's testimony in 1793: AN, DXXV 56, no. 549.
Where Grégoire obtained this money is unclear.

17. See Krieger's analysis of nationalism. Grégoire, *Notice sur la
Sierra-Leona*. Still, he supported the annexation of Savoy and the
Netherlands.

18. Grégoire did not use the argument that a purified church
structure would help missionaries when he defended the Civil Constitution of the Clergy in 1790 and 1791, but in later years he

occasionally mentioned the likelihood that his reorganized Constitutional church would succeed where Roman Catholicism had failed. See, for example, *Actes du second concile national de France, tenu l'an 1801 de J.–C.* (*an 9 de la République française*) *dans l'église métropolitaine de Paris* (Paris: Imprimerie-Librairie Chrétienne, X [1801]), 3:293, 296–300.

19. *Feuille du jour*, 19 Sept. 1791, pp. 646–47; Aulard, *Jacobins*, 3:134; *Courrier des 83 départemens*, 26 Sept. 1791, pp. 411–12; *Spectateur national*, 25 Sept. 1791, p. 1233; *Moniteur*, réimpression, 26 Sept. 1791, pp. 768–70; *Journal des Etats-Généraux* 34:263–78; AP 21:275–79.

20. Motion made by Jean-Louis-Claude Emmery, *Moniteur*, réimpression, 29 Sept. 1791, p. 795; *Spectateur national*, 5 Oct. 1791, pp. 1279–80; *Feuille du jour*, 9 Oct. 1791, pp. 803–4.

21. Grégoire, *Adresse aux députés de la seconde législature*, pp. 9–13.

22. Aulard, *Jacobins* 3:150; AP 21:279; *Journal des Etats-Généraux* 34:263–78; *Moniteur*, réimpression, 24–26 Sept. 1791, pp. 755, 758–60, 763–64, 766, and 768–70; *Spectateur universel*, 24 Sept. 1791, p. 1230. The expulsion of the so-called Triumvirate from the Jacobins was due to their leadership in the Feuillants rather than their procolonial stand, but the egalitarians interpreted and used it for their own purposes: *Patriote françois*, 26 and 28 Sept. 1791, pp. 369 and 378. Perroud, ed., *J. P. Brissot: Mémoires* 2:211–12.

6

The Victory
of the Egalitarians

Grégoire left Paris in October 1791 to assume his position as Constitutional bishop of Blois. This post gave him an opportunity to implement his religious and political theories. Because he regarded the church as an important instrument for developing morality and nationalism, he expected the clergy to help revitalize France's social and cultural institutions. Thus, during his year in Loir-et-Cher he participated actively in the Blois popular society, served as president of the departmental directory, and corresponded with other Constitutional bishops concerning cultural questions. Although he offered to help the local Jews if they should ever need his assistance and occasionally expressed his sympathy for minority groups, there were few Jews or mulattoes in this historic department, and Grégoire had little chance to practice his egalitarian principles.[1]

While Grégoire was in Blois, political conditions changed rapidly in the capital. The Constitution of 1791 failed to end controversy over the nature of the regime, and popular disorders erupted again late in 1791 and in 1792. Deep-seated disagreements among the deputies paralyzed the new regime.

The conservative Feuillants lost control over the Assembly in March 1792, but the radicals were too badly divided among themselves to assert their potential leadership. Hence the country drifted from crisis to crisis.

The issues that arose in 1791 and 1792 aggravated existing divisions among radical deputies, and by early 1792 two rival factions had formed within the Jacobin Club: those who in subsequent history would be called the Gironde and those known as the Mountain.[2] Leaders of the two groups agreed on such policies as further revising the Constitutional church and enfranchising mulattoes, but their differences over diplomatic as well as a variety of domestic issues overshadowed their similarities.

The Gironde proved its strength in March 1792 when the king was forced to appoint several of its members to the ministry. Following Girondin advice, the Legislative Assembly declared war on Austria one month later. But the new ministry, hampered by royal opposition to its program, failed to resolve any of France's immediate problems, be they military, constitutional, religious, social, or colonial.

Influenced by such dedicated abolitionists as Brissot, Pétion, and Condorcet, the Girondins used their temporary ascendancy to achieve civil rights for mulattoes and free Negroes. Under their leadership the Legislative Assembly passed appropriate laws and instructed its troops to repress slave revolts only. Thus, it granted mulattoes the right to fight for civil and social equality without interference. Upon Brissot's recommendation, the Assembly replaced the first civil commissioners with more forceful men and gave very broad powers to the two officials whom it appointed, Léger-Félicité Sonthonax and Etienne Polverel. The commissioners were authorized to restore Saint-Domingue's prerevolutionary administrative structure, to dissolve all local assemblies, and to exercise personal rule over the colony until the legislature could write an imperial constitution.[3]

The laws of April 1792 satisfied all but the most dedicated egalitarians, and even they regarded immediate abolition as a utopian goal. Having achieved citizenship for free Negroes in the colonies and having appointed trustworthy civil commissioners, Brissot found it impossible to hold the Société des Amis des Noirs together. He and the other Girondin abolitionists were preoccupied with national and Parisian affairs, Grégoire was in Blois, while such prominent prerevolutionary egalitarians as Lafayette and Talleyrand had already abandoned politics and would soon leave France.[4] Thus, the society faded out of existence in the spring of 1792 even though colonial conditions remained grave and the more important parts of its program, the abolition of slavery and of slave trading, had not yet been accomplished.

After April 1792 the Legislative Assembly, no longer prodded by abolitionist propaganda, concentrated on defending the empire. The members approved imperial legislation virtually without debate, and the laws that they enacted attracted very little attention. The civil commissioners retained their supposedly temporary powers because the legislators had no time to draw up a new colonial constitution. Indeed, the only institutional change which they made after April 1792 was to abolish the office of colonial apostolic vicar.

The Legislative Assembly's colonial regulations fulfilled part of the Ami des Noirs' egalitarian program even though they contradicted the Girondins' desire to decentralize France's administrative structure. Yet the theoretical centralization that the April laws imposed was never carried out, and, contrary to the abolitionists' expectations, the laws reduced the French West Indies, especially Saint-Domingue, to chaos. They destroyed the power of the white residents, granted absolute authority to metropolitan officials, and enfranchised mulattoes and free Negroes. But because the European war absorbed both supplies and energy, France could not send sufficient soldiers to impose such drastic changes upon an already rebellious population while the mulattoes, from whom the Amis des Noirs had expected so much, proved unable to restore order without metropolitan assistance.[5]

Imperial policy was only one of the areas in which the Girondins found that their program did not restore stability. Attributing their failures to deliberate royal sabotage, some Girondins denounced the constitution as unworkable and recommended deposing Louis XVI. The Assembly first rejected their demand, but on 10 August the deputies suspended royal authority and called a new constitutional assembly, the National Convention.

Elections to the National Convention took place in an atmosphere of impending catastrophe. Prussian troops advanced on French soil while economic conditions and religious conflicts provoked widespread discontent. Although provincial voters rejected conservative candidates, they elected a majority of moderate deputies who were committed to none of the major factions. Since neither the Mountain nor the Gironde controlled the Convention, for several months they struggled to win the allegiance of neutral representatives.

Grégoire returned to Paris as a member of the National Convention. While few legislators had shared his antiroyalist ideas in June 1791, fifteen months later he found widespread republican sentiment among the organized pressure groups of the capital. He no longer represented the views of a small radical minority. "I confess," he wrote many years later, "that for several days my excessive joy" over the suspension of the king "deprived me of both sleep and appetite."[6]

Although pleased with the formation of the Republic, Grégoire found much to criticize in September 1792. In particular, the Constitutional church was threatened by various events that had taken place and decisions that had been made during his absence from the capital. Grégoire was also disturbed by the bitter quarrels among his former friends in the Jacobin Club. Calling it a "factious hell," he sarcastically suggested posting on the door "the opinion one is obliged to have."[7] Finding their quarrels incompatible with his episcopal dignity, he refused to attend the society's meetings and thereafter remained aloof from factional controversies.

During the early months of the Convention, Grégoire's prestige steadily increased because he verbalized the sentiments of many other deputies who also refused to affiliate with either faction. At the Convention's opening session he urged the members to establish a republic. Later, as president of the Assembly, he expressed the delegates' growing imperialism when he recommended the annexation of Savoy.[8] His committee assignments reflected his interests—he was elected to both the Colonial and Public Instruction committees—and in December the Convention sent him as one of its representatives on mission to Savoy.

Grégoire's sojourn in Savoy prevented him from joining the Colonial Committee immediately. Nonetheless, his nomination provoked the planters who had never ceased hating him. Even while he was in Blois, they had concentrated their venom on him, and now they redoubled their attacks. Their charges passed virtually unnoticed, however, because late in 1792 France had such pressing problems to consider as the fate of the king and the prosecution of the war.[9]

The Convention expressed little interest in the empire, and whatever debates it held were less emotional than similar previous discussions. Several reasons can be given for the delegates' disinterest in Caribbean affairs. The European war preoccupied their attention, and domestic crises left little time for peripheral matters. Even the organized abolition movement had ceased agitating for reform because, in the members' opinion, the April 1792 laws had satisfactorily solved the imperial problem.

Although the West Indies required serious attention, neither the abolitionists nor the planters were in a position to campaign for new measures. Although individual Amis des Noirs still wished to achieve complete racial equality, they could exert very little influence in the legislature. For many years their efforts were hampered by the spectre of the old society and the animosities which it had created.

The planters in France had also been weakened by the events of the summer of 1792. Their alliance with the port deputies had dissolved when the merchants lost their colonial trade monopoly. These deputies gravitated towards the Gironde and fell under the influence of that faction's abolitionist leadership. In addition, the conservative landowners left France. Since their society, the Massiac Club, had coordinated anti-mulatto, procolonial strategy, its demise was a serious loss to the landowners.

For a time during the summer of 1792, individual planters could only denounce and accuse the no longer existent Société des Amis des Noirs. They had even less influence than did the individual egalitarians. Yet they soon reorganized under the leadership of three radical republican landowners, Thomas Millet, Pierre-François Page, and Augustin-Jean Brulley. This so-called colonial commission remained alert, waiting for the time when it might demand the complete restoration of white supremacy in the colonies.[10]

The effects of the April 1792 laws were not felt in the colonies for several months. Implementation of the laws was made even more difficult than might have been anticipated by the growing dispute within the Jacobin Club. In November 1792, while the Girondin-appointed civil commissioners were still on their way to Saint-Domingue, the Jacobin Club expelled them along with their mentor, Brissot. Several radical planters, who had recently joined the club, hastened to side with the Mountain, and they used the commissioners' expulsion as grounds for demanding their recall. Sonthonax and Polverel, however, refused to return to France and appealed to the influential Paris Commune for support.[11]

The outbreak of war between England and France further

Jacques-Pierre Brissot,
from Chronique du Mois.

aggravated the mounting tension between planters and abolitionists. As the English threat to the French West Indies grew
more ominous, the landowners in France ignored political distinctions and directed their polemics against all leading egalitarians, be they Girondins, Mountaineers, or neutrals. Using
altered versions of mulatto correspondence to substantiate
their charges, the colonists accused Brissot, Grégoire, Pétion,
and Robespierre of accepting bribes from mulatto spokesmen

in France.[12] Since Brissot and his friends still dominated the Convention in March and April 1793, the representatives ignored the planters' accusations, and the individuals who were attacked did not bother to reply.

The situation changed rapidly as the Gironde-Mountain rivalry reached its height in April and May 1793. Grégoire returned from Savoy during this period, and he tried to maintain his nonpartisan stance. Until the last moment he continued his friendships with prominent members in both factions, but his personal beliefs more closely approximated those of the Mountain. The experiences he had had, both as a youth in a peripheral region of France and as a member of the departmental administration of Loir-et-Cher, convinced him that the nation needed strong administrative and cultural centralization. Like the Mountain, he favored legislation that would improve lower middle-class living conditions. In addition, he disliked the Gironde's belligerent foreign policy, although he would support the war effort later on. Thus, shortly after he returned to Paris, he reportedly said as he pointed to the Gironde: "There are men of state, of virtue, and of talents; but there is disguised counterrevolution." Turning to the Mountain he added: "Here are strong, courageous men, *some of them corrupt*, but here is the Republic."[13]

Grégoire objected to more than mere rumors about corruption within the Mountain's ranks. He opposed the death penalty in theory and had taken an ambiguous stand during the trial of the king.[14] The progressively harsh penalties meted out to political and religious dissenters disturbed him, as did Robespierre's attempts to establish a patriotic, deistic faith completely divorced from Christianity. Yet Grégoire refrained from criticizing any of these policies in public, and fortunately managed not to antagonize either faction because his absence in Savoy enabled him to abstain from several crucial votes.

After his return to Paris, Grégoire adopted the tactic which he would frequently employ in future years; he remained silent even though he twice presided over the Convention during the crisis of 31 May through 2 June. Then, on 4 June he ambiguously asked the assembly to amend its 1 June minutes so as to show "the insults and assaults hurled against the National Convention." Such an emendation, he thought, would reassure the departments that "it had been free" when it proscribed the Girondins.[15]

Grégoire's remarks could have been construed several ways, but his continued friendship with Robespierre and other members of the Mountain insured their proper, innocuous interpretation.[16] The victorious faction left him alone, and throughout the Terror he avoided discussing controversial questions by staying away from the Convention sessions and by commenting only on bills relating to education or agriculture.

The fall of the Gironde had serious consequences for French politics, and it affected questions only peripherally related to the major issues dividing the two factions. Thus, even though prominent members of the Mountain agreed with Girondins on racial equality, both the Mountain and the radical landowners used the crisis in Saint-Domingue as a pretext for discrediting Brissot and his friends. The Mountain saw in the English threat to the West Indies evidence of its almost paranoid belief in a Girondist foreign plot. Consequently, in their official indictments of Brissot, Pétion, and other prominent Girondins, the Mountain focused on the diplomatic rather than the racial aspects of the imperial crisis and did not hold the Girondins responsible for colonial civil war.[17]

The landowners, for their part, ignored the diplomatic issues that so fascinated other members of the Mountain. They equated abolitionism, per se, with treason. During the weeks following Brissot's proscription, flight, and arrest, colonial deputies amused themselves by drawing up formal accusations which they planned to use at his trial. In one such document the first of eight articles charged him with having "carried the spark of civil war, of revolt to the colonies." Brissot, the colonists claimed, had conspired with Lafayette and with English leaders to destroy the French empire by promoting racial reforms. The other egalitarians were simply his dupes.[18]

During his four months' imprisonment, Brissot wrote an elaborate self-defense in which, among other things, he justified his imperial policy and tried to relieve his friends of all responsibility for colonial strife. Rather than concentrate on the Mountain's accusations, he too emphasized the racial issue and denied that he, Pétion, Grégoire, or Clavière had ever been bribed to represent the mulattoes. He showered praise on Grégoire for his "courageous zeal" and his "sentiments of generous anger." Grégoire, according to Brissot, was a "man of courage and virtue, a true patriot, and a pure republican."[19] Although Brissot answered the specific charges concerning domestic and diplomatic issues levied by his enemies, the Revolutionary Tribunal found him guilty and condemned him to death.

Brissot's arrest and eventual execution did not satisfy the planters. In Barnave's trial a few weeks later, they called the Feuillant leader, along with Raimond and Brissot, "the author of all our colonial problems." Again, responsibility for colonial disorder was only one of a number of charges made against Barnave. In this matter, he tried to shift responsibility to his now dead antagonist, but he, too, mounted the scaffold.[20]

Other, less prominent persons were imprisoned simply because they had supported Brissot's colonial program. For example, the Paris Commune was asked to arrest the mulatto leader, Raimond, because as a "confidant of Brissot and Pétion" he must have written to them about the English conspiracy. Throughout the summer, the planters included Sonthonax and Polverel in their wholesale denunciations of Brissot's supporters. Finally in July the Convention enacted a decree of accusation, or indictment, against the two commissioners and dispatched a general to Saint-Domingue.[21]

Although the Mountain used the Caribbean crisis as evidence

of the Gironde's inability to rule, the victorious party did not repudiate the former Amis des Noirs' promulatto policies. Instead of attributing colonial civil war to premature racial reforms as did the planters, the Mountain blamed West Indian disorders on deliberate Girondin treason and mismanagement. Robespierre had enthusiastically supported mulatto rights before the National Assembly, and he now refused to restore the prerevolutionary caste system. Still, he took no steps to make racial equality a reality by ending the slave trade or emancipating the slaves.

Grégoire had been deeply involved in colonial affairs, and he sensed the precariousness of his position. As political repression intensified, and after many of his fellow Amis des Noirs had been arrested, he expected to be called upon to testify and thought that he might be accused along with them.[22] But even though the landowners had concentrated their venom on him as late as March 1793, after May they temporarily ceased attacking him. Perhaps his position seemed too secure; through his service as acting president during the June crisis he had obviously cast his lot with the Mountain, even if he did not enthusiastically support all of its policies. Perhaps the planters did not think that, as an individual, he could be effective without the other Amis des Noirs. Whatever their reasons, the colonists failed to press their earlier charges and only occasionally mentioned him in their accusations against secondary figures.

The West Indian refugees in the United States were less reticent, and they specifically denounced Grégoire to the Convention. The emigrés were out of touch with French politics, however. The deputies ignored their accusations while the landowners in Paris corresponded with Grégoire about ways to improve colonial agriculture.[23]

Grégoire reacted ambivalently to the potential threat posed by the Girondin trials. He hesitated to play an active role in the Colonial Committee, and when the chairman asked him to investigate charges against one of the first civil commissioners, he refused on the grounds that his other committee work consumed too much of his time. His friends had not yet been tried, and he probably thought it unwise to judge a controversy in which he might still be implicated.[24]

Although Grégoire was reluctant to investigate the colonial upheavals, the expulsion of the Girondins made it possible for him to pursue the abolitionist program. Contrary to what the planters probably had anticipated, the leading Amis des Noirs' fall from power divorced the antislavery cause from factional politics, and left Grégoire free to agitate for Negro rights. Thus the planters' halfhearted attempts to implicate him along with Brissot and Pétion discouraged him from defending his former associates but did not keep him from following his egalitarian ideals.

Well before the Girondin trials began, and on the same day as Raimond was denounced before the Paris Commune, Grégoire broke his two years' silence on colonial affairs. His opportunity arose on 4 June when a mulatto delegation paraded through the Convention. This delegation carried a banner decorated with pictures of a white, a mulatto, and a Negro which bore the legend: "Our union will make our strength." Speaking spontaneously as an individual representative and not as a member of the Colonial Committee, Grégoire urged that committee to present a report on the "aristocracy of the skin" because he hoped such a report would convince the Convention to "pronounce the freedom of the blacks."[25]

Once again Grégoire permitted his rhetoric to carry him beyond what was practical at the moment. The Convention ignored his recommendation to abolish slavery and, instead, asked the Colonial and Legislative Committees to report on racial conditions in the colonies. This report never was presented, and Grégoire did not mention emancipation again.

Undaunted by his failure to achieve emancipation, a few weeks later Grégoire asked the Convention to stop subsidizing merchants who engaged in slave trading. The point was a moot one because the Legislative Assembly had already suspended all commercial subsidies. In addition, naval conditions, the state of the French economy, and disorders in the colonies had brought slave trading to a halt. Now, on Grégoire's suggestion and following the free trade ideas of the majority, the Convention permanently abolished the slave trade subsidy, but it refused to outlaw the trade itself.[26]

Grégoire achieved but a small part of what he had hoped to accomplish because the deputies would enact only those reforms that could be justified on practical grounds. Although the spokesman of the Mountain, Robespierre, was closely identified with the antiracist cause, the Convention was no more interested in the principle of complete racial equality than the preceding legislatures had been.

While Grégoire proposed egalitarian legislation in France, the civil commissioners in Saint-Domingue took matters into their own hands. Since the general sent by the Convention could not enforce its indictment against them and had soon withdrawn, the commissioners were free to take whatever steps they could to restore order within the island and to protect it from foreign invasion. Consequently, on 23 August 1793 Sonthonax and Polverel emancipated the Saint-Dominguean slaves.

The commissioners freed the blacks because the whites had used the Convention's decree of accusation as grounds for undermining their authority. Hoping the Negroes would help repel the threatened English invasion, the commissioners only succeeded in further aggravating the situation. While whites and mulattoes appealed to Spain and to England for assistance, the newly liberated Negroes burned the city of LeCap. The whites first assisted the British expedition and then fled en masse to the United States or to the Spanish colonies in the Caribbean.

At almost the same time as the English invaded Saint-Domingue, the Spaniards attacked the North. The civil commissioners managed to hold the English at bay for a few months, but by the end of 1793 the two invading armies captured several important footholds. Under such desperate circumstances, Negro leaders refused to aid the commissioners unless the Convention confirmed their freedom, and the mulattoes refused to help under any circumstances. Thus the civil commissioners had no alternative but to ask the Convention to abolish slavery. Still reluctant to return to the metropolis, they sent a delegation composed of one mulatto, one Negro, and one white that arrived in Paris in January 1794.

The delegates met with a mixed reception in France. Even the Mountain disagreed about emancipation. Several colonial landowners continued to play an important role in the Jacobin Club. They were supported within the Committee of Public Safety by André Jeanbon Saint-André who was primarily concerned with naval affairs. Nonetheless the Convention and the Jacobin Club received the Saint-Dinguean spokesmen with great ceremony. On 4 February the assembly abolished slavery throughout the entire French empire. Thereupon the Convention admitted the three deputies as Saint-Domingue's duly elected representatives.[27]

Grégoire and the abolitionists now had succeeded beyond their fondest hopes, even though slavery had been abolished for pragmatic rather than idealistic reasons and military conditions prevented emancipation from being realized in Martinique and Guadeloupe. None of the egalitarians had participated in the 4 February session, and none of them publicly commented on their victory.

The colonial deputies, for their part, continued to oppose emancipation and repeated all of their old accusations against the abolitionists and against Grégoire. Rather belatedly, they identified Grégoire with counterrevolution by insisting that the emancipation decree had been prepared by a conspiracy conceived in London, operated through Georges-Jacques Danton (who had not yet been executed but who was under suspicion of corruption and treason), and implemented by a faction com-

posed of Grégoire, Brissot, and Jean-Marie Roland. Since both
Girondins had already been executed, two conclusions were
obvious: the 4 February law was Grégoire's work, and he actually was a member of the discredited faction.[28]

The planters' charges served only to irritate the other deputies, who found no grounds for suspecting Grégoire. Wearied
by continued opposition to its now official policy, the Convention accused all the colonial deputies of inciting resistance to
national laws. Thus the leading planters joined the surviving
Amis des Noirs in the jails of Paris.[29]

The Revolutionary Tribunal neither heard nor dismissed
charges against those abolitionists and procolonists who had
not shared responsibility for the discredited Girondin or Feuillant administrations, such as the mulatto leader Raimond and
the various colonial deputies. Even while they waited in prison,
the spokesmen for each side continued to accuse the other of
having conspired with the English. The planters pressed their
charges against Raimond. He, in turn, denied that he had tried
to bribe Grégoire or Robespierre and insisted instead that
Grégoire had loaned him more than seven hundred pounds to
pay for mulatto publications.[30]

During the period of uncertainty which followed Robespierre's fall, the existence of these numerous prisoners embarrassed the Convention. When Sonthonax and Polverel finally
returned to France a week after 9 Thermidor, the Convention
was forced to decide what action it wished to take. The majority now favored emancipation and was unwilling to prosecute
the men who had first freed the blacks. Therefore the representative who had demanded the commissioners' arrest one
year before now recommended leaving them free to prepare
their defense, while the Jacobin Club, which had called Sonthonax a "vile intriguer" the previous year, in August 1794
welcomed the two commissioners to the capital.[31]

Rather than try the commissioners before the Revolutionary Tribunal, the Convention asked the Naval and Colonial

committees to investigate all cases connected with the Saint-Dominguean disaster. When the combined committees procrastinated, the Convention appointed a special nine man commission to study all of the upheavals in the French West Indies. This commission included Grégoire and was presided over by Jean-Philippe Garran de Coulon, an abolitionist who had championed mulatto enfranchisement in both the Paris General Assembly and the Legislative Assembly. The composition of the commission foretold what its conclusions would be.[32]

The planters protested against the membership of the Colonial Commission, especially against Grégoire's nomination to it. Since the commission had been authorized to investigate recent disorders in Saint-Domingue and Martinique, they argued, a man who had been "implicated by name in the Saint-Dominguean affair" should have the delicacy to refrain from sitting "among those who must investigate it," for he could not be both "judge and party" to the case. Grégoire readily admitted holding opinions which were "not those held by other people," and he offered to resign rather than discredit the work of the Colonial Commission "in the eyes of prejudiced or evil-minded people." He also cited overwork and ill health as reasons for withdrawing from the commission.[33]

Although Grégoire's colleagues in the commission refused to consider his resignation, the colonists personally approached him and threatened to disclose damaging evidence against him unless he voluntarily withdrew. Certain the other deputies would support him, he called the planters' bluff by asking them to present their evidence immediately. When the colonists failed to do so, Grégoire appealed to the Convention, and the members voted to ignore all accusations against him. Grégoire's "sentiments of humanitarianism and justice," said one member, provided a sufficient reply to his critics.[34] The Convention's refusal to consider charges against Grégoire temporarily ended the planters' protest against the commission and Grégoire's membership on it.

The Colonial Commission's hearings were important for planters and abolitionists alike, because they provided the two sides with a less hazardous arena in which they might continue their controversy without risking a formal and possibly fatal court appearance. If the commission managed to settle the bitter disputes which the egalitarians' campaign had provoked, then perhaps the Convention would be able to devise a permanent and coherent imperial policy.

Both the colonists and the egalitarians regarded the current status of the West Indies as temporary. The planters wished to restore slavery and white rule over the colonies. The abolitionists, for their part, took the planters' threats seriously and hesitated to develop a complete reform program until they were certain that the Negroes would remain free.

The abolitionists had good reason for being concerned about the future. Although at the moment France could not spare any more troops for the West Indies, on the continent the immediate threat of invasion had passed. Once France defeated her European enemies, she obviously would try to reconquer her Caribbean possessions. The abolitionists feared that when the time came, the planters might persuade the Convention to reassert white rule over Negroes along with French rule over her shattered empire. Hence Grégoire and his friends could not ignore the planters' propaganda, and they paid careful attention to the Colonial Commission's proceedings.

For the first months of the Colonial Commission's existence, Grégoire participated actively in its work. He, too, hoped to discover the truth about the Caribbean disasters. Only when the dust of past controversy had settled could he begin to rebuild the colonies' shattered social and cultural institutions. Anxious to help in whatever way he could, he regularly attended the commission's sessions and performed such trivial services as hiring stenographers for the hearings and preparing catalogues of the papers that it had seized.

But Grégoire's enthusiasm passed after the Convention

granted limited religious toleration in February 1795. Shortly thereafter Garran asked him to write a report on Martinique. He was deeply involved in reorganizing the Constitutional church, however, and he evidently did not comply with Garran's request.

The Colonial Commission spent several months listening to various witnesses who blamed West Indian disorders on the abolitionists, the white planters, and/or the civil commissioners. The planters testified often and at great length. Although they frequently mentioned Grégoire's name, they failed to present concrete evidence against him, and they qualified many of their earlier accusations.

The most likely reason for the planters' restraint lay in the attitude of the president, Garran de Coulon, who pointedly ruled that "there can be no question of representatives of the people in this discussion." Sonthonax, moreover, forced planter spokesmen to retract some of their more violent statements by threatening to bring a libel suit against them.[35] Not unexpectedly, the commission ignored adverse testimony against Grégoire and the other surviving abolitionists.

Despite frequent meetings and occasional reminders from the Convention, the Commission wandered further and further from its original task of investigating the sources of colonial strife. Circumstances rather than satisfaction with the testimony laid before it forced the members to reach a preliminary decision. Polverel died on 10 April 1795, and ten days later the Convention released Raimond from prison and named him as one of the new civil commissioners for Saint-Domingue. Obviously the Convention did not believe the planters' charges against the mulatto leader, but because he still was under indictment, Raimond could not leave France before the commission presented its report. Finally on 15 May the commission cleared the mulatto and incidentally denied the most serious charges against Grégoire.[36]

After Raimond was released, the planters made one last

attempt to condemn all who had participated in the formula-
tion of imperial policy. In particular, they accused Grégoire of
suppressing evidence which they had compiled concerning the
abolitionists' complicity in the English conspiracy, but Garran
prevented the planters from pursuing the matter.

When the colonists realized the hopelessness of their case
they lashed out against the National Convention and reproached it for having followed "the illusion and the sublimity
of an ill-considered philanthropy." In addition, the editor of
one paper described the accused civil commissioners as perpetrators of "the most destruction during the course of the
Revolution."[37]

Throughout 1794 and 1795 the abolitionists had ignored the
colonists' polemics. Now, as the Colonial Commission prepared
to terminate its work, they finally counterattacked. But their
charges lacked the bitterness which characterized the colonists'
statements, and they preferred to cite documents written by
others rather than fabricate their own accusations. The president, Garran de Coulon, permitted them to speak freely.

The abolitionists presented several different explanations for
the West Indian disorders. Sonthonax accused the colonists of
having conspired with the English as early as 1791, well before
mulatto enfranchisement or Negro emancipation might have
justified their treason. Grégoire read a letter from a Martinique
refugee who attributed uprisings in that colony to the selfish-
ness of the French chambers of commerce rather than agitation
by "the Brissots, the Grégoires, and others such as the Grand
Devil." Indeed, this writer insisted, civil war might have been
averted if the Assembly had followed Grégoire's advice in 1790
and 1791.[38]

Neither side in the hearings discussed the real source of
colonial upheavals, the multisided social and economic conflict
among Negroes, mulattoes, and colonial whites and among the
whites, the absentee landowners, and the ministers. These tensions had been aggravated by the National Assembly's failure

to establish a consistent policy enforced by adequate troops. Ignoring these fundamental problems and sharing revolutionary logic, planters and abolitionists alike attributed all disasters to conspiracies and deliberate treason.

But the abolitionists no longer cared and did not press their charges. They had nothing to gain from being vindictive; they were anxious to maintain rather than revise existing colonial legislation; and they were in the process of formulating plans for restoring the Caribbean islands to their former prosperity without reimposing slavery. Interested in bringing the hearings to an end, they presented just enough favorable testimony to prevent the planters from appealing the commission's verdict to the Convention. Thus when Garran presented his report on 22 October 1795, four days before the National Convention closed, the majority accepted the president's conclusions, and two days later they formally cleared Sonthonax of all suspicion.

The Colonial Commission's report ended the Jacobin planters' unsuccessful attempt to achieve judicial revenge against those whom they blamed for colonial civil war. The colonists had added to the clamor against Barnave, Brissot, Condorcet, and Pétion because, during the summer of 1793, their denunciations had suited the Mountain's domestic plans. By linking the colonial disaster to factional politics, however, the planters failed to reach all of their enemies. They could not effectively press charges against such men as Grégoire or Raimond, who, however close they might have been with the Girondins, were not responsible for that faction's diplomatic and domestic decisions and had not openly opposed any of the Mountain's important policies.

Even during the Terror, the planters could not use Brissot's fall to discredit his egalitarian ideals or to forestall further reforms. Robespierre, at least, prevented a thorough investigation of colonial disorders as long as the Committee of Public Safety controlled the Convention. Although he had abandoned the racial cause after 1791 and gave no sign of renewing it in 1793, he could not refuse the opportunity to emancipate the slaves once the civil commissioners presented it to him.

Robespierre's refusal to placate the radical planters was based on more than egalitarian ideology. Imperial centralization and a broad application of the Declaration of Rights were more compatible with Mountain than with Girondin philosophy. Although one member of the Committee of Public Safety, Jeanbon Saint-André, sided with the planters on the abolition issue, emancipation and complete subordination of the colonies to metropolitan rule were logical by-products of the Mountain's victory in June 1793.

After 9 Thermidor the planters tried to shift responsibility for colonial disorders from Brissot to Robespierre, but neither the Colonial Commission nor the Convention listened to them. Egalitarian ideals transcended factional differences, and emancipation was rapidly incorporated into the revolutionary tradition. Thus the Thermidorians saw no reason for restoring white supremacy in the colonies. They did not regard the men who had freed the slaves as criminals unless they had committed other sins within France, and they made no attempt to reverse the Convention's radical colonial policy. Emancipation, therefore, was secure as long as the Republic lasted.

NOTES

1. Minutes of the Blois popular society, BM Blois; minutes of the Directory of the Department of Loir-et-Cher, AD, L&C, L 106 and L 118; and Grégoire's ecclesiastical correspondence in the archives of the bishopric of Blois, 1 D 7 A. His comments on mulattoes and Jews are in the minutes of the popular society, 14 Nov. 1791 and 2 Feb. 1792. As late as 1808 there were only two Jewish families in Blois; Hertzberg, *French Enlightenment*, p. 15n.

2. This and the subsequent description of the political con-

troversy between 1792 and 1794 adheres to the traditional characterization of the Gironde as a loose but identifiable group of deputies and their supporters. Although Sydenham's discussion is thought provoking and useful, this is not the place to defend or refute any such thesis, and employing the term "Gironde," which is readily understood by most readers, permits a simplified but hopefully valid sketch of the background against which the most striking colonial reforms were enacted; Sydenham, *The Girondins*.

3. *Moniteur*, réimpression, 24 and 26 March and 8 Aug. 1792, pp. 705–7, 723–24, and 350. The law enfranchising mulattoes was enacted on 4 April 1792; AN, DXXV 3, dos. 30, p. 13. There actually were three commissioners, but the third, Ailhaud played only a minor role in subsequent events.

4. Since the leading Amis des Noirs were all Girondins, the society was identified with that faction, but to consider its members as exclusively Girondist is a deliberate misrepresentation fostered by the Jacobin landowners in 1793.

5. French forces were estimated at six thousand; *Moniteur*, réimpression, 16 April 1792, p. 134. Sonthonax's complaints about the inadequacy of his troops: letter to Brissot, 4 Jan. 1793 in Perroud, ed., *Brissot, Correspondance*, p. 333. See also Stoddard, *The French Revolution in San Domingo*, p. 180.

6. *Mémoires*, 1:410.

7. Ibid., 1:388. Before he left Blois he still respected the Jacobin Club; "Sociétés populaires," 16 Sept. 1792, BM Blois.

8. [Lallement], ed., *Choix de rapports*, 10:17, 21, 22; ibid., 11: 41–54; *Annual Register*, 1793, pp. 79, 136–37; *Mémoires*, 1:410, 413.

9. Examples of the planters' charges: Tarbé, *Réplique a J. P. Brissot*, pp. 14–15; *Moniteur*, réimpression, 27 Oct. and 16 Nov. 1792, pp. 229 and 477.

10. Garran de Coulon, *Rapport sur les troubles de Saint-Domingue*, 4:471, 476, 491; Maurel, *Saint-Domingue et la Révolution française*, pp. 33–49.

11. *Moniteur*, réimpression, 17 March and 17 July 1793, pp. 716 and 143; Sonthonax to the Paris municipality, 12 Feb. 1793, BN, NAF 22,819, p. 86.

12. They published a *Lettre de Raimond, mulâtre*, see p. 6, esp.

They also included long extracts in [Page and Brulley], *Développement des causes des troubles et désastres des colonies françaises*, pp. 58–59, 73–74. See also Garran de Coulon, *Rapport sur les troubles*, 4:162, 471, 489, 491; Raimond, *Lettre au citoyen D****, p. 8.

13. J. J. Delorme, *Histoire de la ville de St.-Aignan* (Saint-Aignan: Chez l'Auteur, 1842), 1:271; [Grégoire, et al.], *Lettre pastoral des évêques réunis*.

14. On 15 Nov. 1793 Grégoire urged the Convention to condemn Louis XVI "to live"; *Journal de Paris National*, 16 Nov. 1792, pp. 185–86. For his stand on the execution of Louis in Jan. 1793 see Introduction, fn. 5, and *Journal des Amis*, 2 Feb. 1793, pp. 198–99.

15. *Moniteur*, réimpression, 6 June 1793, p. 563; *Gazette du jour*, 4 June 1793, p. 3.

16. The Girondins regarded this as support for their cause; minutes of the Committee of Public Safety of Moulins, 10 June 1793, in Perroud, ed., *Brissot, Correspondance*, p. 347; Perroud, *La proscription des Girondins*, pp. 49ff.

17. Palmer's *Twelve Who Ruled*, pp. 299 and passim, does not mention the colonies in connection with the foreign plot, but the colonists frequently accused the abolitionists of having betrayed the West Indies to the British.

18. "J'accuse Brissot," undated, anonymous, AN, F⁷ 4443, no. 18, plaq. 4, p. 186; [Page and Brulley], *Développement des causes*, pp. 58–59, 73, 89, 137.

19. Montrol, ed., *Mémoires de Brissot*, 3:101; Perroud, ed., *Brissot, Mémoires*, 2:90. Actually the first life to be sacrificed in the Saint-Dominguean trials was that of Governor Blanchelande who was executed on 15 April 1793; see AN, F³ 198, colonies.

20. Villigegeth [?] to Antoine-Quentin Fouquier-Tinville, 3 Frimaire year 2 (23 Nov. 1793) and Page's testimony at Barnave's trial, 7 Frimaire year 2 (27 Nov. 1793), AN, W 298, dos. 285; Bérenger de la Drôme, ed., *Oeuvres de Barnave*, 2:367.

21. Extract from the register of the General Council of Paris, 4 June 1793, AN, BB³; decree of accusation against Sonthonax and Polverel, 16 July 1793, AN, DXXV 11, no. 102, p. 17.

22. In his *Mémoires* Grégoire claimed that he expected to be

arrested momentarily, but his fear was based on religious rather than colonial issues; see draft in Arsenal 5290, p. 224; *Mémoires*, 1:88–91; Touchard-Lafosse, *Histoire de Blois*, pp. 313–14.

23. *Conspiration découverte par le représentant du peuple Creuset-Pascale*, pp. 3, 7n; Commissioners to the Committee of General Security, 26 Sept. 1793, AN, W 292, dos. 204, pt. 2, p. 68; [Raimond], *Lettre d'un Citoyen*, p. 10; Garran de Coulon, *Rapport sur les troubles*, 4:410, citing letter to Larchévêque Thibaud, 27 Sept. 1793; Jer. Littée to Brulley, two letters of 6 Oct. 1793 noting his correspondence with Grégoire, AN, DXXV 71, dos. 714, pp. 40, 41.

24. Various letters of Philippe-Rose Roume and St. Léger to the National Convention and to the Committees of the Navy and Colonies, dated 30 Aug., 2 and 5 Sept. 1793, AN, DXXV 3, dos. 31.

25. AP 66:57.

26. AP 69:580; *Moniteur*, réimpression, 29 July 1793, p. 252.

27. On 3 Sept., for example, Saint-André demanded enforcement of the decree against Sonthonax and Polverel; *Moniteur*, réimpression, 4 Sept. 1793, p. 559. The imprisoned planters were pleased to learn of Saint-André's return to Paris; Page and Brulley to LeGrand, 14 Prairial [year 2] (2 June [1794]), AN, DXXV 72, dos. 720, p. 17. For emancipation see: Maurel, *Saint-Domingue*, pp. 52–54; Aulard, *Jacobins*, 5:651; *Moniteur*, réimpression, 17 Pluviôse year 2 (5 Feb. 1794), pp. 387–88; Caron, ed., *Paris pendant la Terreur*, 3:319.

28. Garran de Coulon, *Rapport sur les troubles*, 4:236; Thomas Millet to the Committee of Public Safety, 29 Floréal and 20 Thermidor year 2 (18 May and 7 Aug. 1794), AN, DXXV 81, no. 793, p. 3 and AN, DXXV 82, no. 800, p. 14; Page, Brulley, and LeGrand, *Adresse à la Convention Nationale*, p. 5.

29. Page and Brulley to LeGrand, 13 and 14 Prairial [year 2] (1 and 2 June [1794]), AN, DXXV 72, dos. 720, pp. 14, 17.

30. Raimond's trial: AN, DXXV 56, no. 549 and AN, DXXV 110, no. 867; Saint-Domingue colonists to Page and Brulley, 26 Frimaire year 2 (16 Dec. 1793), AN, DXXV 68, no. 670, p. 35; Thomas Millet to the French Legate in Baltimore (Edmond Genêt), 8 Dec. 1793, AN, DXXV 69, no. 682, p. 1.

31. *Le Cri de l'innocence révolutionnaire*, p. 12; *Moniteur*, réimpression, 5 and 16 Aug. 1794, pp. 394 and 490.

32. The main sources for the Colonial Commission are the published reports by Garran de Coulon (his two *Rapport* and his *Débats*), and the minutes included in the DXXV series of the AN. Specific references will be given for direct quotations or for sources other than the DXXV series.

33. *Moniteur*, réimpression, 18 Vendémiaire year 3 (9 Oct. 1794), pp. 170–71; see their complaints regarding another member in Thomas Millet to the committees of Public Safety and General Security, 20 Thermidor year 2 (7 Aug. 1794), AN, DXXV 82, no. 800, p. 14. Grégoire's health supposedly was injured by his year's residence in the damp climate of Loire-et-Cher, but his longevity indicates that he was stronger than he thought; see Gazier, *Etudes*, p. 85.

34. *Moniteur*, réimpression, 18 Vendémiaire year 3 (9 Oct. 1794), p. 171; Garran de Coulon, *Rapport sur les troubles*, 4:589–90; papers of the Colonial Commission, AN, DXXV 57, dos. 560, p. 2.

35. Garran de Coulon, *Débats*, 3:18 and meeting of 1 Aug. 1795, AN, DXXV 57, dos. 565, p. 37.

36. Garran [de Coulon], *Rapport sur Julien Raimond*, p. 35; Raimond, *Lettre d'un citoyen*.

37. Gouly, *Opinion et réflexions*, p. 7; *Journal de Bonhomme Richard*, 7 Fructidor year 3 (24 Aug. 1795), pp. 317–18. C. L. R. James' assertion that the planters had more influence under the Thermidorian Regime is not justified by the evidence; *The Black Jacobins*, pp. 178–79.

38. LeRoy to the Colonial Commission, 3 Thermidor year 3 (21 July 1795), read on 1 Aug. 1795, AN, DXXV 57, dos. 565, p. 37.

PART TWO

Towards a New Imperial System

7

Bishop Grégoire and the Colonial Church

The men who overthrew Robespierre on 27 July 1794, the so-called Thermidorians, unwittingly began the counterrevolutionary trend which would end with the Bourbon Restoration two decades later. Not all of the Thermidorians' decisions were reactionary, however, and some of them had far-reaching consequences for Grégoire, in particular the Convention's vote in February 1795 to modify its dechristianization policy and to grant limited religious toleration. Relieved, as were so many others, by the end of the Terror, and unable to foresee how far the pendulum would swing, Grégoire applauded the new government's policies.

Grégoire had always regarded religious reform as a fundamental part of his egalitarian program. But he had reacted ambivalently to the Civil Constitution of the Clergy. Although he had argued against many of its provisions, he had first supported the Constitutional church and had abandoned the Jews in order to ensure its acceptance. Two years later he had decided against martyrdom when the Terrorists closed most of the churches.[1] Finally in February 1795, when Constitutional

worship again became legal, he grasped the opportunity to introduce additional innovations. Since the church was now a
private voluntary organization, free from papal interference and
subject only to external governmental control, certain parts of
its structure which had displeased him in 1790 could be revised.
Hoping to put some of his rather unusual theories into practice, he joined several other Constitutional bishops and began
to reorganize the church.

Still, Grégoire was not completely free to carry out his ideas
because he had to cooperate with other clerics. In addition,
even though dechristianization had passed, anticlericalism survived, and many administrators still distrusted all Catholics. As
the most prominent member of the Constitutional clergy, and
as an unquestioned republican, he could effectively plead the
church's cause by demanding the same freedom for Catholics
as the National Assembly had granted to religious minorities
four years before. Thus, for the next two years he served as an
intermediary between frightened priests and overzealous officials, and he had little time to implement his ecclesiastical
theories.

As Grégoire's ideas about church reform gradually emerged
after 1795, they showed striking similarities with several of the
assumptions which lay behind Robespierre's religious program.
Both Robespierre and Grégoire hoped to create a model republic founded on virtue. Convinced that the political revolution
would not succeed unless Frenchmen also underwent a moral
revolution, both used religious institutions to encourage civic
morality, to develop a national culture, and to promote social
equality. Yet they disagreed over what form their religion should
take. Grégoire rejected Robespierre's state-supported deistic cult
and insisted upon maintaining an organized, traditional church.
Although the Civil Constitution of the Clergy had fallen short
of his ideal, he thought that the reorganized post-Terror Constitutional church would be an excellent instrument for incul-
cating patriotism, morality, and respect for law and order.

Rescuing the Constitutional church from the chaos into which it had fallen during the Terror was only a beginning for Grégoire. Much as he believed that France had to undergo a moral revolution, he regarded the colonial need as far greater and more urgent. Consequently, he proposed to incorporate at least the Caribbean territories within his new church. This project was, in one respect, an extension of his earlier campaign for Negro rights. Now that slavery had been abolished and now that he had a controlling position within the Constitutional church, he hoped to further assist the blacks by using ecclesiastical institutions to hasten their assimilation to European religious, social, and political customs.

According to Grégoire, the Constitutional church was uniquely qualified for colonial service. Since the next phase of imperial development would involve drastic social, economic, and cultural changes, it demanded the services of educators and technicians who were prepared to Europeanize the Negroes and teach them practical skills. During the preceding seven years, civil and military administrators had amply demonstrated their inability to handle social tensions in the colonies; hence they could not be expected to instruct the former slaves in the rights and duties of citizenship. But the metropolis could spare very few lay teachers and technicians. Because the church had provided many prerevolutionary educators and because some priests had tried to promote scientific agriculture, Grégoire thought they were equipped for the task and felt justified in concentrating upon recruiting missionaries for the West Indies.

The problem was most acute in Saint-Domingue because Negroes had failed to gain their complete freedom elsewhere.[2] Even more than in the other French West Indian territories, six years of revolution had shattered Saint-Dominguean social, political, and economic institutions. British and Spanish military successes completely undermined metropolitan authority, and after Sonthonax and Polverel returned to Paris, the French general, Etienne Laveaux, was the only significant French official left. By 1795 Laveaux had won over the rising Negro leader François-Dominique Toussaint L'Ouverture. Indeed, without Toussaint's aid, Laveaux was powerless either to continue the war against Britain or to govern the island. Thus developed what, for France, was an unfortunate situation which would never be reversed—in reality, if not yet in law, Saint-Domingue had become a black republic with only tenuous ties to France.

But even Toussaint could not restore Saint-Dominguean stability and tranquillity. The blacks, ever fearful of reenslavement, readily turned against the few whites who remained in the island. Old tensions between blacks and mulattoes reemerged, while continued military campaigns hindered any program designed to restore agriculture and commerce.

Aware that the blacks would not long remain free unless they were persuaded to resume their work and were gradually educated to their rights and responsibilities as citizens, Toussaint devised a harsh labor system and tried to encourage the resumption of regular religious services. He was anxious to gain whatever assistance the French were willing to give, but, although Saint-Domingue was considered to be the most important colony, members of the French legislature demonstrated no interest in helping the Saint-Dingueans restore the old and develop new social and economic institutions. Consequently Toussaint had to rely on private organizations, including the Constitutional church.

For their part, most Frenchmen were willing to leave colonial rehabilitation to others, and few challenged Grégoire's desire to Europeanize the Negroes. Yet his adherence to traditional Christian doctrine aroused the suspicions of deputies who, disregarding the differences between Constitutionals and Romans, considered Catholicism (or Christianity) as a bastion for antirepublicanism. Since appeals to the legislature would be fruitless, Grégoire at first hesitated to devise a coherent plan for an imperial church and tailored his program to suit the rapidly shifting political conditions under the Thermidorian Reaction and the Directory.

Fortunately for him, some of Grégoire's motives for sending missionaries were shared by Etienne Laveaux who, despite his own anticlericalism, discovered that many Negroes, including Toussaint, had remained loyal Catholics and wished to attend religious services. Although the blacks preferred Constitutional priests whom they identified with Grégoire and hence with their freedom, most of the Constitutional clerics had left in 1793. Thereafter the Negroes had the choice of attending no services at all or of frequenting churches served by Roman Catholic missionaries who had come under the auspices of the British invaders and had spread throughout the unoccupied parts of the island. Since these missionaries were anti-French and antirepublican, Laveaux asked the Convention to send fifty republican priests to the colony.[3]

When Grégoire learned of Laveaux's request he wrote to several priests who had been expelled from the Caribbean during the Terror. Although the Catholic church in the West Indies was in a desperate condition—it was described as "the most pitiful, the most ramshackle in the world"—the former missionaries hesitated to return to their posts.[4] Grégoire finally found a few priests who volunteered for colonial service because they wished to escape anticlericalism in France. Too much time had elapsed, however, for the Convention had disbanded in the meantime, and the Directory, which ignored Christianity whenever it could, refused to provide transportation for the clerics.

Failure did not discourage Grégoire. He again drew up plans for a colonial church when in 1796 Toussaint L'Ouverture publicly urged the few remaining Catholic clerics to resume their traditional functions. Indeed Toussaint probably had persuaded Laveaux to ask for republican priests in 1795. After the Directory failed to provide passage for the missionaries, Toussaint wrote directly to Grégoire and asked this "superior minister of the most holy of religions . . . worthy pastor of the faithful," to help him by sending twelve priests whose "exemplary conduct [and] patience beyond all proof" would enable them to "lead the erring sheep back to the fold."[5]

Grégoire did not immediately act upon Toussaint's request. The Directory's earlier refusal to provide transportation for missionaries had taught him a lesson; now he tried a different approach. Overconfident because of a recent decline in official dechristianization and overestimating his own influence, he tried to exert pressure on the government by arousing the National Institute's interest in establishing a republican colonial church. In order to gain his colleagues' support he had first to combat their anticlerical prejudices, a task which required far more tact than he possessed.

Grégoire's prestige in the Institute at least ensured him a hearing there. But the members were intransigent anti-Catholics who adhered to anticlericalism long after the rest of France returned to orthodoxy. Consequently, Grégoire could not persuade his friends that the church had been responsible for abolishing ancient slavery and feudal servitude. "Christian maxims," he asserted, had "mitigated man's miseries, comforted the poor, freed the captives, and emancipated the slaves." He pointed out how the planters, anxious to keep Negroes in bondage, had tried to prevent their conversion to Christianity.[6] Rather unsurprisingly, this speech was not even mentioned in the Institute's records, and Grégoire realized that he could convince neither the Institute nor the legislature of the Negroes' need for religious instruction.

Early 1796 was an inappropriate time for Grégoire to broach any question relating to the empire. Although the Colonial Commission had absolved the Amis des Noirs of all responsibility for colonial civil war, suspicions lingered on, and some people would forever regard the abolitionists as traitors. They blamed the egalitarians because English troops still occupied part of Saint Domingue and because military conditions remained chaotic in the rest of the French West Indies. On the whole, most egalitarians preferred to avoid provoking the planters by proposing new reforms.

The planters, playing upon French disillusionment with Jacobinism, urged the Legislative Bodies to restore prerevolutionary social and economic institutions in the colonies. Throughout the Directory they published a steady stream of propaganda. A few writers demanded the restoration of slavery because, they insisted, the colonies could not produce a profit unless they employed unfree non-European labor. Reviving old accusations against the original abolitionists, they shifted responsibility from Brissot to Robespierre. In addition, they paid special attention to Grégoire's role in the recent Colonial Commission. His ignorance about the colonies, they claimed, had created greater evils than his moralizing had alleviated because, as a result of his activities, where once a few slaves had been maltreated, now the entire white population was being assassinated.[7]

The Directory and the Legislative Bodies ignored the planters' charges, but they followed an even more contradictory policy than the National Assembly had. When in 1795 the deputies decided to restore civilian rule in Saint-Domingue, they chose the mulatto leader Raimond and the emancipator Sonthonax to serve as civil commissioners. Nonetheless, at the same time they appointed several proslavery men to the new Colonial Committee. Thus future policy would be devised by planters and enforced by abolitionists. Such a divergence between the legislative committee and its supposed agents guaranteed that colonial strife would continue.[8]

Ignoring the legislature and its Colonial Committee, Grégoire tried a new approach which would not require political sanction. Since he regarded religious instruction as essential and since French priests could not get to the island, he decided to transcend sectarian differences by appealing to American abolitionist societies. The philanthropists, he thought, might at least advise the newly appointed French commissioners on ways to rehabilitate the colony's social and moral institutions. In addition, he prepared a set of instructions for the residents of Saint-Domingue which Commissioner Raimond promised to print as soon as he reached the West Indies. But the civil commissioners found they could not follow Grégoire's advice when they arrived in Saint-Domingue. Although Sonthonax encouraged at least one priest to resume public services, strained military conditions prevented the commissioners from either corresponding with the American abolitionists or undertaking any broad reform program.[9]

Even while the civil commissioners were trying to impose their authority on Saint-Domingue, French voters returned a conservative majority to the Legislative Bodies. The new deputies, not bothering to disguise their proslavery sentiments, accused both Sonthonax and Toussaint of fermenting civil war and were not unduly disturbed when the Negro general forced the commissioners to leave Saint-Domingue.

Civilian rule having proved insufficient in Saint-Domingue, the Directory replaced Sonthonax and Raimond with Gabriel-Marie Hédouville, a general who had pacified the counter-revolutionary Vendéen rebels two years before and had thereby paved the way for Catholic toleration in France. Hédouville, conservatives assumed, would easily defeat Toussaint. Then metropolitan authority would be reasserted and traditional institutions would be restored.[10] Since the abolition of slavery had not been carried out completely in the other islands, the destruction of Negro leadership in Saint-Domingue would be an important step towards reestablishing prerevolutionary conditions in the French West Indies.

Dissatisfaction with the Directory's Caribbean policy played only a minor role in the 1797 election. French voters were more interested in restoring traditional institutions in France than in the colonies. They particularly wanted to practice their customary religious rites without any restrictions. Pressured by such a widespread demand, the Directory was forced to ease its antireligious policies. Since, as far as the government was concerned, the Constitutional church was still better than orthodoxy, Grégoire's organization profited from the conservatives' victory in 1797. Among other concessions, the government suddenly agreed to provide free transportation for colonial missionaries whom it called "public teachers." The Directory authorized Grégoire to handle recruitment and to judge the applicants' qualifications.[11]

As in 1795, Grégoire delayed too long because none of the priests who previously had served in the colonies were willing to return. He therefore made a public appeal for new missionaries. The response to his appeal was so great that Grégoire could not answer the individual letters, and he was forced to establish stringent requirements, paying special attention to the candidates' political sentiments. In the meantime, he named as unofficial vicar a priest who had remained in Saint-Domingue during the revolutionary upheavals.[12]

Grégoire had an additional reason for not sending priests immediately. According to him, Constitutional missionaries by themselves could not save the empire from royalist intrigues. Since the colonies were mission districts, the pope, who never had bothered to disguise his antirepublican sentiments, would probably interfere with the revolutionary priests. Grégoire could only circumvent papal influence by creating an imperial hierarchy loyal to republican ideals. Consequently, he thought that sending clerics to the colonies would be impractical unless a sympathetic bishop presided over the French West Indies.

Grégoire had already tried to provide episcopal services for Saint-Domingue in 1795 when Spain ceded her part of Hispaniola to France. Shortly thereafter he inquired whether the Spanish archbishop of Santo Domingo would extend his jurisdiction over the French colony. Although the prelate reportedly was interested and several French legislators offered to sponsor appropriate laws, he advised them to wait because he doubted whether the Directory would interfere in religious affairs by recognizing the status of archbishop.[13]

By 1797 the government had become more friendly towards the Constitutional church, but the archbishop of Santo Domingo had been transferred to a new see and could no longer supervise potential missionaries. Hesitant to select a prelate himself, Grégoire waited until the summer when the Directory permitted him to convoke a National Council of the Constitutional church. Taking advantage of this assembly, as soon as the Council opened, Grégoire asked the members to create colonial dioceses, to appoint bishops, and to sponsor his missionary program.

The National Council readily agreed to send missionaries to the colonies, but Grégoire's proposal to nominate an imperial hierarchy was endangered by a serious controversy within the Constitutional clergy. The issue at stake was a fundamental one which concerned ecclesiastical organization. Some members, including Grégoire, wanted to strengthen episcopal control within the church, while representatives of the lower clergy, joined by a few bishops, hoped to decentralize church authority. This latter group hesitated to found colonial dioceses because they opposed any numerical increase in the size of the episcopacy.[14]

Several clergymen had other, less theoretical objections to Grégoire's imperial program. Some opposed because, they said, the Constitutional church could not spare bishops for colonial service as long as such important French dioceses as Paris and Lyons remained vacant. Curés and bishops alike questioned whether the Council could erect new dioceses without papal or civil approval, and others thought that the people in the colonies should choose their own prelates.

The controversy over ecclesiastical organization was important because it jeopardized Grégoire's domestic as well as his imperial program. Grégoire, himself, never admitted the changes which had taken place in his own opinions. Ten years before he had begun his career by opposing episcopal tyranny; now he wanted to centralize the church in order to maintain his version of dogmatic and ritual purity. His ideas about religious organization probably were influenced by his recent political experiences. During the first years of the Revolution he had supported the Paris oriented Mountain over the provincial Gironde and imperial centralists over colonial autonomists; now he wished to institutionalize both the control exercised by himself and several other bishops—the self-styled United Bishops—over the French church and the authority of the French church over colonial priests. Therefore, throughout the Council he tried to prevent the so-called presbyterian or Richérist priests from further democratizing the Constitutional church.[15] His fight to establish colonial bishoprics was only one part of this overall struggle, and by emphasizing what to other priests was an insignificant issue, he exacerbated the divisions within the church.

Grégoire pursued his colonial program with his well-known stubbornness, employing all the arguments which he could devise, be they religious, pragmatic, nationalist, or egalitarian. For the first time, he was able to discuss fully the role which he thought that the church might play in encouraging social reform, and his several speeches on the colonial church illuminate his subsequent attitudes towards the problem of Negro assimilation.

In response to the opposition's practical arguments, Grégoire appealed to the priests' obligation to save souls. The French West Indies, he reminded his colleagues, contained one million inhabitants who must be saved from atheism and/or paganism. But, he insisted, the colonies could not be served adequately unless they had their own bishops.[16]

Admitting that French ecclesiastics were in short supply, Grégoire explained how a handful of colonial bishops could train and ordain a sizeable mulatto and Negro ministry similar to that which he thought existed in the Spanish colonies. He could see no other means of preparing Negro priests who, he thought, would be important for egalitarian and secular as well as religious reasons. They would prove Negro and European equality before God. In addition, by their mere existence they would erase the traces of the prerevolutionary caste system, they would hasten the former slaves' acculturation to European morés, and they would thus serve as instruments for developing French patriotism in the colonies.

Yet more than anything else, Grégoire stressed the church's moral obligation towards the empire. The colonies were integral parts of France. Moreover, he proclaimed, reverting to his earlier cosmopolitanism, bonds of charity united all men "whatever their color or place of birth." In the peroration of one of his speeches, he exhorted the Council members: "Let us plant, and, if possible, let us water, in the hope that God will provide the harvest."[17]

Grégoire's arguments silenced the opposing priests, none of whom wished to be accused of racial prejudice or of failure to support the national interest. The Council reluctantly established colonial sees and elected candidates for four of the newly created dioceses. Somewhat hostile because of the means that Grégoire had employed and fearing to condone prerevolutionary abuses by naming absentee bishops, the members insisted upon postponing consecration until the nominees could leave for the West Indies. They decided not to notify the pope about this new colonial hierarchy because they feared he might intervene. For the same reason, the Council failed to include the decree which established colonial sees in its official records.[18]

The National Council was a great personal triumph for Grégoire, but its work would be meaningless unless the government approved of and assisted in implementing its decisions. Even before the National Council terminated its sessions, Grégoire's entire colonial project seemed to be doomed by the coup d'état of 18 Fructidor Year 5 (4 September 1797) which temporarily retarded the course of counterrevolution. Now strident anticlericals replaced the moderate members of the Directory. The new minister of police advised the Directors against providing transportation for missionaries under any guise, and the government withdrew its offer.[19]

Despite the Fructidor coup, prospective missionaries continued to apply for colonial duty. For a time Grégoire held his religious projects in abeyance while he tried to maintain the priests' enthusiasm and searched for a way to get them to the Caribbean. Bishops and priests who were anxious to go to the colonies did not realize his powerlessness, and they urged him to make the necessary arrangements. Finally, during a brief lull in official anticlericalism, he asked the minister of the interior to provide transportation for the clerics. Anticipating a favorable decision, he and the other United Bishops published an epistle to the French colonies in which they belatedly announced the National Council's decision to establish imperial dioceses.[20]

The United Bishops addressed their epistle to a sophisticated audience rather than to laymen. In it they tried to prove the National Council's jurisdiction over the imperial church and its right to appoint a colonial hierarchy. Masking the continued schism in France between Constitutionals and Romans, they fraudulently claimed to have convinced the papacy concerning their orthodoxy. The United Bishops thereby implied that anyone who rejected their authority was schismatic. The nominated Constitutional missionaries and bishops, they asserted, were the only legitimate clergy in the colonies.

Besides justifying their jurisdiction, the United Bishops urged toleration for all Christians and tried to dissuade the blacks in Saint-Domingue from declaring their independence. In order to preserve their newly gained rights, the authors explained, Negroes and mulattoes must faithfully fulfill all of their duties as citizens. Since France had granted them freedom, the blacks owed a debt to the mother country which they could only repay by recognizing the sacred bonds linking the colonies with the metropolis.

Even if Grégoire's epistle had circulated widely in the colonies, its arguments were too complicated and its distinctions were too esoteric for it to have had much influence on colonial residents. It evidently was written for Toussaint and his advisors because the general was rumored to be indifferent to the distinction between Roman and Constitutional clergy. Grégoire's remarks about loyalty to France also applied to Toussaint whose foreign and commercial policies were becoming increasingly incompatible with metropolitan strategy.[21]

Whether because of Grégoire's epistle or for other reasons, Toussaint continued to prefer Constitutional priests during the next two years. Still, the Directory ignored the epistle and failed to answer Grégoire's request for permission to send missionaries to the colonies. The government remained silent because it first had to make a decision on what action it wished to take in order to curb the most recent episode of civil war in the French West Indies, especially since this outbreak involved religious as well as racial and political issues.

Throughout its existence the Directory neither recognized colonial autonomy nor took effective steps to impose its rule over the West Indies. As a result, the most important territory, Saint-Domingue, slipped further and further from its grasp. By October 1798, Hédouville's mission there had ended in failure. Although the last English forces withdrew that year, they surrendered their territory to Toussaint rather than to the French general. Toussaint refused to cooperate with Hédouville, partly because the Frenchman objected to Toussaint's pro-Catholic policies. The general also enraged Toussaint by encouraging mulatto opposition to Negro domination, and the Negro leader forced Hédouville to return to France. Before the general left, he guaranteed further anarchy in Saint-Domingue by delegating his authority to the mulatto leader, André Rigaud, rather than to Toussaint.[22]

In April 1799, as Hédouville perhaps had anticipated, civil war erupted again in Saint-Domingue. The conflict between Rigaud and Toussaint arose from religious as well as racial differences. Rigaud was anticlerical while Toussaint still wanted to reestablish either Roman or Constitutional Catholicism. The Directory, finding little to chose between the two leaders, adopted a strictly neutral stance.[23] Since any decision concerning Constitutional missionaires, favorable or otherwise, might be construed as support either for Rigaud or for Toussaint, the Directory did not dare answer Grégoire's letters. It did not replace Hédouville but waited to see who would emerge victorious from the latest civil war in Saint-Domingue. In the meantime, Grégoire had also to postpone his missionary program.

NOTES

1. Failure to be executed by the dechristianizers was not, for a man in Grégoire's position, equivalent to apostasy. Robespierre did not approve of the spectacles encouraged by other Terrorists, and since Grégoire had severed his relations with his episcopal council in 1792, the issue did not arise. Of course, he could have denounced the closure of churches and the execution of priests on questionable accusations, but he preferred to maintain his disapproving silence. What he actually said when asked to abdicate is open to doubt: Necheles, "The Abbé Grégoire," pp. 12–14; Palmer, *Twelve Who Ruled*, pp. 117–22; Duport to Grégoire, 27 Jan. 1793, BPR, L&C I.

2. Victor Hugues had emancipated the Negroes in Guadeloupe, but many remained with their previous owners: McCloy, *The Negro in the French West Indies*, p. 83; Roberts, *The French in the West Indies*, pp. 225–27.

3. Guerrier's letters, 3 Aug. 1795 through 9 April 1799, BPR, MNO; Etienne Laveaux to the Convention, 29 Frimaire year 4 (20 Dec. 1795), copy in AN, F³ 199, colonies.

4. Guerrier to anon., 3 Aug. year 3 (1795); BPR, MNO.

5. Toussaint to Grégoire, 29 Nov. 1796 in *Annales de la religion,*

23 Sept. 1797, pp. 495–96; Laurent, *Toussaint Louverture*, p. 369; Toussaint to Laveaux, 25 Germinal year 4 (14 April 1796), BN, MSF 12,104, fo. 186; Sonthonax to Besson, 24 Prairial and 19 Messidor year 4 (12 June and 7 July 1796), BN, MSF, 8986, I, fo. 6, 20.

6. Quoted in Grégoire's "De l'influence du Christianisme sur l'abolition de l'esclavage," chap. 4 of unpublished MS in BPR, Rév. 177, p. 1. This work was completed in 1813 according to Grégoire's letter to Grappin, 17 June 1813, BM Besançon, 622, fo. 340–41.

7. Barbé-Marbois, *Réflexions sur la colonie de Saint-Domingue*, 1:75 and passim; [Chastenet-Desterre], *Considérations sur Saint-Domingue*; Col. Venault de Charmilly, *Lettre à M. Bryan Edwards*; Limochel, *La France demandant ses colonies*; Creuze, *Lettre*, pp. 6, 65–66; *Le Télégraphe*, 15 Nov. 1796, p. 63. Grégoire's friends answered the planters' attacks; see: *Journal des patriotes de 89*, 17 Ventôse year 4 (7 March 1796), pp. 818–19; Gaterau, *Réponse aux libelles*, p. 17.

8. Bourdon de l'Oise, *Rapport au nom de la Commission des colonies*.

9. Raimond to Grégoire, 28 Ventôse year 4 (18 March 1796), BPR, CD; "Journal historique de la Société Libre et Littéraire de Philosophie Chrétienne," entry for 28 July and 5 Aug. 1796, anon. private collection in Paris; *Merchants' Daily Advertiser* (Philadelphia), 13 July 1797; J. Bloompist to the Société des Amis des Noirs, 9 May 1797, BPR, TUVWXYZ; Sonthonax to Besson, 24 Prairial and 19 Messidor year 4 (12 June and 7 July 1796), BN, MSF 8986, I, fo. 6, 20.

10. The conservatives were more interested in slavery than in religion. Hédouville actually was anti-Catholic, and although his victory in the West had paved the way for the resumption of religious services first in the Vendée and then in the rest of France, he was reluctant to grant the same privilege in Saint-Domingue; see Hédouville to Toussaint, 12 Thermidor year 6 (30 July 1798), AN, F³202, colonies.

11. *Annales de la religion*, 15 July 1797, pp. 251–53.

12. *Nouvelles ecclésiastiques*, 12 Sept. 1797, p. 74; Constantin to Grégoire, 6 July 1797 in Cabon, *Notes sur l'histoire religieuse*

d'Haïti, p. 37n. This is identical with Guerrier's letter to Grégoire, 7 July 1796 and similar to his letter of 12 July 1797 in BPR, MNO. See also: Jacquemin to anon., undated, BPR, TUVWXYZ; "Journal historique," entry for 21 July 1796, anon. private collection in Paris; *Annales de la religion*, 15 July, 5 Aug., 2 and 23 Sept. 1797, pp. 241–53, 325–27, 429, and 493–98; Carayon to editor of the *Annales*, 18 Aug. 1797, BPR, TUVWXYZ.

13. His name was Fernando Postillo y Torres; see *Annales de la religion*, 2 Jan. 1796, p. 237; Grégoire, *Compte rendu*, pp. 37–38; Rallier, *Suite des observations sur Saint-Domingue*, pp. 20–21. Why Grégoire thought that the archbishop would be less pro-Bourbon than the rest of the hierarchy is unclear, although some eighteenth-century Spanish bishops were influenced by Gallicanism.

14. This quarrel and its connection with Grégoire's colonial plans is described in Chapter 8 of this volume. The minutes and rough drafts of the National Council are in BPR, Concile national 1797, I.

15. Edmond Richer, a seventeenth-century theologian who advocated increased rights for the lower clergy. His followers during the Revolution were called "presbyterians" because they wanted to limit the bishops' authority by creating powerful episcopal councils, or presbyteries; Préclin, *Les Jansénistes*, pp. 529–31.

16. Grégoire's various speeches on the colonial church: *Journal du Concile national*, 20 Oct. and 8 Nov. 1797, pp. 122 and 159; draft in BPR, Concile 1811, "autographes,"; minutes of the council for 5, 10, and 20 Oct. 1797, BPR, Concile national 1797, I; Grégoire, *Compte rendu*, pp. 31–42.

17. *Journal du Concile national*, 8 Nov. 1797, p. 159.

18. Minutes of the Council, 20 and 28 Oct. 1797, BPR, Concile national 1797, I; *Annales de la religion*, 28 Oct. and 5 Nov. 1797, pp. 606 and 45–46; *Journal du bon sens*, 10 Nov. 1797; *Journal du Concile national*, 8 Nov. 1797, pp. 146–47; minutes of the assembly of bishops and priests, 14 Nov. 1797, BPR, Concile national 1797, I.

19. Minister of police to minister of the navy, 23 Ventôse year 6 (13 March 1798), AN, F[7]3449.

20. Roussel to Grégoire, 1 Vendémiaire year 6 (22 Sept. 1797) and 19 Nov. 1797, BPR, EFGH; Capelle to Grégoire, 4 Oct. 1797, BPR, TUVWXYZ; Beauchessne to Grégoire, 10 Oct. 1797,

BPR, Loir-et-Cher; Jacquemin to Grégoire, 7 April 1798, BPR, TUVWXYZ; Grégoire et al., *Epître des évêques réunis*.

21. Edward Stevens to Timothy Pickering, 30 Sept. 1799, 13 Feb., and 16 March 1800, in "Letters of Toussaint-L'Ouverture and of Edward Stevens," pp. 84, 93, 94, 96; Jordan, *White Over Black*, p. 377.

22. Toussaint to anon., Oct. 1798 in *Annales de la religion* (1798), pp. 138–39, 142–44; Pierre Cun to Toussaint, 21 July 1798, and Hédouville to Toussaint, 12 Thermidor year 6 (30 July 1798), AN, F³202, colonies.

23. Tonnelier, *De la nécessité*, p. 3; *Moniteur*, réimpression, 27 April 1799, p. 660. Roume, who represented French authority in Saint-Domingue after Hédouville's departure, also was anticlerical, but he unsuccessfully urged the Directory to support Toussaint against Rigaud; see his letters to the minister of the navy and colonies from 2 Frimaire year 7 (22 November 1798) through 22 Prairial year 8 (11 June 1800), LC, Roume Papers, no. 28.

8

The New Amis des Noirs

Grégoire's revolutionary experiences taught him to pursue his goals through as many channels as he could find. He also learned to divide his projects into different stages or aspects. Thus, although he was most interested in restoring colonial religious institutions, he also considered the Negroes' secular problems and worried about slaves in the other parts of the new world. The success or failure of emancipation in the French empire, he thought, would influence the fate of slavery throughout the Western Hemisphere. Yet the West Indies could hardly prosper unless their political and economic institutions were drastically reorganized. Consequently, whenever opposition to his ecclesiastical projects seemed overwhelming, he became active in various secular associations which were dedicated to promoting imperial reform and indirectly to proving that abolition would work.

By 1795 the imperial problem was primarily an economic one. Grégoire understood very little about such matters, but he realized their importance. For example, he saw the need to replace the technology and capital which had left the Caribbean when the whites fled in 1793. Somehow land had to be reapportioned and Negroes had to be persuaded to produce an export crop. In addition, social and economic institutions which had been shattered by civil war, by foreign occupation, by emigration of wealthy planters, and by demoralization of the labor force had to be restored.

Because the government seemed incapable of providing the Caribbean territories with adequate assistance and because he knew so little about such matters himself, Grégoire brought together some of his friends who also hoped to make the French empire a model for the rest of the world. Although he could offer few concrete suggestions, he could encourage his friends and serve as coordinator and errand boy. He could also lend his prestige to the projects devised by such associates as Charles Bernhard Wadstrom, a Swedish naturalist, whose interest in Africa dated back thirty years, and Dr. Francis Lanthénas, a founding member of the defunct Société des Amis des Noirs, a colleague in the Colonial Commission, and a commissioner of the Paris Directory.[1]

Grégoire, Lanthénas, and Wadstrom agreed only in their concern over the French empire. Their interests and even their analysis of what problems actually confronted the colonies differed significantly. Lanthénas, for example, devised plans for using free labor on the plantations. Wadstrom, for his part, worried more about diplomatic problems. England so far had refused to abolish even the slave trade. Consequently the scientist feared that once the European war came to an end, renewed commercial rivalry between the two countries might force France to reestablish slavery and resume slave trading.[2]

Grégoire undoubtedly approved of Lanthénas' projects, but he disagreed with Wadstrom. Throughout his life, Grégoire underestimated the power of material interests and judged all questions according to ethical standards. He regarded English statesmen as moral men, and he accepted their antislavery pronouncements as sincere. Anxious to resume prerevolutionary ties with the English Slave Trade Committee, he hoped to restore diplomatic relations with Britain as soon as possible. Rather unrealistically, he assumed that Wadstrom, as a citizen of a neutral state, would serve as a liaison between philanthropists in both countries. But Wadstrom's scepticism concerning British motives prevented him from acting as an intermediary.[3]

Faced with many obstacles, at first Grégoire and his friends worked as private individuals, making no effort to coordinate their activities or to reconcile their differences. Then, early in 1796, they decided to expand their membership and to become a legally recognized organization which they called the Société des Amis des Noirs et des Colonies. They invited those members of the previous Amis des Noirs "who had constantly adhered to its true principles" to join their work. Allaying potential fears, the new society pledged to avoid political entanglement in factional disputes. This was a wise move because many of the Terror restraints on private associations remained in force.[4]

Grégoire informed the National Institute about the creation of the new Amis des Noirs while Lanthénas formally asked the government for permission to organize. The Directory, satisfied with the members' declaration of principles, authorized Grégoire and his friends to establish their society, and it held its first official meeting in March 1796.[5]

Of all the members of the new society, only the three founders really were committed to resolving colonial problems. During the following year, therefore, the membership proved too busy to meet regularly, and they saw each other on social occasions only. Nonetheless they drew up a vague but optimistic program which expressed faith in their ability to encourage other nations to liberate their Negroes. Slaveholding countries would follow France's lead, they thought, if the society demonstrated how colonial agriculture, trade, commerce, and industry would be advanced by using free labor. The members also planned to investigate the various scientific, medical, and legislative problems peculiar to the Western Hemisphere. Grégoire, unqualified to elucidate any of these topics, probably insisted upon including the moral and physical improvement of colonial citizens among the society's goals.[6]

The society remained inactive for another year. Then, perhaps coincidentally, shortly after the National Council closed and the time Grégoire devoted to the Constitutional church decreased, the society finally began to hold regular meetings and to keep records.

As it developed in late 1797 and in early 1798, the new society differed significantly from its more famous predecessor. Although it included several government officials among its members, it remained very cautious. Anxious to avoid publicity, for a time it refused to identify its pamphlets with the still suspect name, the Amis des Noirs, and very few outsiders were even aware of the society's existence. More importantly, it eschewed factional politics and devoted itself to promoting colonial industries and to proposing techniques for organizing free Negro laborers. The members steered clear of controversial issues and refrained from discussing moral problems. For example, they refused to sponsor a history of slave trading which Grégoire proposed. Perhaps fearing to praise the national enemy, and, in any case, admitting how much they depended on English information, the members asserted that they "did not want anything which would be mediocre or imperfect" in comparison with British publications on the same subject.[7]

Few people regularly attended the society's meetings, and, in March 1798, frustrated by their inability to complete any of their projects, they decided to expand their membership. In the process the society became a public association and underwent a significant transformation. It now adopted the vague humanitarian and egalitarian goals proclaimed by its predecessor. Meeting more frequently so as to increase its productivity, the society broadened its program to include the promotion of universal free trade, the establishment of experimental colonies, and the expansion of educational institutions within the existing empire.

Several people of contemporary importance joined the new Société des Amis des Noirs, such as the young economist Jean-Baptiste Say, the emancipator, Sonthonax, and the director of the colonial office, Granet. By November 1798 the society had sixty members, including seven representatives (Grégoire's term in the Council of Five Hundred had expired in May 1798), six government officials of varying importance, eight colonial residents, and six foreigners. Some mulattoes joined but were not identified as such on the membership roll.[8]

As reorganized in 1798, the society was more congenial to Grégoire's interests and outlook. Other members, however, felt uneasy with the new program. Fearing involvement in another political debacle, they urged the rest not to take sides on controversial questions. Although the society naturally attracted radicals, it did manage to avoid identification with any political faction, and it had no serious difficulties with the government.

Grégoire probably approved of the society's neutral policy since he scrupulously maintained the nonpartisan stance which he had adopted in 1792. Yet he was not unduly worried about planter agitation, and he permitted the society to use his address for correspondence. He also arranged to publicize the society's treatises in the *Décade philosophique*, a journal with which he had vague editorial connections. This same journal issued inexpensive reprints for the society.

Despite his practical services and despite his regular attendance after November 1797, Grégoire usually remained silent during the society's discussions. At one point he tried to outline a plan devised by another member for liquidating the colonists' debts and for purchasing whatever slaves remained in the colonies. He also read parts of, and the members agreed to collect material for, his history of slave trading.[9]

Expanded membership and increased publicity did not guarantee the official support which the society needed if it wished to undertake any significant colonial reforms. In the summer of 1798 it circulated memoranda to members of the legislature and asked the Directory for special privileges. At least the minister of the navy sympathized with the society's goals and provided the members with a room in which they could hold their meetings. But the society's schemes for expansion in Louisiana, Africa, and India were far too ambitious for France to undertake in 1798, and its plans remained little more than vague dreams.[10]

On 4 February 1799 the Société des Amis des Noirs et des Colonies celebrated the fifth anniversary of Negro emancipation by holding a public meeting in honor of the man directly responsible for abolition, Sonthonax. A large crowd attended and was treated to diverse entertainment. Grégoire provided the appropriate romantic note when he related "sentimental anecdotes which greatly moved the audience." The members were introduced to a young Negro who was being educated in France in preparation for returning to Africa. Say spoke, as did another member, on the "usefulness of admitting women into philanthropic societies."[11]

Sonthonax's speech, however, was the high point of the evening. Praising himself and the National Convention for fulfilling the promises contained in the Declaration of the Rights of Man, he pointed to those parts of the world where slavery and slave trading still flourished. He exhorted his audience to fight for complete Negro freedom so that, eventually, France's example would spread to the rest of the world. "You are still the [Negroes'] brothers and [their] friends even though they now are free," he reminded the assembled crowd. Sonthonax's speech implied that the society intended to embark upon a new aggressive campaign, and the audience disbanded in a self-congratulatory mood.[12]

The success of the 4 February celebration encouraged the

Amis des Noirs to undertake more venturesome projects. Yet memories of the old Société des Amis des Noirs still haunted individual members. Some thought that an increased publication program might "forestall or destroy the prejudices which might arise against us in one part of the public and perhaps among members of the administration and the government." Reversing their earlier, more cautious policy, the members decided to print both their debates and scholarly treatises concerning colonial problems. They even considered sponsoring annual essay contests similar to those organized by prerevolutionary scientific societies.[13]

Perhaps the prejudices noted in mid-1799 succeeded in destroying the society, but more probably it disintegrated after its two most active members, Wadstrom and Lanthénas, died earlier that year. Grégoire could not replace the leadership provided by his two collaborators, and after September he evidently did little to prolong the society's life.[14]

The new Amis des Noirs' brief history showed how superficial the French intellectuals' concern over the colonies actually was. Wadstrom, at least, had realized this, and he had exhorted the members to show more zeal and perseverance in making Negro freedom a practical reality. But, satisfied with congratulating themselves for having achieved emancipation before any other country, the Amis des Noirs failed to take the time to investigate seriously the complex problems which abolition had created, and during its four years the society produced only meagre results.[15]

For Grégoire the society was only one of several means whereby he tried to rebuild the Caribbean colonies, and he adopted a passive role in it. Since the members were not interested in his moral, religious program, he never contributed significantly to their creative activities, and after he made one feeble attempt in 1798 to present a technical report, he remained silent during its meetings and expressed his own ideas elsewhere. The collapse of this society did not seriously disturb him, and after it disbanded he, almost alone among its surviving members, continued to devote his attention to colonial problems.

Even before the Société des Amis des Noirs et des Colonies began to disintegrate, Grégoire first presented to the National Institute the various reports which he prepared on subjects relating to Negroes and to slavery. The Institute was imperialistic and belligerently nationalistic; both Talleyrand and Bonaparte, for example, used it as a sounding board for their Egyptian scheme. The members were also strongly anticlerical, and after his experience in 1796 Grégoire tried very hard to tailor his reports to this audience. Contrary to his earlier practice, he scrupulously avoided discussing his religious plans, and he even went so far as to characterize the English antislavery movement as Machiavellian. In addition, he attributed French emancipation to enlightenment ideology rather than Christian influence.[16]

Grégoire's reports to the National Institute covered several subjects. He traced the history of slavery, answered the planters' charges against the old Amis des Noirs, and suggested general methods of helping Negroes use their freedom wisely. In May 1799 he read a paper on what was to become his favorite subject, the intellectual, spiritual, and technical achievements of liberated Negroes. In this speech he reverted to the theory, first discussed in his Essai sur la régénération, that intellectual and moral characteristics depended on environmental rather than hereditary or racial factors. He promised to use all the evidence he could find to destroy "certain unfavorable theories" about Negroes and to prove that "their vices are the work of tyranny; their virtues belong to them."[17]

Grégoire faced the same obstacles in the National Institute as he did in the Société des Amis des Noirs et des Colonies. The members were unconcerned about the humanitarian and moral issues which interested him. In their eagerness to expand the empire as a means of combatting England, they ignored the existing colonies and cared little about the former slaves. Consequently, they disregarded most of Grégoire's moralistic appeals and did not bother to print his speeches in their records.[18]

Grégoire's attempts to bring about the physical reconstruction and moral regeneration of the colonies came to naught under the Directory. Neither the politicians nor the intellectuals were really interested in making the French empire into a model for the rest of the world. Indeed, when Bonaparte assumed power in November 1799, the empire served foreign egalitarians more as a warning than as a source of encouragement.

The outbreak of revolution in France and the subsequent emancipation of slaves created severe dislocations in all of the French colonies, but Saint-Domingue suffered the most severely. Although the French finally expelled the English from the island, neither military nor civilian officials succeeded in reasserting metropolitan authority. Despite the efforts of Grégoire and his associates, racial civil war, now between Negroes and mulattoes, continued unabated. Schools and churches remained closed, and the Saint-Dominguean economy reverted to subsistence agriculture.[19]

Between 1795 and 1799 military and political conditions as well as general apathy prevented Grégoire from sponsoring a complete program of colonial reform. Still, he played a more constructive role during the Directory than he had under previous regimes. His work was, in part, conservative; for several years he helped combat the landowners' attempts to reimpose a racial caste system upon the colonies. At the same time he defended the early abolitionists' reputations. But, most important of all, he and his friends began what would prove to be a long and frustrating process of readjusting colonial institutions to an egalitarian society. While his practically-oriented colleagues considered social, economic, and administrative questions, he, more than before, limited himself to problems which he understood, primarily religious and educational ones.

Throughout the Directory Grégoire avoided many of the errors which had marred his earlier legislative career. He not only limited himself to areas in which he was competent, but he tempered his rhetoric, refrained from making vicious personal attacks, worked directly with the appropriate government officials, and resisted the temptation to appeal over their heads to public opinion. When a proposal proved impractical, he abandoned it until a more propitious time while he found new outlets for his superabundant energy. Grégoire would never show exceptional political ability, but his activities between 1795 and 1799 indicate that even he profited from the experiences of the Terror.

Grégoire's major goal during the Directory was to restore the Constitutional church. In his dealings with the colonies he was more concerned about establishing a black ministry than about solving any of their other problems.

Grégoire's emphasis on religion is understandable. Yet, although his motives were partially sectarian, his program had an element of disinterestedness as well. If it had succeeded, it would have hurt rather than helped the Constitutional church. This institution could ill afford to send any of its personnel to the colonies because it needed all available ecclesiastics to train priests who could fill vacant posts in France. Grégoire was concerned about the shortage of continental priests, but he regarded colonial needs as even more pressing. Unless steps were promptly taken, he feared, Christian Negroes would lapse into paganism and pagan ones would never learn the truth. He did not think that France was as seriously threatened by apostasy as were the West Indies.

Grégoire's sectarianism did not lessen the egalitarian intention of his program. Instead, his willingness to sacrifice the interests of the French Constitutional church indicates how sincere his concern for the Negroes actually was. Evidently, even where the church was involved, he believed that moral principles outweighed practical considerations.

Grégoire justified his interest in colonial religion on secular as well as religious grounds. As long as the colonies remained French and continued to send deputies to the metropolitan legislature, the inhabitants had to be educated, assimilated to French life, and persuaded to accept European institutions. Because most white residents had fled the West Indies in 1793, only the church could help absorb mulattoes and Negroes into European society. The church's secular, cultural role became even more important after the Société des Amis des Noirs et des Colonies disbanded in 1799. When Bonaparte came to power, therefore, Grégoire determined to create West Indian bishoprics, no matter what the cost to him or his church might be.

NOTES

1. Minutes of the Société des Amis des Noirs et des Colonies for early 1796, BPR, TUVWXYZ. Grégoire performed similar functions for the Société de la Philosophie Chrétienne which he helped to found at the same time; see "Journal historique" in anon. private collection in Paris.

2. Wadstrom, *Adresse au Corps législatif*; Lanthénas to the Directory, 20 Pluviôse year 4 (9 Feb. 1796), BPR, TUVWXYZ.

3. Grégoire's remarks on 22 Jan. 1796 in the *Décade philosophique*, 10 Ventôse year 4 (29 Feb. 1796), p. 411.

4. "Règlemen de la Société," undated, BPR, TUVWXYZ; Wadstrom to friend, 8 Messidor (26 June [1797]), BPR, Paris Presbytery.

5. *Décade philosophique*, 10 Ventôse year 4 (29 Feb. 1796), pp. 402–12; Lanthénas to the Directory, 20 Pluviôse year 4 (9 Feb. 1796), BPR, TUVWXYZ.

6. "Règlemen de la Société," undated, BPR, TUVWXYZ;

Charles-Philbert Lasteyrie to Grégoire, 10 Aug. 1797, anon. private collection in Paris.

7. Aussy, Mentor, and Bayard, "Rapport," undated, BPR, TUVWXYZ. (Unless otherwise noted, all information concerning the Société des Amis des Noirs et des Colonies comes from this collection.) Still, the society did receive letters of encouragement from the Philadelphia convention of abolitionist societies; see: J. Bloompist, 9 May 1797, in BPR, TUVWXYZ, and *Merchants' Daily Advertiser* (Philadelphia), 13 July 1797.

8. Minutes, 10 and 20 Pluviôse year 6 (29 Jan. and 8 Feb. 1798), BPR, TUVWXYZ; Lanthénas to Bancal-des-Issarts, 20 Ventôse year 6 (10 March 1798), BN, NAF 9534, p. 303; Wadstrom, [*Note présentée à la Société des amis des noirs*]; printed letters in BPR, Rév. 171, no. 35, 38, and answers from Tournelier, Jean-Baptiste Say, and Gaillard, all dated May 1798, in BPR, Rev. 171, no. 72, 77, 78; LePays to Lanthénas, 17 Messidor year 6 (5 July 1798), and Braid to the Amis des Noirs, 14 Vendémiaire year 7 (5 Oct. 1798), ibid., no. 73, 76.

9. Minutes for 25 and 29 Germinal (14 and 18 April), 10 and 20 Floréal year 6 (29 April and 9 May 1798), and 20 Frimaire year 7 (10 Dec. 1798), BPR, TUVWXYZ.

10. Antoine Vallée to Lanthénas, 18 Prairial year 6 (6 June 1798), and Lescallier to Lanthénas, 10 Messidor year 6 (28 June 1798), in BPR, Rév. 171, no. 75, 74; minutes for 20 and 30 Floréal (9 and 19 May), 20 Fructidor year 6 (6 Sept. 1798), 20 Frimaire year 7 (10 Dec. 1798), and 30 Pluviôse year 7 (18 Feb. 1799), BPR, TUVWXYZ.

11. *Chronique universelle*, 29 Pluviôse year 7 (17 Feb. 1799). The society invited the wives of all of its members to join as well as the English poetess, Helene Williams.

12. Sonthonax, "Discours," 16 Pluviôse year 7 (4 Feb. 1799), BPR, TUVWXYZ. His statement was a paraphrase of the English abolitionists' motto. See also *Chronique universelle*, 29 Pluviôse year 7 (17 Feb. 1799).

13. Lasteyrie, Théremin, and Say, "Rapport fait," undated, BPR, TUVWXYZ; report on regulations by Wadstrom, Dugout, and Lepage, 30 Brumaire year 7 (20 Nov. 1798), BPR, Rév. 171, no. 67.

14. The events of mid-1799 might have intervened. Grégoire was embroiled in a controversy with the Paris Constitutional church, see Necheles, "The Abbé," pp. 292–93.

15. Wadstrom, [*Note présentée*]. Jordan asserts that secular abolitionists in America, who based their egalitarianism on natural rights philosophy, were almost uniformly incapable of pursuing their ideas beyond the act of emancipation, and that only the Quakers who, just as Grégoire, were religious egalitarians, considered the problems involved in assimilating ex-slaves. This was not quite true in France; the mere existence of the Société des Amis des Noirs et des Colonies indicates that a few Frenchmen felt some obligation towards the Negroes in the colonies which they were incapable of translating into concrete or sustained action, however. Jordan's theory might help explain their inactivity in contrast with Grégoire's continuing concern about the fate of the Haitians: Jordan, *White Over Black*, pp. 353–62.

16. *Mémoires de l'Institut*, year 4 (1796); vol. I, pp. 552–66. Also *Moniteur*, réimpression, 14 April 1796, p. 198.

17. *Magazine encyclopédique*, 1 Prairial year 7 (20 May 1799), p. 116; 1 Ventôse year 7 (19 Feb. 1799), p. 370; minutes of the Société des Amis des Noirs, 10 Germinal year 7 (30 March 1799), BPR, TUVWXYZ; Gruvel to Grégoire, 14 Messidor year 7 (2 July 1799), BPR, Concile 1811; Münter to Grégoire, 9 May 1799, Arsenal 5290, p. 157 verso. Grégoire tried the same approach in justifying Jewish rights; see "Sur la littérature des juifs," *Correspondance sur les affaires du temps* 3 (1797): 88–91.

18. One of the few exceptions was Philippe-Rose Roume, a French agent in Saint-Domingue who belatedly joined the abolitionist cause and who encouraged Grégoire's study of African intellectual and cultural life; see Roume to Grégoire, 28 Pluviôse year 10 (17 Feb. 1802), LC, Roume Papers, no. 29, pp. 54–59.

19. For contrary evidence see J. B. Deville to Société des Amis des Noirs, undated but read during the session of 30 Pluviôse year 7 (18 Feb. 1799), BPR, TUVWXYZ.

9

Grégoire and
the Anti-Bonapartists

Guided by Bonaparte, the Consulate accelerated the counterrevolutionary trend begun by the Thermidorians and continued
under the Directory. Most Frenchmen readily accepted the
domestic stability and international prestige which Bonaparte
promised in exchange for innovations which had little impact
on their daily lives—the right to participate in government and
the equal status of non-Christian religions, for example. They
did not care whether privileges were extended to such people
as Jews, West Indian mulattoes, and Negroes, whom they
regarded as foreigners in any case.

During the Consulate, resistance to Bonaparte's program
came from a small clique of doctrinaire republicans, professional and frequently corrupt politicians, and men who had
personal or sectarian reasons for dissent. Grégoire joined this
opposition because the government gradually reversed all the
reforms which he had promoted during the preceding decade.
The First Consul restored many aspects of prerevolutionary
Catholicism including papal jurisdiction over the French
church. In addition, he reimposed slavery in the colonies

and violated the principle of universal equality by creating a new aristocracy and by imposing special restrictions on northeastern Jews.[1]

Throughout his years in opposition, Grégoire retained his interest in religious and social equality, concentrating upon two problems which seemed to him to be related: defending the so-called Gallican Liberties and helping the Africans in their homeland and in the new world. Although his activities were insignificant, his writings during the Napoleonic era are interesting because he finally had sufficient leisure to analyze the theories which lay behind his earlier political activities. The books which he wrote after 1799 shed considerable light on his thought, and they illustrate the limitations of his moralistic and sectarian approach to egalitarian problems.

Throughout the Napoleonic regime Grégoire pursued his antiracist and pro-Jewish campaigns simultaneously; but in public he divorced one issue from the other and both from his political opposition to imperial institutions. Although he tried to discuss the various aspects of egalitarianism separately, they were united in his mind by his long-range goal of preparing all men for the millennium. Now the chiliastic aspirations which underlaid his secular and religious policies became apparent, and he increasingly showed that he wanted to assist persecuted minority groups, especially Jews and Negroes, because he hoped to bring God's plan a little closer to realization.

Steadily embittered by contemporary events, Grégoire became obsessed with a sense of decay. Occasionally he speculated whether the disasters which occurred during the latter part of the Empire did not foretell the apocalypse. Such pessimistic ideas never completely supplanted his revolutionary optimism, but he became less and less confident of his or anyone else's ability to save his countrymen from their own folly, particularly after they repeatedly rejected his advice. Although he never considered his personal success or failure to be a matter of great significance, he regretted his loss of political influence at just the time when his most important programs were being reversed. Despairing about Europe's future, he predicted that moral leadership would be transferred from the old to the new world. He therefore hoped to advise those countries in the Western Hemisphere where his prestige had not been tarnished by French political controversies.[2]

Contrary to Grégoire's optimistic and this-worldly outlook during the early, promising days of the Revolution, his writings after 1799 were permeated with a sense of personal urgency. He was growing older while so much remained to be accomplished. In order to concentrate his diminishing energy, he became even more sectarian and dogmatic, although after the Concordat of 1802 which disbanded the Constitutional church he no longer had an organized church through which he could operate. Prevented by his republicanism from assuming an important political role, and finding himself increasingly excluded from intellectual circles, Grégoire fell back upon his position as retired bishop of Blois and saw little opportunity for helping any of his protégés save through religious institutions.

Still Grégoire was not unduly disturbed by Bonaparte's seizure of power in 1799 because the First Consul only gradually unveiled his program. Bonaparte at first appeared ready to maintain certain revolutionary reforms, and his early actions, especially those involving imperial affairs, were encouraging. In 1800 he reappointed the mulatto Raimond as civil commissioner for Saint-Domingue and confirmed Toussaint's usurped authority there. In addition, he offered Guillaume Mauviel, Grégoire's former secretary and bishop-designate of Saint-Domingue, free transportation to the Caribbean.

Since Bonaparte did not permit the bishop-designate of Cayenne to go to his diocese, Mauviel's mission assumed great significance for Grégoire. This diocese, he optimistically assumed, eventually would serve as a base from which the Constitutional church, or at least a national rather than a

Roman church, could be extended throughout the French West Indies.[3]

Shortly after Grégoire learned that Mauviel would be permitted to depart for Saint-Domingue, he decided to use the debate concerning Bonaparte's Concordat negotiations to arouse interest in the bishop's mission. Now, he thought, was the time to answer the anticlericals' criticism of the church and to repeat his earlier arguments concerning the role which Christianity had played in the antislavery movement.

One of the examples which anticlericals cited to justify their animosity towards Catholicism was the legend of Bartolomé de Las Casas. This sixteenth-century Spanish bishop supposedly had suggested using African slaves rather than Indians in the new world colonies. Hence, according to anti-Catholics, the church was directly responsible for Negro degradation. Grégoire, however, unearthed evidence which discredited the tale, and in 1800 he presented this new information in a paper, an *Apologie de Las Casas*, which he read before a public meeting of the National Institute. The Spanish prelate, he insisted, along with "all benefactors of mankind," had considered "men of all countries to be members of a single human family, obligated to love and to assist one another and endowed with the same rights."[4] Consequently it was not, as anticlericals claimed, religious fanaticism which had enslaved Negroes, but religious charity which had tried to save and to protect them.

Grégoire praised other Christians besides Catholics. He asserted that devout members of all sects shared the same ideals, and he cited a long line of pious opponents of slavery which stretched from Las Casas to Thomas Clarkson. In later years his friends added his name to the list and gave him the title, "the new Las Casas," but at the moment Grégoire could not overcome anti-Catholic sentiment among leading members of the National Institute, and this paper had greater popularity outside France than it had in his own community.[5]

Grégoire hoped to persuade his friends in France to assist

him in providing the colonies with religious institutions, but he was even more interested in guaranteeing Mauviel a favorable reception in Saint-Domingue. He wrote letters of introduction to Toussaint and to the French commander in the island. He also advised the bishop as to how he should behave and urged him to pursue sectarian and egalitarian goals simultaneously. Mauviel, Grégoire suggested, could combat civil strife by preaching relevant parts of the gospel and by disseminating Constitutional literature throughout the island. This, he assumed, would seriously undermine the Romans by highlighting their failure to campaign against racial prejudice.[6]

Despite Grégoire's letters of introduction, when Mauviel arrived in Saint-Domingue in 1801 Toussaint refused to recognize him as bishop. The Negro leader originally had asked Grégoire for Constitutional priests, but by the time the prelate arrived in the West Indies, Toussaint had openly espoused Roman Catholicism. Naively expecting the pope to side with him against the French government, Toussaint adhered to orthodoxy. But the Concordat negotiations frustrated his scheme, and when he realized that Rome would never recognize his regime, he tried to force Mauviel to acknowledge his rule over the island.

At first Mauviel proclaimed his loyalty to the Negro general, but after a few months he became disillusioned with the chaos created by emancipation, and, calling Toussaint "infamous" and a "monster," he fled to the Spanish part of the island. There he joined the French expedition when it landed in January 1802. Events in France, particularly the conclusion of the Concordat, made his position increasingly tenuous, however.[7]

The Concordat negotiations, which eventually terminated the schism within the French church, took almost a year to complete. Well before Bonaparte and the pope agreed to terms, Grégoire, who had been consulted earlier, knew enough about the probable provisions of the Concordat to understand the threat that it posed to his domestic and colonial schemes. He vigorously opposed the Concordat but was unable to save the Constitutional church at home. Nonetheless, he tried to salvage at least the French controlled colonial church from the wreckage of his dreams, and together with three other Constitutional bishops, he urged Bonaparte to include the newly established West Indian dioceses in the Concordat. Repeating the arguments which Grégoire had employed during the National Council in 1797, they recommended Mauviel and the bishop-designate of Cayenne, the former apostolic vicar Nicolas Jacquemin, as candidates for two of these sees.[8]

Under other circumstances, Grégoire's logic might have convinced Bonaparte, who, in the future, would freely infringe upon papal jurisdiction. But in 1801 the First Consul refused to jeopardize the delicate Concordat negotiations by insisting on a peripheral matter. Although the minister of religion wrote Grégoire a polite reply, the government avoided taking any stand whatsoever concerning the colonial church, and it was not mentioned in the final version of the Concordat. Thus Bonaparte implicitly recognized Roman jurisdiction over the West Indies.[9]

Grégoire's political power steadily diminished after 1801, and he could do no more than petition the government. This decline was not obvious to outsiders because the Brumaire coup d'état had permitted his reelection to the legislature (the Legislative Body) after a two years' absence, and during the Consulate and Empire he received several honorific titles. Nonetheless, Bonaparte's progressively authoritarian regime emasculated the representative bodies and gradually stifled all independent political action. Despite Grégoire's impressive titles and despite Bonaparte's early attempts to win his allegiance by consulting him, Grégoire found he could no longer influence policy decisions and was, instead, relegated to the harmless position of symbolic leader of the small and ineffectual group of anti-Bonapartists.

Much against his will, after 1800 Grégoire again became involved in factional politics. Primarily because of his outspoken stand on the Concordat, anti-Bonapartists nominated him to the Senate early in 1801, and his election by the senators in December, over Bonaparte's repeated objections, made him a prominent member of the opposition. The senatorial revolt against the Concordat failed, however. During the next six months Bonaparte completed his negotiations with the pope, reimposed slavery, and in many other ways convinced Grégoire that his position as senator was an empty honor.

Grégoire's evaluation of the Senate's power was vindicated when in 1802 Bonaparte neglected to consult either the Legislative Bodies or the Council of State about his decisions to launch an expedition against Saint-Domingue and to restore slavery. Instead of asking his advice, as he had done during the Concordat negotiations, Bonaparte publicly taunted Grégoire for his pro-Negro reputation.[10]

Grégoire was more seriously affected when, as the expedition to Saint-Domingue began to falter, Bonaparte forbade the publication of all works remotely related to colonial affairs. This was a sharp and sudden reversal of a government policy which had permitted a lively debate on all aspects of the colonial controversy during the two years which had preceded the expedition. During this time the planters had freely advocated the restoration of slavery and had renewed their old attacks on the Amis des Noirs, including Grégoire.[11] Then, suddenly, Grégoire found himself unable to defend his past career, to say nothing of proposing future reforms.

Prevented from criticizing Bonaparte's colonial policy by censorship regulations and by the impotence of the Senate, Grégoire tried to use his personal influence with prominent members of the government. News that the French expedition in Saint-Domingue had abolished civil rule there distressed him, and he expressed his concern to Charles LeClerc, Bonaparte's brother-in-law and commander of the expeditionary force. Military government, Grégoire protested, was "a monstrosity contrary to healthy fundamental principles of all good government and especially of ours" because, he postulated, "the separation of powers is an inviolable rule for social organization."[12]

Grégoire refrained from explicitly criticizing the reinstitution of slavery either in his letter to LeClerc or in his published works. For the next few years he found no opportunity to discuss the matter in public although he did insert remarks concerning the evils of slavery and the innate equality of all men into some of his publications. In addition, he continued to collect material for the project which he had begun in 1798, a study of Negro intellectual capacities.[13]

Grégoire became interested in Africa as such and sponsored at least one society dedicated to exploring that continent. But he did not perceive how imperialism intensified what he regarded as outstanding contemporary problems, race prejudice and military despotism. Fearing these evils would outlive him, in his first will he set aside funds for a prize contest on the topic "What is the best way to erase the white man's unjust and barbaric prejudice against African and mulatto skin color?" and he endowed another contest on ways to prevent military authority from usurping civilian rights.[14]

Disgusted with events in France and convinced he need not attend the Senate's sessions, in June 1802 Grégoire took advantage of the temporary truce provided by the Peace of Amiens and fled to England. From the British point of view his visit was undesirable. For a decade French emigré priests had bitterly denounced the members of the Constitutional church, especially Grégoire. Hence the Constitutional bishop met with a mixed reception in London. The anti-Jacobin editor William Cobbett, for example, condemned the prelate's supposedly anti-Catholic behavior during the Terror. Justified or not, other Englishmen shared Cobbett's views and disapproved of his visit.[15]

Even some prominent British abolitionists greeted Grégoire without enthusiasm. Although the patriarch, Granville Sharp, still admired him, others blamed him for the severe setback which the disastrous events in Saint-Domingue had caused the English antislavery movement. The most prominent abolitionist, William Wilberforce, who was even more antirevolutionary than some of his colleagues, found Grégoire both too Catholic and too radical for his evangelical and socially conservative tastes. "I do not much effect the Abbé," he confided in his diary. He summed up Grégoire's personality: "La Religion, Humanité [sic], La Liberté. That is my object."[16]

For the moment Wilberforce kept his opinions to himself and invited Grégoire to visit a school for African youths which he and other abolitionists had established. He also presented Grégoire with a collection of records which he hoped Grégoire would use in his publications.[17] Impressed by his courteous reception, Grégoire would never understand Wilberforce's unfavorable reaction to him.

Grégoire remained in England for only a short time. When he returned to Paris, he found that Mauviel's position in Saint-Domingue had improved considerably. The initial French invasion of the island had proved successful. Although the future king of Haiti, Henry Christophe, opposed LeClerc's landing, the French soon conquered most of the coast line. Some of Toussaint's subordinates submitted, and by April Toussaint and Christophe began negotiations with the French. Even the most vigorously anti-French general, Jean-Jacques Dessalines, was forced to recognize LeClerc's authority early in May. One month later, the French kidnapped Toussaint and sent him to Europe. Toussaint's most powerful generals, Dessalines and Christophe, refused to aid the man who they believed had betrayed them, and only isolated uprisings occurred.

Confident that black resistance had been destroyed, LeClerc began to prepare for civilian rule. He appointed a provisional assembly to advise him on domestic affairs. In addition, he encouraged the Constitutional bishop, Mauviel, to exercise his episcopal functions and granted him a prelate's salary. The pope neglected to provide apostolic vicars for the West Indies, and the French official, praising Mauviel's loyalty, urged Bonaparte to confirm the bishop's jurisdiction and to send additional priests.[18]

Mauviel, encouraged by the French general's support, petitioned Bonaparte to provide formal organization for the colonial church. The First Consul evidently took his commander's advice more seriously than Grégoire's and he publicly repeated his general's statements. Yet when he asked the opinion of one of his advisors, he received an unfavorable response. Since Mauviel had been selected by the abolitionist Grégoire, the official commented, the bishop must be a Negrophile and, therefore, probably disapproved of Bonaparte's now official policy to reinstitute slavery. Emphasizing the illegality of Mauviel's mission, the official characterized it as incompatible with the Concordat.[19]

By October 1802 the French expedition began to falter. Mulatto and Negro leaders mutinied, and LeClerc died soon thereafter. General Donatien-Marie Rochambeau, who succeeded LeClerc, followed an earlier, anticlerical tradition. Distrusting the bishop's loyalty, he soon quarreled with Mauviel. The bishop regarded him as worse than any of Robespierre's officials, while Rochambeau objected to the prelate because he supposedly had encouraged Negro resistance to reenslavement. Moreover, he considered priests to be a divisive influence and saw no need to have any in the colony. Rochambeau's successor was even more critical of Mauviel, and the bishop left Saint-Domingue in 1804, after the Negro leader, Dessalines, had proclaimed Haitian independence and the French had lost effective control over most of the island.[20]

During his four years' stay, Mauviel failed to accomplish any of his more important tasks, such as establishing a seminary and creating a complete educational system for Saint-Domingue.

He did, however, spread Grégoire's reputation as an egalitarian, and he encouraged antipapal sentiment among the Negro population there.[21]

Even before Mauviel left Saint-Domingue, however, his friendship with Grégoire began to cool. Mauviel became increasingly disillusioned when faced with the reality of emancipation. Yet Grégoire could view events in the Caribbean with the equanimity provided by five thousand miles of intervening ocean. For example, he continued to regard Toussaint as an outstanding example of what Negroes might accomplish if given an opportunity, even though he later admitted some of the general's shortcomings. But Mauviel could not view Toussaint so dispassionately. When he returned to Paris, he and Grégoire did not renew their earlier close friendship, and Mauviel occasionally accused Grégoire of having abandoned him.[22]

By the time that Mauviel returned home, Grégoire had retreated into semiretirement. Bonaparte, confident of his power within France, followed a lenient policy towards his opponents and left them alone as long as they proved to be ineffective. The few whom he regarded as potentially dangerous, such as Mme de Staël, were sent into exile, but Grégoire did not receive even this dubious distinction. Caution and his long-standing friendship with the minister of police, Joseph Fouché, saved Grégoire from anything more discomforting than political oblivion. This remained true even after he dramatically severed relations with Napoleon by alluding to Caesar when he voted against establishing an hereditary empire. Grégoire distrusted Fouché's continued benevolence, however. It was impossible, he commented to one of his friends, "to do good safely in the midst of so many sots and perverse people."[23]

By 1807 Napoleon had so revised the constitution that the Senate became what Grégoire disparagingly called a "bureau for registering Bonaparte's will."[24] As far as Grégoire was concerned, the only way France could be saved was by overthrowing the

Empire. When he reached that conclusion, he joined another unsuccessful plot against Napoleon's regime. Although he thereafter retreated to the suburbs, hoping to lead the quiet life of writer and retired bishop, he could not resist returning to the capital for crucial votes in the Senate. For example, in 1809 he not only voted against Napoleon's divorce but also admonished the emperor: "Such conduct does not agree with conscience," he reportedly said.[25] Napoleon ignored Grégoire's disapproval, which was shared by more orthodox clerics, and Grégoire sank further into disfavor.

Following Grégoire's complete break with Napoleon, the censors vigilantly scrutinized his manuscripts. Grégoire used his connections in Germany to print some of his pamphlets there, and he took special precautions with what he expected to be a very controversial book, his *Littérature des Nègres*. Both the deliberately misleading and cumbersome title and an, even for him, unusually pedantic style were designed to confuse the censors. Fouché, despite his friendship, might have had to seize the book if he thought it explicitly criticized imperial policy. Insofar as the book's entire thesis, "Negroes are capable of virtues and talents," denied any racial justification for slavery, it did indeed attack the government, but Grégoire carefully left his readers free to draw their own conclusions. He limited himself to asserting that the Negroes' intellectual accomplishments provided "irrefutable arguments against [their] enemies."[26]

Grégoire's *Littérature des Nègres* discussed far more than literature. It is interesting because in it he indicated a new approach to social problems. He used still unsystematic anthropological observations to achieve a scientific definition of race which would disprove the "curse of Ham." In addition, he employed Montesquieu's concepts concerning the relationship between environment and institutions to demonstrate how the same people, exposed to different physical conditions, would develop divergent social patterns. Thus, for example, he attributed to climatic conditions the African Negroes' failure to attain the cultural heights achieved by European societies. Africa, he insisted, had a too congenial environment which permitted men to survive without forcing them to create an advanced civilization. Throughout his book he cited examples of how Negroes who had been transported to the new world and placed in favorable (or less favorable) circumstances demonstrated the same talents and virtues common among whites. Indeed, he sarcastically compared Haitian and French history during the preceding twenty years and challenged his readers to discern evidence of greater stability or higher civilization in French events.

Although Grégoire tried to use social science methods, his *Littérature des Nègres* shows, even more than his writings on Jews, the extent to which he and his contemporaries judged other civilizations in European terms exclusively. Jews, after all, lived as a minority within European society and had to conform to their cultural environment if they were to survive. Negroes and mulattoes, however, made up a large part of the African and Caribbean population, and it no longer is as evident to us as it was to eighteenth-century Frenchmen that they must adopt western civilization before qualifying as equals.

Grégoire did not—could not, for all his efforts to be tolerant —find any virtue or evidence of civilization in non-Christian Africa. That continent, according to him, had reached its highest level of development under the early North African church; thereafter it had lapsed into barbarism and paganism which, for him, were synonymous. Failing to recognize the existence of values and cultures different from the European model, Grégoire later could not understand Haitian needs, and his relations with the population there, despite his great sympathy, became increasingly strained. If one accepts his criterion, as did his contemporaries, then Grégoire was correct in attempting to impose European Christianity on Africans (and Jews), but in actuality his desire to impose cultural conformity denied the very tolerance which he so fervently proclaimed.

Grégoire's *Littérature des Nègres* could not alter the opinions of those who either regarded slavery as a necessary evil or who firmly believed in racial inequality. The book was tedious and encyclopedic, but it still "excited [the planters'] just indignation." Fouché lifted the ban on literature concerning the colonies and permitted several procolonialists to answer Grégoire's work.[27] Disturbed by the planters' charges, Grégoire bitterly accused the French press of transforming "the literary scene into a gladiatorial arena." "Between virtue and crime," he insisted, "there can be neither peace nor truce; it is an interminable war." Fouché also permitted a few of Grégoire's friends to defend the work, and Grégoire, ostensibly ignoring his enemies and encouraged by his acquaintances' response, began to plan a supplementary work describing what he termed the slave trade among whites.[28]

At first Grégoire had doubted whether he could publish his *Littérature des Nègres* in France, and, in any case, he expected more from foreign than from French readers. Consequently he also arranged for German and English translations when he submitted the manuscript to a French publisher.[29] Even when publication in France was assured, he continued his plans for foreign editions. He wanted to spread his ideas throughout as many countries as possible because he believed that emancipation would be permanent only if it were achieved through international agreement.

Grégoire regarded the English translation as most important. Britain and the United States had outlawed slave trading in 1808. But anticipating that egalitarians would be satisfied with this victory, Grégoire hoped, through his *Littérature des Nègres*, to encourage pro-Negro forces to continue their fight until slavery itself came to an end in both empires.[30] He therefore urged the American consul in Paris, David Bailie Warden, to render his work into English.

Rather tactlessly, but expecting to win the patronage of such an important man, Grégoire sent a manuscript copy of Warden's translation to Thomas Jefferson. Jefferson, whom

Grégoire had criticized in this work for postulating innate Negro inferiority, was unconvinced by the author's logic and enraged by the former bishop's unintentional involvement in American political feuds. Although he wrote a polite reply to Grégoire, Jefferson privately charged him with gullibility and was unwilling to do any more for the American abolitionist cause for the moment. Lacking Jefferson's support, for two years Warden could not find a publisher in the United States.[31]

Jefferson's irritation with Grégoire arose out of a ludicrous but typical incident. In 1809 Grégoire wrote a letter attacking an engraving in Joel Barlow's long epic poem, the *Columbiad*, which he regarded as anti-Catholic. Jefferson's and Barlow's enemies, the Federalists, used Grégoire's letter as political propaganda. Barlow thought it necessary to mollify his old friend by printing a reply. If other Catholics had been like Grégoire, he wrote, "the world at this day would all be catholics." Grégoire regretted the Federalists' publication of his letter, and although Barlow readily forgave him, the incident deeply antagonized Jefferson.[32]

Unaware of Jefferson's real reaction to his book, and cut off from both the United States and England by the events which preceded the War of 1812 (which coincided with Napoleon's Russian campaign), Grégoire turned again to his French readers. Fouché's willingness to permit the circulation of his *Littérature des Nègres* apparently encouraged Grégoire to broaden his indirect attack on imperial institutions, and he published a *Histoire des Sectes* in 1810.

The subject of Grégoire's newest book, the theological errors into which various schismatic churches had fallen, was in itself unobjectionable. In the process of describing these groups, however, Grégoire strayed far from the point and implicitly criticized Napoleon's proslavery and anti-Jewish policies. He scattered references to the abolitionist activities of various Protestant sects and substantiated the assertion which he had first made in 1796 and had repeated in 1800: a religious man, no matter what his creed, could not tolerate slavery. He showered praise on Wilberforce, the Quakers, and the American abolitionists for their long and only recently fruitful fight against the slave trade.[33]

Grégoire's indiscretions were too much even for Fouché. Despite his friendship with Grégoire (who, after all, had persistently ignored the minister of police's private warnings), he seized and destroyed all of the copies of the *Histoire* which he could find. A short time later Napoleon established a separate censorship bureau beyond Fouché's jurisdiction.[34]

After the police seized his *Histoire des sectes*, Grégoire was effectively silenced and had to mark time until the ban against him was lifted. Nonetheless, he tried to rescue what he could by publishing some of his works in Germany. He also incorporated part of his condemned book into a paper which he read before the small circle of the National Institute. In this report he described discrimination in France, attacked all forms of social stratification, and reserved his harshest remarks for religious persecution, especially of Jews. This report evidently led to further censure, because subsequent installments were innocuous, and Grégoire never fulfilled his promise to investigate anti-Semitism more thoroughly.[35]

In view of French apathy and increasingly restrictive censorship, Grégoire was unable to publish anything more about slavery for the duration of the Empire. Yet he did not relinquish his pen, and in 1812 he arranged to print a *Histoire de la domesticité* in Germany.[36] Although his agent there asked him to write a general study comparing slavery and servitude, Grégoire preferred to concentrate on the problems of unfree labor and racial inequality. He prepared a supplement for his *Littérature des Nègres*, which he circulated among his friends, and collected material for a biographical dictionary of men who had played a prominent role in the struggle for freedom.

By 1813 Grégoire completed his "Doctrine du Christianisme," a manuscript which he never published. Later, however, he did incorporate parts of it into other works on Christianity and slavery. Because, according to him, God made "no exceptions among people," in this manuscript he characterized Christianity as "a veritable declaration of rights and duties." Slave owners, he asserted, had refused to teach religion to Negroes because they feared its egalitarian principles would destroy the racist basis upon which slavery rested.[37]

Grégoire's literary activities never really satisfied him, and he spent his years as an "anchorite" in Sarcelles waiting for a chance to renew his conspiracies against the Empire. Thus, immediately after Napoleon's defeat in Russia, he and his friends drew up an act of abdication in which they declared themselves, as a rump senate, to be France's legitimate government. Their activities remained clandestine until the Empire collapsed in March 1814. The liberal senators who had plotted for so long now had their opportunity, and on 30 March Grégoire addressed their last secret session. Exactly what they planned is not clear because the Bourbonites, lately reinforced by Talleyrand's adherence to their cause, proved more adept than they. After numerous intrigues, on 6 April the Senate, purged of Bonapartists, voted to restore the Bourbon dynasty, and Grégoire, along with the few other republicans, had to accept reality.[38]

NOTES

1. See Chapter 2 for Bonaparte and the Jews. His proclamation reestablishing slavery is printed in Anderson, *Constitutions and documents of France,* p. 339.

2. See his correspondence with Gulian Verplanck in the NYHS and his *Noblesse de la peau,* pp. 22–23.

3. Jacquemin to Grégoire, 28 Floréal year 8 (18 May 1800), BPR, TUVWXYZ; Jacquemin to the minister of the navy, 20 Pluviôse year 11 (9 Feb. 1803), AN, F¹⁹6201; Bonaparte's proclamation to the citizens of Saint-Domingue dated 25 Dec. 1799

declared that "the sacred principles of black liberty and equality will never suffer violation or modification in your country," *Correspondance*, 6:42.

4. Grégoire, *Apologie de las-Casas* [*sic*], p. 14; mentioned in the *Magazin encyclopédique*, Thermidor year 8 (July-Aug. 1800), p. 263.

5. Cournand was the first to compare Grégoire with Las Casas; see his *Réponse* (1790?), p. 7. Neither Grégoire's contemporaries nor subsequent scholars found Grégoire's evidence concerning Las Casas convincing, although his *Apologie* is cited in studies of the Spanish bishop. See, for example, Hanke, *Bartolomé de Las Casas*, pp. 62–64 and Aimes, *History of Slavery in Cuba*, pp. 66, 71, which shows eighteenth-century attitudes toward the bishop.

6. *Annales de la religion* (1800): 423–32; Grégoire to Cit. General, undated, Arsenal 6339, fo. 1–2.

7. Mauviel to Grégoire and Eléonore-Marie Desbois, 1 April 1802, *Annales de la religion* (1802): 126; Mauviel to Grégoire, 17 Sept. 1803, "Correspondance de Guillaume Mauviel," pp. 51–53; Mauviel to Toussaint, 25 March 1800, *Annales de la religion* (1801): 141–43; Toussaint speech, 28 Ventôse year 8 (17 March 1800), copy in Schomburg Collection of the New York Public Library, C–4; Guerrier to the United Bishops, 28 Floréal year 9 (18 May 1801), BPR, MNO; Saint-Rémy des Cayes, *Pétion et Haïti*, 3:4.

8. Petition by Grégoire, Jean-Baptiste Demandre, François-Xavier Moyse, and Eléonore-Marie Desbois, 26 Oct. 1801, printed in the *Annales de la religion* (1801):79–83.

9. *Annales de la religion* (1800): 423–32; Jean Portalis to Grégoire, 19 Brumaire year 10 (10 Nov. 1801), BPR, Loir-et-Cher.

10. Leconte, *Henri Christophe*, p. 123. Others also tried to persuade Bonaparte to preserve racial equality in the colonies; see Roume to Admiral Bruix (minister of the navy), 4 Nivôse year 10 (25 Dec. 1801) and to Grégoire, 28 Pluviôse year 10 (17 Feb. 1802), LC, Roume Papers, no. 29, pp. 53–59. Later Bonaparte blamed Josephine for his decisions relating to Saint-Domingue, but his correspondence of 1801 does not indicate her responsibility; Herold, ed., *The Mind of Napoleon*, pp. 186–87, 189.

11. Ardouin, *Etudes*, 4:463n; Pamphile de Lacroix, *Mémoires*

de la Révolution de Saint Domingue, 1:231; Barruel, *Abrégé des mémoires du Jacobinisme*, 2:252; Bertrand de Moleville, *Histoire de la Révolution*, 8:380–82; René-François Chateaubriand, *Génie du Christianisme*, cited in Martin, *Histoire de l'esclavage*, p. 247.

12. Grégoire to Cit. General, undated, Arsenal 6339, fo. 1–2.

13. See, for example, Grégoire, *Essai historique sur l'état de l'agriculture en Europe*, pp. 6, 27, 28, 33; Grégoire's correspondence with the Barlows in Harvard Library, AM 1468.

14. *Mémoires*, 1:306; "Titres et diplomes," in BM Nancy 1134 (536).

15. *Cobbett's Weekly Political Register*, 10 July 1802, p. 20.

16. Diary entry for 25 Aug. 1802 in Robert and Samuel Wilberforce, *The Life of William Wilberforce*, 3:65. Sharp at least sent Grégoire a manuscript copy of his "Remarks on 1 Timoth. IV" concerning the marriage of priests (BPR, Rév. 180). For a similar American reaction to the events in the French West Indies, see Jordan, *White Over Black*, p. 380.

17. Grégoire, *An Enquiry*, p. 155.

18. LeClerc to Mauviel, 14 Feb. 1802, *Annales de la religion* (1802): 131 and (1801): 478; Grégoire to Cit. General, undated, Arsenal 6339, fo. 1–2; Mauviel to Grégoire, 24 Sept. 1802, "Correspondance de Mauviel," pp. 31–32.

19. Report of the prefect of police, 4 Germinal year 10 (25 March 1802), AN, F⁷3830; "Rapport aux Consuls," c. 13 Messidor year 10 (c. 2 July 1802), AN, F¹⁹6200; Mauviel to Grégoire, 24 Sept. 1802, "Correspondance de Mauviel," pp. 31–32.

20. Mauviel, "Aperçu de la situation de St-Domingue," 20 Floréal year 11 (10 May 1803), AN, AF⁴1213; "Exposé," 1 Prairial year 13 (21 May 1805), ibid.; Mauviel to the minister of religion, 25 Floréal and 21 Fructidor year 13 (15 May and 8 Sept. 1805), minister's note on Mauviel's letter, and the minister of the navy to the minister of religion, 25 Fructidor year 13 (12 Sept. 1805), AN, F¹⁹6201.

21. Mauviel to Grégoire, 24 May 1803, "Correspondence de Mauviel," p. 50; Pamphile de Lacroix, *Mémoires de la Révolution*, p. 302; Leyburn, *The Haitian People*, pp. 117–18; Cabon, *Notes d'Haiti*, pp. 31–55; Matinée, *Anecdotes de la révolution*.

22. Grégoire, *An Enquiry*, pp. 104–5; Mauviel to Grégoire, 17

Sept. 1803, "Correspondance de Mauviel," pp. 51–53; Mauviel to Grégoire, 19 Aug. 1807, BPR, TUVWXYZ.

23. Grégoire to Barlow, 26 Oct. 1807, Harvard, AM 1468 (606). Lady Morgan thought that Grégoire made these comments about Caesar when he voted against the new nobility (1804); see Morgan, *France*, 1:185. See also Grunebaum-Ballin, *L'abbé Grégoire et les juifs*, p. 15; Grégoire, *Mémoires*, 1:124–25, 364; d'Hautrive, ed., *La police secrète du premier empire*, 1:349.

24. *Mémoires*, 1:124. They were written in 1808.

25. Manuscript summary of Grégoire's life by Debussy in BPR, Loir-et-Cher II; Thiry, *Le Sénat de Napoléon*, pp. 280–82.

26. Grégoire, *An Enquiry*, p. 248, published in French as *De la littérature des Nègres*.

27. [Tussac], *Cri des colons*, p. 16; *Journal de l'Empire*, 20 Oct. 1808, pp. 1–4; *Le Publiciste*, 9 Sept. 1808, pp. 1–2.

28. Grégoire to anon., 9 April 1810, Arsenal 13,990, fo. 10; Grégoire to Barlow, copy, 28 Feb. 1810, Yale Library, Pequot Collection, M 981; Pierre-Toussaint Durand-Maillane to Grégoire, 18 June 1809, BPR, AB; *De l'opinion de M. Grégoire, ancien évêque de Blois et sénateur, dans le Procès de Louis XVI*, p. 2; Lanjuinais, *Notice de l'ouvrage de Grégoire*; supplement not published until 1814; Grégoire to anon., 25 Sept. 1808, AD, L&C, F 592, fo. 23; Verdet to Grégoire, 20 April 1809, BPR, MNO; Grégoire's correspondence with Blessig, Dec. 1803 and after, BPR, AB.

29. John Pinkerton to David Bailie Warden, 20 May 1808, MHS, David Bailie Warden Papers.

30. Jordan, *White Over Black*, pp. 373–74.

31. Jefferson to Grégoire, 25 Feb. 1809, LC, Thomas Jefferson Collection, 33125, reprinted in Koch and Peden, eds., *Life of Thomas Jefferson*, pp. 594–95; Barlow to David Bailie Warden, 10 Dec. 1808, LC, DBW Collec. II; Jefferson to Barlow, 8 Oct. 1809, LC, TJ Collec., 33511, reprinted in Ford, ed., *Writings of Thomas Jefferson*, 9:261–62.

32. Barlow, *Letter to Gregoire* [sic], p. 7; Grégoire, *Critical observations on THE COLUMBIAD*. Both Barlow's and Grégoire's letters were printed in *The Monthly Anthology and Boston Review* 7 (1809): 2–11, 290–98; Barlow to Warden, 18 March 1809, LC,

DBW Collec. II; Grégoire to Barlow, copy, 28 Feb. 1810, Yale, Pequot, M 981; Warden to Judge Jacob, 1 Oct. 1809, in "Reminiscences by Dr. John W. Francis, Extended to thirteen volumes by the addition of drawings, engravings and autographs," (New York, 1895), 3:345, in NYHS. Noah Webster, for example, expressed similar criticisms of Barlow's poem: Herbert M. Morais, *Deism in Eighteenth Century America* (New York: Columbia University Press, 1934), p. 139. Just as the French emigré priests had aroused English public opinion against Grégoire, so the refugees from the West Indies in the United States had attacked revolutionary religious and egalitarian policies: Frances S. Childs, *French Refugee Life in the United States, 1790–1800: An American Chapter of the French Revolution* (Baltimore: The Johns Hopkins Press, 1940), pp. 150–56.

33. *Histoire des sectes* (1810), 1:123–24, 32–33, lxxi, lxxvi, 240.

34. Fouché to Grégoire, 11 Jan. 1810 in *Mémoires*, 1:139–40 and Maggiolo, "L'abbé Grégoire," p. li n; Grégoire to anon., 9 April 1810, Arsenal 13,990, fo. 10. Napoleon already had criticized one of his books, the 1809 edition of his *Ruines de Port-Royal:* Bn de Pommereaux to Grégoire, undated, BM Nancy 957 (533), p. 87 verso; Maggiolo, "L'abbé Grégoire," p. xiv n.

35. Blessig to Grégoire, 30 Dec. 1809, BPR, AB, published by A.M.P. Ingold, ed., "Lettres de Blessig à Grégoire," *Revue d'Alsace* 12 (1911): 215; *Magazin encyclopédique* (1810): vol. 4, pp. 251–58.

36. Published in France as *De la domesticité chez les peuples anciens et modernes* (Paris: A. Egron, Imprimeur-Libraire, 1814). There is no evidence that the German edition ever appeared, although a manuscript copy of the translation is in the Bibliothèque Universitaire of Strasbourg (MS 3901) along with the French draft completed in 1804 (cf. p. 186 for the date). Grégoire published his *Geschichte des Theophilanthropismus* (Hannover: Gebr. Hahn, 1806), but his correspondence with Blessig and others indicates the difficulties which he encountered; see Stendlin to Grégoire, 25 March 1806, anon. private collection in Paris; Grégoire to LeCoz, 3 May 1806, Pingaud, pp. 53–54; letters to Blessig published in the *Revue d'Alsace* 12 (1911).

37. "Doctrine du Christianisme," pp. 4, 10, BPR, Rév. 177. Norman Ravitch lists *De l'influence du christianisme sur l'abolition*

de l'esclavage among Grégoire's works published during the Empire, but there is no evidence that it ever was printed; see his "Liberalism, Catholicism, and the Abbé Grégoire," p. 426. See also: Grégoire to Mauviel, 24 April 1810, AD L&C, F 353; Grégoire to the Ionian Academy, 22 July 1812, copy, BM Nancy 1134 (536), no. 23; Grégoire to Grappin, 17 June 1813, BM Besançon 622, fo. 340–41.

38. Grégoire to Bauche de Neuville, 2 Dec. 1814, and to Chevalier Huzard, 8 April 1809, Bibliothèque de l'Institut, MS 2325, XXIV, p. 9, and MS 1976, XVI; Grégoire, *Mémoires*, 1:166–79; *Journal de Paris*, 3 and 9 April 1814; Thiry, *Le Sénat*, p. 327.

PART THREE

Grégoire
in Opposition

10

Grégoire and
the Bourbon Restoration

Grégoire briefly reemerged on the political scene during the interregnum between Napoleon's fall and Louis XVIII's arrival in Paris, but his ideas were anachronistic, and royalists hopelessly outnumbered the small band of republicans. Thus, when Grégoire was named to the Senate's Constitutional Committee, he could not influence the draft which it prepared and disliked many of its provisions. But he signed it because he agreed with his colleagues' desire to write a constitution before the king arrived.

Even before Louis entered France, he rejected the proposed constitution and promulgated his own charter. Grégoire thereupon unleashed his bitterness against both monarch and Senate. Angrily denouncing the king's failure to guarantee popular sovereignty and to divide power explicitly among the various branches of government, he demanded that the Charter be altered immediately.[1]

Grégoire's short-lived return to political affairs reopened long forgotten wounds. Moderates and conservatives alike took issue with his rigorous republican stand, while conservatives reserved their choicest invective for his prominent role in past egalitarian movements. Since Grégoire expected the real decisions concerning slavery and the slave trade to be made by the Congress of Vienna rather than by the French government, he did not bother to answer the conservatives' charges.

The political balance had long since shifted against the abolitionists, and the egalitarians apparently were condemned to silence in 1814. Sadly depleted in numbers, those who had survived the vicissitudes of the Revolution were, like Grégoire, politically ostracized, and they could not hope to win any show of strength against the colonial landowners who were now in a powerful. position. Allied with conservative royalists (the Ultras), and, appealing to French patriotism, the planters accused the abolitionists of having assisted the English in defeating their country. Playing on French hopes and fears, they depicted the reconquest of Haiti as a patriotic duty and adamantly opposed recognizing Haitian independence. They also insisted upon preserving slavery and slave trading.[2]

Faced with a coalition composed of colonial landowners and conservative royalists, only a few prominent people in France besides Grégoire—Lafayette, Duke Achille-Charles-Léonce-Victor de Broglie, Benjamin Constant, and Auguste de Staël, for example—dared to campaign for Negro rights. They were supported by others who for practical rather than ideological reasons opposed an expedition against Saint-Domingue and recommended using free labor in the remaining French colonies.[3]

But suspect of republicanism, few in number, and lacking an organization, the egalitarians could accomplish very little unless they received outside aid. Most of all, they suffered from insufficient funds. French journals, they discovered, refused to print their articles because the leading abolitionist, that is Grégoire, supposedly was a regicide. Consequently, they had to rely on foreign, primarily English, subsidies in order to print their publications as separate pamphlets.

Weak as they were, the Restoration abolitionists vowed to

start from the beginning and to avoid the mistakes made by their predecessors, the members of the Société des Amis des Noirs. Modeling themselves on the English Abolition Society, Parisian philanthropists deliberately eschewed emotionalism, political radicalism, and references to suspect principles of natural rights. Although they naturally appealed to liberals rather than conservatives, they tried to establish ties with such moderates as de Broglie and François-Pierre Guizot and steadfastly refused to associate with dogmatic republicans. They preferred to work directly with the appropriate ministers rather than engage in parliamentary debates, and for eight years they hesitated to organize a society. Since they did not have access to the statistical information which the Abolition Society had used so successfully in its campaign against British slave traders, they frequently translated and issued English publications instead of writing their own propaganda.

Throughout the first decade of the Restoration the abolitionists not only suffered from identification with the old Amis des Noirs, but they also were criticized for their links with England and with evangelical Protestantism. Here, at least, they did not succeed in circumventing their predecessors' errors. Despite their cautiousness, moreover, they eventually would have to engage in political action, and they would not be able to exclude Grégoire completely from their work.

Primarily interested in blocking the planters' schemes, the abolitionists focused on three issues: outlawing slave trading, emancipating slaves, and recognizing Haitian independence. Mulatto status would not become a serious question for several more years. Although the abolitionists discussed all three of these topics, outlawing the slave trade seemed to be both the most urgent problem and the one most likely to be resolved during the first restoration if only because they could rely fully on English support.[4]

The British philanthropists based their entire campaign against the slave trade on the assumption that ending it would gradually and peacefully destroy slavery. According to them, the trade was the key point of the slavery system, at least in the currently crucial Caribbean colonies. Although they thought that such slave-owning countries as the United States, which had temperate climates and vast space, might rely on natural increase to maintain their stock of slaves, they were convinced that limited space, expensive land, and high mortality rates would require the continuous importation of fresh labor into the West Indies. Once plantation owners no longer could bring Africans to the Caribbean, they either would have to modify their slavery system or would have to employ an increasing number of free workers. One way or another, Caribbean slavery, as it then existed, would end shortly after slave trading was outlawed.

On the basis of these and other arguments, the British Parliament had outlawed English participation in the slave trade in 1808. At that time, naval warfare had excluded other countries from the African trade. Now, the philanthropists feared, other slave-owning countries would import Africans on a far greater scale than ever before in order to fulfill the long accumulated demand for colonial labor. Unless the British planters smuggled in slaves, they would face overwhelming competition from the colonies where labor costs would rapidly decline. Thus the planters' protests probably would convince Parliament to rescind the ban on slave trading and would thereby destroy any progress towards abolition which had been achieved so far.

French and British abolitionists alike were dismayed when the Anglo-French treaty of 1814 permitted France to import Africans for another five years. Although the British foreign minister, Viscount Castleraegh, had tried to persuade Louis XVIII to terminate the trade immediately, he finally had accepted this clause because the king's tenuous political position prevented him from antagonizing his most fervent supporters, the aristocratic planters. The colonial landowners insisted that they needed to replenish their labor force, which had been decimated by a quarter-century of foreign and civil war, before they permanently renounced the trade. As far as the abolitionists were concerned, this clause was unnecessarily heartless towards those Africans who would be kidnapped to sustain what, to them, was a doomed institution.

Recognizing the abolitionists' weak position in France, the British sent Zachary Macaulay, a former treasurer of the African Institute and a colleague of Wilberforce and Clarkson, to Paris in May 1814. Macaulay hoped to persuade Louis XVIII to renounce even a temporary renewal of the trade by signing an international declaration against it. The French abolitionists tried to help by introducing him to all appropriate cabinet members. But the ministry could not reach a decision because it was divided between the minister of the navy, the aging proslavery publicist Pierre-Victor Malouet, and the minister of foreign affairs, the long time opponent of slavery, Talleyrand.

In August Clarkson came to assist Macaulay. Although he received commitments from Tsar Alexander I, the Duke of Wellington, and Minister Talleyrand, he also wanted to stimulate interest among the French public. Otherwise, he rightly feared, the French would never really terminate slave trading even if the king adhered to the declaration and the chambers enacted appropriate legislation.[5]

Anxious to increase the abolitionists' influence, the British urged their continental friends to form a society. There were serious obstacles, however. As soon as Macaulay arrived in France, his superior, Wilberforce, received a warning. "Grégoire and all the old amis-des-noirs men are in exceedingly bad odor" he was informed. "No respectable persons will have anything to do with them." The English abolitionists were advised to cooperate with Lafayette (also in "bad odor" at the moment), Mme de Staël, the German naturalist Alexander Humboldt, and the Swiss writer Jean-Charles de Sismondi.[6] Wilberforce probably needed no encouragement to avoid associating with Grégoire, but three of the people recommended to him were foreigners who could hardly be expected to influence French opinion.

The Parisian egalitarians who had cautioned Wilberforce refused to form any permanent organization because, they argued, it would have to include those who were "detested for political reasons."[7] Yet some English abolitionists were less afraid of radical contamination than were Wilberforce and their continental colleagues. Despite Wilberforce's admonitions, Clarkson and Macaulay consulted Grégoire as to strategy and asked him to translate English abolition tracts. They also introduced him to other Britishers in Paris. One described the former bishop as "a kind-hearted benevolent man, with no great strength of understanding, and somewhat of a petit-maître in his habits."[8] Obviously he was neither a great asset nor a liability for their cause and could safely be ignored.

Acting with or without British encouragement, as soon as the Napoleonic censorship was lifted Grégoire prepared to publish some of the manuscripts on slavery and Negro equality which he previously had composed. But political isolation and unofficial press censorship continued to plague him. Although he wanted to denounce the Anglo-French treaty, for several months no printer was willing to accept his work. Finally in January 1815 he managed to publish an anonymous essay, *De la traite de l'esclavage des noirs et des blancs*.

Grégoire devoted most of this pamphlet to refuting religious and racially based arguments for slavery. These, after all, constituted the greatest challenge to his ideas concerning the universal brotherhood of man and the egalitarian nature of Christianity. Consequently, he attacked the planters where they were most vulnerable, in the newly found piety which swept over France during the early years of the Restoration. Appealing to this religiosity, Grégoire insisted that for the past one hundred and fifty years the Catholic church had opposed slave trading because it preferred to proselytize free men in Africa rather than exiled men under a coercive regime. This was a point to which he would frequently return in future works.

Turning to the French public as a whole, Grégoire character-ized it as being "without character and without fixed opinions," and he criticized his countrymen for having left egalitarianism to the "phases of national versatility."⁹ Now he recommended the creation of a well-organized abolition society and urged the government to remove all restrictions on publications and pub-lic associations. In connection with the latter point, he blamed colonial interests for the recent expulsion from the renamed Royal Institute of its one mulatto member and predicted that they would also demand his ouster because of his abolitionist reputation.

The censors forbade any discussion of Grégoire's De la traite in French journals, but Clarkson translated and printed it in English. Because Grégoire had made some irrelevant and tact-less remarks concerning both the territorial settlements of the Congress of Vienna and English persecution of Catholics, the work antagonized British abolitionists as well as French plant-ers. Still Clarkson refused to take Grégoire's comments on the ill-treatment of British Catholics seriously and disregarded his suspect political beliefs. Indeed the Britisher characterized Grégoire as one of the few revolutionary figures worthy of "respect and affectionate esteem."¹⁰

Unfortunately for the French abolition movement, Wilber-force was not as understanding as his subordinate was. Because Grégoire's De la traite once again demonstrated his tendency to employ reckless rhetoric, it provided an additional argument against establishing the society which he and others thought they must have in order to wage a successful campaign against slavery.

The abolitionists' hopes rose during Napoleon's brief return to power between March and June 1815. The former emperor was anxious either to separate England from her continental allies or to convince the Congress of Vienna that his govern-ment would be more stable than a Bourbon regime. Conse-quently, he tried to win radical and liberal support by outlaw-ing slave trading and offering the Haitian government de facto recognition in the form of commercial and military treaties.

Grégoire approved of the emperor's new colonial policy, but he did not convert to Bonapartism. He failed to participate in the Chamber of Peers and expressed his disapproval by inscribing a negative vote against the Constitution of the Hundred Days in the records of the Royal Institute. Upon reflection, he decided that Napoleon probably would not abide by his decision to end slave trading. The emperor, Grégoire feared, would reopen colonial ports to slave vessels and perhaps would launch a new expedition against Haiti as soon as he had consolidated his control in France.[11]

As the prospect of a second restoration loomed closer, Grégoire became even more anxious because he expected Louis XVIII to ignore all of Napoleon's proclamations. Grégoire wanted to ensure the abolition of slave trading by incorporating it into the constitution, thereby placing it beyond the jurisdiction of either the king or the legislature. One day before the French armies capitulated, he wrote to the Chamber of Deputies asking it to insert a clause in the constitution which would outlaw slave trading. Instead of acting on this petition, the Chamber sent it to the Constitutional Committee where it died with the assembly. Its only tangible result was to increase, if possible, the planters' antipathy for Grégoire because in it he had referred to the "Republic of Haiti" rather than Saint-Domingue.[12]

The planters were free to voice their dislike for Grégoire after Louis XVIII returned to Paris for the second time, and a new reactionary wave, known as the "White Terror," engulfed France. Once again as they had done during the first terror, colonial landowners took advantage of the latest political shift. This time they allied with the extreme conservatives who won an overwhelming majority in the Chamber of Deputies. Presumably the Ultras would uphold the prerevolutionary racial caste system in the West Indies and probably they would prevent effective enforcement of the ban on the slave trade. The colonists also hoped to use the purges of 1815 to punish those enemies who had remained beyond their grasp in 1793 and 1794.

Louis XVIII, fearing both republican and Ultra extremists, tried to govern through a coalition of moderate and liberal royalists. This group eventually won the reluctant support of such Negro sympathizers as the Duke de Broglie and Benjamin Constant. Surrounded by moderate advisors, Louis resisted Ultra pressure in regard to the colonies and, after his second restoration, confirmed Napoleon's recent decision to outlaw slave trading. Louis' proclamation was reinforced by the new treaty with England which obligated France to abolish the trade immediately. Still, French officials failed to implement either the treaty or the proclamation and, indeed, did not even publish them.

Louis rejected the Ultras' plans concerning the colonies, but he proved either unable or unwilling to restrain the conservatives' hostility towards the regicides. Those who had gone over to Napoleon during the Hundred Days were also persecuted, and mobs in the provinces attacked many who they feared would escape judicial proceedings.

Even though he had neither voted for Louis XVI's execution nor supported Napoleon, Grégoire numbered among those who suffered during the second restoration. He now became more isolated than before, and, although not imprisoned or exiled, his income and influence steadily declined. For a short time he contemplated voluntary exile, but he decided against abandoning his country during such a difficult period. At the age of sixty-five he could not transplant himself, and the next few years were difficult ones. Special occupation taxes reduced him to poverty, and after they passed, he was dropped from the Royal Institute. Denied the pensions due to him as a former senator and member of the Institute, he now had to live from his salary as commander of the Legion of Honor.[13]

Despite his misfortunes, Grégoire continued to fight for his most important causes and found funds for friends who had even less than he. Surrounded by what one visitor described as a jumble of books on moral philosophy and devotions, a crucifix, a model slave ship, and a bookcase full of works by Negro authors, he received numerous foreign visitors and carried on an extensive international correspondence.[14]

Grégoire's exclusion from the Royal Institute, which he attributed to his pro-Negro sentiments, was a serious blow because he had been one of its founding members. Refusing to accept his ostracism from intellectual circles, he drew up a charter for an international community of scholars. This association, contrary to the French one, was to accept members of all races because, he claimed, "reason has relegated the nobility of the skin into the archives of foolishness." This society never was formed, but Grégoire henceforth served as an unofficial center for antislavery, antiracist, and antipapal propaganda.[15]

Still fighting the isolation to which the Ultras had condemned him, Grégoire made one attempt to refute his colonial critics. In 1816 he wrote a vigorous and, as he admitted, rude reply to the most vicious and influential attack written by the man who had served as minister of the navy in 1791, Antoine-François Bertrand de Moleville. Since French censors forbade the publication of this letter, Grégoire had to insert it in foreign journals. Bertrand's and Grégoire's polemics added nothing to the slavery controversy—calling one's critics "a class of privileged assassins more guilty than those who seek to kill" only provoked Grégoire's enemies and cast discredit upon the entire abolitionist movement.[16]

Censorship applied only to newspapers, but several French printers refused to handle Grégoire's manuscripts.[17] Thus, the cost of publishing books and pamphlets limited what he could print until the easing of government restrictions during the following years permitted him to assist in founding two journals, the *Constitutionnel* (1817 to 1825) and the *Chronique religieuse* (1819 to 1821). Avoiding any direct discussion of French policy, he used both papers to promote the Negroes' cause by publishing material calculated to demonstrate their literary abilities. For example, he printed their letters, edited their manuscripts, and reviewed relevant books.

Proving Negro intellectual ability, however, would not solve the most serious problem facing these people, the continuation of the slave trade. Despite Louis XVIII's reluctant acceptance of abolition in 1815, England had not been able to attain a meaningful international declaration against the trade either at the Congress of Vienna or of Aix-la-Chapelle in 1818, and she had to negotiate bilateral agreements with the major slave trading powers.

By 1818 the most important participants in the slave trade had agreed to one form of restriction or another. Still, trading continued and the philanthropists shifted their attention to demanding stricter enforcement of existing agreements. France was one of the chief offenders. The apathy of that country's officials in the face of flagrant violations indicated the ministry's unwillingness to comply with her treaty obligations. Since few French legislators objected to the trade, the abolitionists tried to create outside pressure on the ministry, either through diplomatic channels or through arousing public opinion. But they faced a difficult task. Although a few French philanthropists were interested in giving direction to the humanitarian movement, they hesitated to make a popular appeal. Understanding their reluctance, Grégoire devised a strategy which he hoped might prove effective.

The contrast between Protestant concern and Catholic apathy towards the fate of kidnapped Africans had disturbed Grégoire since the early days of the Revolution. Between 1789 and 1802 controversy over ecclesiastical innovations had frustrated his attempts to channel Christian feelings against the barbarity of the trade, but now Catholic unity had been restored, and he hoped to use France's revived religiosity against colonial landowners. Realizing, however, how little influence he had with devout Catholics, he asked papal officials to condemn slave trading. Such a statement, he asserted, would not only influence Frenchmen, but it also would help abolitionists in all predominantly Catholic countries. Adding sectarian to humanitarian reasons for recommending such a declaration, he claimed that it would mitigate non-Catholic prejudice against their faith and thereby would both assist English Catholics in their struggle for enfranchisement and facilitate missionary activity among Moslem and pagan Africans.[18]

Grégoire's appeals to Rome were based on more than mere wishful thinking because in 1816 one member of the Congregation of Propaganda had written a friendly letter comparing him with Las Casas. Misinterpreting a direct communication from Rome as a sign of his improved status there, Grégoire wrote to the director of the Congregation of Propaganda, Cardinal François-Louis Fontana.

Ostensibly Grégoire wanted a copy of a condemnation of slave trading written by Cardinal Alderan Cybo,[19] who had directed this congregation during the seventeenth century. Much as Grégoire wanted this document, however, he was even more interested in persuading Fontana to speak out against the current trade. Reminding the cardinal that missionaries in Africa who preached against slave trading were still being persecuted, he asked the prelate to take a firm stand by republishing Cybo's two-hundred-year-old instructions to Catholic clerics in Africa.

Fontana hesitated to comply with Grégoire's request for several reasons. In France the people who supported slavery were also the most fervent "Romans." Even if the pope wished to denounce slavery and to recognize Haiti, such actions would jeopardize his still delicate position in France.[20] Moreover, the church, in contrast with individual ecclesiastics, regarded Grégoire as schismatic because he persistently refused to admit the errors contained in the Civil Constitution of the Clergy. Hence the church could not afford to grant him any sign of official recognition.

Despite all of these cogent reasons, which Grégoire should

have understood, he was embittered by Fontana's silence. He repeated his request for a copy of Cybo's instructions and claimed to have considered writing to the pasha of Egypt. Mohammed-Ali, Grégoire sarcastically insisted, at least would have answered his letter.[21]

Even while Grégoire was writing his futile appeals to the Congregation of Propaganda, his position in France began to improve, and it appeared as though his political ostracism might soon come to an end. Although he still inspired fear and dislike among certain moderate and liberal circles, as the postwar reaction subsided, some French Radicals, as well as a few English abolitionists, began to regard him as an asset rather than a liability. For a short time it even appeared as though he might once again hold public office.

NOTES

1. Grégoire, *De la Constitution française.*

2. [Grégoire], *Première et dernière réponse aux libellistes;* Dillon, *Mémoire sur l'esclavage colonial,* written in 1802; Delmas, *Histoire de la révolution de Saint-Domingue,* 1:69, 161, written in the United States in 1793–94.

3. Malenfant, *Des colonies,* pp. ii–vii. A few writers envisioned the future of the Western Hemisphere in terms of capital rather than labor exploitation, but such writers found little response in France; see Stein and Stein, *Colonial Heritage of Latin America,* pp. 124–25.

4. In Dec. 1814 the abolitionists established an international committee to work for the abolition of the North African trade in whites and blacks. This committee was supported by representatives of Alexander I, Frederick William III, Ferdinand II, and numerous other monarchs and aristocrats: "Souscription au fonds charitable," Arsenal 6339, fo. 93–94 verso. The list was revised through Oct. 1816.

5. For discussion of the need to arouse French public opinion:

Ninth report of the African Institution, p. 11. For English diplomacy see Fladeland, "Abolitionist Pressures on the Concert of Europe."

6. Wilberforce's diary for 15 May 1814, in Wilberforce, *Life,* 4:182. See also: ibid., p. 202; Lafayette, *Mémoires,* 5:539–40.

7. Humboldt to Wilberforce, 28 Sept. 1814, in Wilberforce, *Life,* 4:213–14. Nonetheless, Grégoire did attend Mme de Staël's salon before her death in 1817; see draft of letter, undated, in Schomburg Coll., C–4.

8. Robinson's reminiscences, entry for 2 Sept. 1814 in Sadler, ed., *Diary of Robinson,* 1:441, 447; Wilberforce to Macaulay, 25 Oct. 1814 in Wilberforce, *Life,* 4:213; Griggs, *Thomas Clarkson,* p. 117.

9. [Grégoire], *De la traite de l'esclavage des noirs et des blancs,* pp. 25,19; Grégoire to Bishop John Carroll, 1 Feb. 1815, Baltimore Archdiocese, 4 B 7.

10. Clarkson's introduction to Grégoire's *On the slave trade & on the slavery of the blacks & of the whites,* p. ix.

11. Grégoire expressed more optimism concerning Bonaparte's intentions in a letter of 15 April 1815 in BN, NAF 24,910, fo. 288. See also report to ministère de police générale, 25 March 1816, AN, F⁷ 6707, plaq. 1, p. 40.

12. Lafayette, *Mémoires,* 5:409; *Journal universel,* 10 June 1815; Grégoire, *Mémoires,* 1:190–92; [Delbare], *Histoire des deux chambres,* p. 273; Morgan, *France* 2:330; Ardouin, *Etudes,* 8:136 n.

13. Bertier de Sauvigny states that the excluded peers were granted an annual pension of 36,000 francs, but Grégoire was one of the few exceptions; see Bertier de Sauvigny, *Bourbon Restoration,* p. 72; undated circular by David, included in Grégoire's letter to Verplanck of 23 Oct. 1826 (NYHS). For Grégoire and the trial of Louis XVI see above, Introduction, fn. 5. The issue of whether Grégoire was morally guilty for condemning the king to death would plague him for the rest of his life, but a ministry of police report declared him to be legally innocent; ministère de police générale, 25 March 1816, AN, F⁷ 6707, plaq. 1, p. 40.

14. He was almost a tourist attraction for liberal Anglo-American visitors; Morgan, *France* 2:332; Grégoire to Jennart, 9 Oct. 1815, BM Nancy, autographes, reprinted in Cosson, ed., *Lettres de l'abbé Grégoire.*

15. Grégoire, *Plan d'association générale*, p. 49. See: James Stevens to Grégoire, 7 Sept. 1815, Grégoire's note, Arsenal 6339, fo. 59 verso; W. E. Channing to Benjamin Vaughn, 13 May 1822, American Philosophical Society, Benjamin Vaughn Papers, BV 46. Grégoire had suggested the formation of such a society as early as 1796; see *Mémoires de l'Institut*, year 4 (1796): vol. 1, pp. 564–66. He also served as a center for an international antipapal, neo-Jansenist group.

16. Printed in *L'Abeille Heytienne*, 1 Feb. 1818, pp. 11–13; *Lo Spettatore*, 1817, pp. 246–48, and *Journal of Edinbourg*, 1817, p. 266. Grégoire noted his inability to publish it in France in a letter to Warden, 19 Oct. [1816], MHS. This letter was a specific response to Bertrand de Moleville, *Mémoires particuliers*, 1:190–204. See also Grégoire to Jennart, 14 Oct. 1816, BM Nancy, autographes.

17. Grégoire complained of difficulties in finding printers willing to publish his works; letter to Degola, 8 March 1817 in Gubernatis, *Eustachio Degola*, pp. 358–59.

18. The English abolitionists did campaign for Catholic enfranchisement at home. In 1822 Macaulay convinced Canning to ask the pope to publish a bull against the trade, but the English pleas were equally unsuccessful; Fladeland, "Abolitionist pressures," p. 371 and note. See also Brunschwig, "The Origins of the New French Empire, "from *Mythes et réalitiés de l'impérialisme colonial français, 1871–1914* (Paris: Armand Colin, 1960), in George H. Nadel and Perry Curtis, eds., *Imperialism and Colonialism* (New York: Macmillan, 1964), p. 115.

19. Grégoire called him Cardinal Cibo. See: Grégoire to Eminence, 7 Dec. 1818, copy in Arsenal 6339, fo. 48–50; Grégoire to Chancellier, 2 Sept. 1816, AN, AB XIX 3195, dr. 1; to Chancellier, 1 April 1819, AD, L&C, F 353. Papal bulls against the trade had been issued in 1557, 1639, and 1741; Aimes, *History of Slavery*, p. 140 n.

20. During the early years of the Restoration, the papacy was trying to negotiate a new, more favorable concordat to replace the one signed with Napoleon. Liberals and Radicals opposed these negotiations.

21. Grégoire, *Des peines infamantes à infliger aux négriers*, p. 29. The Arabian slave trade was the last to be suppressed.

11

The Election
of 1819 and Its Aftermath

By 1817 a number of radicals, too young to be identified with revolutionary upheavals and unafraid of Grégoire's reputation, began to seek his assistance in various projects. Some were rebellious Catholics; others were nonreligious intellectuals who admired his republicanism and his opposition to Roman ecclesiastical domination as well as his egalitarian career.

At first Grégoire collaborated with the young men on two journals, the *Constitutionnel* and the *Revue encyclopédique*. Exactly what his connections with the first paper were is unclear. The second, the *Revue encyclopédique*, did not list Grégoire's name as a member of the editorial staff and hesitated to publish articles signed by him. Still, from 1819 onwards, it printed favorable reviews of his recent works and mentioned his antislavery and pro-Jewish activities whenever appropriate and sometimes when not. The editors were anxious to clear his name and reputation. In return Grégoire established direct communications between the editor of the *Revue* and President Boyer of Haiti and provided the journal with information concerning the other countries in the Western Hemisphere.[1]

In addition to his young admirers, Grégoire also worked closely with Lafayette. Both had been members of the Société des Amis des Noirs in 1790, but their paths had diverged during the Revolution. Their common hatred of Napoleon had affected a reconciliation, and they corresponded regularly during the Restoration, but their mutual interest in Haiti proved their most important bond. In addition, they both disliked the Charter of 1814, although Grégoire would prove to be a more intransigent republican than the old hero of two worlds.[2]

Several developments encouraged the radicals, young and old alike, by facilitating their struggle against Ultra political domination. The first shock of the Restoration wore off. More important, during 1818 the government paid the indemnity levied upon France by the allied powers, and the withdrawal of occupation forces enabled Louis XVIII to ease censorship regulations.

As political opinions were more easily expressed, differences became increasingly obvious, and party lines began to emerge. Yet individuals passed freely from one group to another, and French parties would never assume the rigid structure which gradually developed in Britain and the United States. Prejudice against "factions," in the sense that the word was used in the *Federalist Papers*, and a very narrow franchise made mass political organization impossible and unnecessary.[3] Instead, interested Frenchmen coalesced around prominent figures and formed alliances of fluctuating stability.

The Ultras were the first group of deputies to meet regularly and to draw up a common legislative strategy. Later the Liberals organized several clubs, including the Société des Amis de la Presse, which paved the way for future electoral campaigns by fighting remaining censorship restrictions and by publicizing their ideas.

Four major coalitions emerged by 1818: the Ultras organized around Louis XVIII's brother and heir, the Count d'Artois; the Ministerials, moderate royalist bureaucrats united by a vested

interest in the present government and led by Duke Armand-
Emmanuel Richelieu and Elie Decazes; the constitutional mon-
archists, or so-called Liberals, led by Benjamin Constant, who
did not hold political offices or bureaucratic posts, but who
otherwise had only minor ideological differences with the Ministerials; and the Radicals, few in number, mostly but not exclusively republican in outlook, and more apt to engage in
clandestine organizations similar to the Italian Carbonari than
to participate in electoral campaigns. The most famous Radicals were Lafayette, Marc-René-Marie Voyer d'Argenson, and
Jacques-Antoine Manuel. In 1818 they too turned to public
political activity, even while they secretly continued to conspire
against the government.[4]

Of these groups only the Radicals and Ultras advocated
significant changes in the status quo. The other two parties
criticized the fashion in which the Charter was implemented
but were satisfied with the general form of the regime. Indeed,
the sometimes bitter internecine warfare between Ministerials
and Liberals arose from family quarrels and rivalry for political
offices rather than from important ideological differences.

The election of 1818 was the first to be held in many years
with a relatively untrammeled press. The Radicals nominated
Lafayette, Manuel, and Grégoire that year.[5] The first two were
elected, and although Grégoire's candidacy in the Moselle received scant attention, Lafayette's victory showed Radical
strength. The abolitionists also regarded Lafayette's election as
a significant achievement, and they were temporarily encouraged
by it.

The Radicals hoped to cap their success in 1818 with an even
more dramatic victory. In the following spring Lafayette and
two leaders of the Carbonari forerunner, the Union, decided to
send Grégoire to the Chamber of Deputies. They selected the
department of the Isère because a three-year-old incident between French soldiers and a group of citizens had caused widespread dissatisfaction in that distant region. Evidently Lafayette

had consulted Grégoire before he announced the scheme, and, despite the candidate's noncommittal reply, the Radicals drummed up enthusiasm among the members of the Union and the disenfranchised artisans of Grenoble.[6]

Grégoire's nomination unleashed a political holocaust. Liberals were horrified. Even though they did not dare oppose Grégoire's candidacy publicly, Constant feverishly tried to prevent the former bishop's election. The Liberals' dismay proved justified as right-wing parties tried to foist Grégoire upon them.[7]

Since the Liberals were more likely to win seats in the legislature than the Radicals were, the Ultras chose to hold the former responsible for Grégoire's nomination. The conservatives accused them of forming a faction, a dictatorial electoral committee (actually the Société des Amis de la Presse). This society, according to conservatives, was plotting to seduce unsophisticated French electors into choosing unsuitable deputies by drawing up a national slate of candidates.[8]

The conservatives' assumptions seemed to be confirmed when a Liberal, Louis-Saturnin Brissot-Thivars, published a detailed electoral guide reviewing the various candidates' qualifications. The author devoted eight pages to Grégoire, claiming that the retired bishop's past guaranteed his future career. Brissot-Thivars, a nephew of the revolutionary abolitionist, attributed to Grégoire reforms actually introduced by other legislators. Summarizing his qualities, Brissot wrote: "One rarely finds so much religion, virtue, tolerance, firmness of character, wisdom, and philosophy as in Mr. Grégoire."[9]

Most Liberals lacked Brissot-Thivars's enthusiasm for Grégoire. Nonetheless, such a public defense of the revolutionary bishop convinced conservatives that they would have to attack the candidate directly rather than concentrate on blaming the Liberal party for supposedly having nominated this unsavory person. The conservative press resurrected the hyperbolic tone popular three decades before. Grégoire, one editor said, was such a "great protector of the children of Israel that he would trade twenty whites for a Jew, and such an ardent friend of Negroes that he would trade twenty whites for a black." The Ultras criticized his egalitarian career, his republicanism, his dogmatic belief in the Declaration of the Rights of Man, and his denial of papal supremacy. This man, they insisted, could never be a loyal servant of a monarchical regime.[10]

As the furor mounted, the Liberals supposedly offered (not very reluctantly, one can imagine) to abandon Grégoire's candidacy if the Ministerials would support their other nominees, but Radical intransigence made any such compromise impossible. Much against their will the Liberals, several of whom were abolitionists, had to defend Grégoire's reputation. In their publications, therefore, they minimized his role in the Constitutional church, his questionable stand during the trial of Louis XVI, and his friendship with Robespierre. They emphasized instead his uncompromising opposition to Bonaparte, his fight for mulatto rights, and his work for Negroes during the Restoration.[11]

Grégoire's victory further confused matters. Reports that the Ultras of Isère had cast their votes for Grégoire in hopes of discrediting the Charter led to an official investigation which proved embarrassing for the prefect of the department and for the Ministerial party. While the artisans of Grenoble celebrated and both the local press and the electoral college of Isère congratulated their new deputy, liberal, moderate, and conservative politicians elsewhere exchanged recriminations. Everyone blamed everyone else, and even some Radicals began to doubt whether Grégoire's election had been a prudent move.[12]

In Paris only Negroes and mulattoes expressed real satisfaction with their old friend's victory. Supposedly they flocked to congratulate Grégoire, and they certainly had good reasons for rejoicing. Expecting him to defend Negro interests and to press for effective enforcement of the ban on slave trading, a few offered concrete suggestions as to what legislation he should propose when he entered the Chamber.[13]

Once Grégoire's election became known, the men who still claimed land in Saint-Domingue formed their own society. The landowners organized with the express purpose of devising strategy against this *"noble and loyal"* deputy whose presence in the Chamber might possibly destroy whatever remained of their wealth and would certainly jeopardize their hopes for an expedition against Saint-Domingue. Already disgruntled because the king had taken no steps to recapture the lost colony, the planters became even more enraged when the government refused to loan them public facilities. They therefore founded a periodical, the *Défenseur des colonies,* to protect the remaining empire from Grégoire's anticipated onslaught.[14]

The planters received the conservatives' enthusiastic support. Like the Liberals, the Ultra press now ignored Grégoire's political and religious career and focused instead on his egalitarian activities. Although only a few of them had any real interest in the colonies, they evidently thought this issue would arouse a greater amount of public outrage because of the sensational images which it evoked. Besides depicting revolutionary horrors in Saint-Domingue, they revived old rumors by implying that Grégoire was still being paid by the English. According to them, the British government had promised to establish a Constitutional church in Bengal if he would continue to advocate complete abolition. Last but not least, the Ultras used Grégoire's election to prove the worthlessness of the Charter and the ineffectualness of the moderate ministry which had permitted such a disaster to occur.[15]

Grégoire had refused to participate in the campaign—candidates usually did not—and now he stayed home, working on a revision of his *Littérature des Nègres.* He finally broke his silence when, two weeks after his election, he thanked the electoral college of Isère and denied any intention of renouncing his seat. Justifying his reluctance to discuss his revolutionary career by citing Louis XVIII's four-year-old amnesty, he refused to answer his recent critics and left the burden to others.[16]

The Liberals could not escape their dilemma so easily. As they had anticipated, conservatives used Grégoire's election as grounds for discrediting the constitutional monarchy. If Liberals vindicated the former bishop's past, they risked identification with his republicanism. But if they abandoned him completely, the Ultras might construe their silence as evidence of their inability to uphold the Charter. Consequently, they halfheartedly supported Grégoire. Avoiding the real issues, they tried to show his ecumenicism by mentioning how he had defended "persecuted priests, Protestants, Jews, Frenchmen imprisoned in foreign countries, mulattoes, Negroes, serfs, Fribourg Swiss, Spaniards, Irish, and still others."[17] Such a man could not be entirely evil.

Behind the scenes the Liberals searched for a way out of this embarassing and potentially dangerous situation. Auguste de Staël asked Grégoire to resign in order to preserve peace and the constitution. The danger appeared obvious to him because shortly beforehand the European powers had reacted to the liberal movement in Germany by forcing the Confederation to enact the repressive Carlsbad Decrees. In France, only Louis XVIII's frail health stood between the Charter and the Ultra leader, his brother Charles d'Artois.[18]

Intended as a private communication, de Staël's letter found its way into the press where its effect was contrary to the author's intention. The Radicals immediately denounced de Staël. Constant, for his part, feared the Liberals would be soundly defeated in the next election if they openly deserted Grégoire.

Publicly the Liberals tried to make the rights of free representation and of free speech into the key issues of the controversy over Grégoire's election. Ignoring the deputy-elect as much as possible, they asked for a moratorium on thirty-year-old quarrels. Still, they unbent sufficiently to distribute portraits which honored Grégoire's "disinterested philanthropy, his universal tolerance, his courage in defending all who are oppressed, and his love for men of all countries and of all colors."[19]

In private the Liberals now tried to persuade Grégoire's friends, Lafayette and Jean-Denis Lanjuinais, to help them by convincing Grégoire to resign. The former reluctantly agreed. Yet Lanjuinais, who in 1794 had blamed Grégoire for deserting him along with the rest of the Gironde, steadfastly refused to abandon the old republican.[20]

At almost the last moment the ministry discovered a technicality under which it might exclude Grégoire from the Chamber without increasing Ultra influence. Combing the Charter carefully, it stumbled upon a clause which required one-half of any delegation to reside in the department which it represented. Grégoire obviously lived in Paris. Since another of the four deputies chosen in the Isère clearly lived elsewhere and the status of still another was questionable, the ministry decided to circumvent acrimonious debates by nullifying Grégoire's election on the grounds of nonresidence. Charles Sapey, the deputy whose residence was questioned, protested, however, and insisted that the legislature must judge Grégoire's nomination on the deputy's merits.[21]

On the day before the Chamber of Deputies was scheduled to debate Grégoire's election, the Liberals held a caucus with the Radical leaders. Until two in the morning Lafayette, Voyer d'Argenson, and three others insisted upon fighting for Grégoire, but finally they agreed not to speak against the ministry's proposal. Voyer then was deputized to tell Grégoire the caucus' decision and to request his resignation. Grégoire remained firm and, refusing to withdraw at this late date, denounced the Liberals as cowards. This forced the Liberals to go through with the farce.[22]

As soon as the 6 December session began, the Credentials Committee recommended nullifying Grégoire's election on the grounds of nonresidence. Liberals urged the other deputies to accept this report without debate. The majority refused; Grégoire, they insisted, must be excluded as unworthy of serving in the legislature. Constant and Manuel concentrated on defeating the "unworthiness" clause. As during much of the campaign, Grégoire's personality was forgotten while spokesmen for all sides debated the constitutional issues. Finally the question was put to a vote, and the members, with one exception (Grégoire's fellow dissenter in the Imperial Senate, Count Charles-Joseph Lambrechts), decided to exclude Grégoire without giving cause and without passing on the validity of his election. The grave political implications of this vote were obvious to moderates, liberals, and radicals alike.[23]

Grégoire reacted to his exclusion from the Chamber of Deputies with bitterness and characteristic pomposity. "On the day when we all appear before the Grand Judge," he exclaimed, "let him not find [the representatives] more unworthy than me!" But, he added in a more Christian spirit, "I will pray for them and pardon them."[24]

Grégoire's bitterness was only temporary. When the Radicals decided to renominate him in 1820 he consented to their plans on the grounds that France was approaching a new political crisis. According to him, he had to clear his own reputation by running again because the Ultras were using his first election as a pretext for undermining the existing form of government. Leaving personal considerations aside, he feared that the Ultras would destroy what little remained of revolutionary progress unless the Charter underwent fundamental revision. As it now stood, church-state relations were poorly defined, political liberty was insecure, and the ban on slave trading was not being enforced. Consequently, Grégoire believed, he must try to become a member of the legislature in order to fight for necessary reforms.[25]

Others agreed with Grégoire's interpretation of the conservatives' campaign against his admission to the Chamber of Deputies. It was, they thought, merely one part in the Ultras' general attack on the principles of constitutional monarchy which were embodied in the Charter and in the moderate ministry.[26] But Grégoire's election soon was superseded as an issue, because the assassination in February 1820 of the king's nephew, the Duke de Berry, led the conservatives to redouble their assault upon the Charter.

The assassination of the one man capable of carrying on the Bourbon dynasty seemed to confirm what the Ultras had insisted all along: Liberal and Radical agitation threatened the foundations of Restoration government. Consequently they demanded and received new censorship laws. By the summer of 1820, they achieved another important victory when the king appointed an increasing number of conservative councilors and the center alliance upon which the Richelieu ministry depended collapsed. The Liberals now were completely isolated politically, and the Radicals, faced with renewed suspicions and stricter press restraints, did not dare renominate Grégoire.[27]

By mid-1820 the Ultras, no longer finding his name a useful issue, turned their attention away from Grégoire. Yet the election of 1819 was not the last of his personal humiliations and trials. Benjamin Laroche, one of his young admirers, was forced to flee to England because he had published some of Grégoire's letters. In addition, in 1822 Grégoire was maneuvered into resigning from the Legion of Honor, which for a time had provided his only income.[28]

Although overshadowed by de Berry's assassination, Grégoire's election had serious consequences for Restoration politics. As far as abolitionism was concerned, the widespread publicity given to his egalitarian career during the campaign reinforced the reluctance of such men as the Duke de Broglie, Auguste de Staël, and Benjamin Constant to form an abolition society and thereby to risk contamination by Grégoire's disgraceful reputation.

Frightened by the growing political reaction, the abolitionists proved obstinate. Late in 1819 when Macaulay finally convinced the various Negrophiles to meet, the gathering disbanded after one person nominated Grégoire for the presidency of the unborn society. This threat was too great, especially for de

Broglie. Even one year later when they had two petitions before the Chamber and Macaulay again tried to organize the abolitionists, the moderates refused to support such a hazardous undertaking.[29]

The 1819 election cleared the air for other egalitarians, such as Lafayette, who were too unpolitic or too old to worry about their reputations and who valued a man's present virtues over his past sins. For them Grégoire was a martyr. Yet the Radicals were too few and too uninfluential to form an abolitionist society on their own, and they had to wait until the moderates recovered from their panic of 1819.

The colonial landowners, for their part, failed to maintain the momentum which had been generated by their immediate shock over Grégoire's election. Their new organization soon passed out of existence. Yet as individuals they continued to campaign for the reconquest of Haiti and for a complete return to prerevolutionary conditions in the West Indies, including the legalization of slave trading. They still were optimistic about their eventual success because they expected further assistance from the now apparently firmly entrenched Ultras.

Only Grégoire seemed relatively unaffected by the traumatic events of December 1819. Despite his increased poverty and bitterness, and despite the renewed censorship of 1820, he managed to publish almost all of his abolitionist tracts. Somehow he found sufficient funds not only to survive and to write, but he also provided money for impecunious friends and enemies. "We all age," he wrote a friend, "but my courage is forever young." Forced to withdraw within himself even more than before, he would spend most of his remaining years watching over the interests of his Haitian protégés and ignoring day-to-day politics in France.[30]

NOTES

1. Grégoire to Julien, 17 Oct., no year, AD, L&C, F 592, fo. 41; Grégoire to Antoine Métral, 10 March 1819, AD, L&C, F 353. See also: *Revue encyclopédique* 1 (1819): 313, 526; *L'Abeille Heytienne*, 28 April 1819, p. 25; Joseph George to Grégoire, undated, Arsenal 6339, fo. 105–6, reprinted in Cook, "Document: A Letter from a Haitian to Abbé Grégoire," pp. 438–39.

2. Lafayette's letters to Grégoire in anon. private collection in Paris.

3. "Federalist" no. 10 by Madison in *The Federalist: A Commentary on the Constitution of the United States, Being a Collection of Essays Written in Support of the Constitution Agreed upon September 17, 1787, by the Federal Convention*, Edward Mead Earle, introduction (New York: Modern Library, 1937), pp. 52–63. Electors in France had to pay 300 fr. ($60) annually in direct taxes. This excluded 99 percent of the adult male population according to Bertier de Sauvigny, *Bourbon Restoration*, pp. 68–69.

4. This description differs somewhat from the standard classification of Restoration parties which usually describes only three groups —Ultras, Constitutionals (with the Doctrinaires as a subgroup), and Independents. Lafayette, Constant, and Manuel are included in the latter, which is characterized as anti-Bourbon. I believe this classification confuses an essential distinction. Men like Constant —contrary to Lafayette, Manuel, and Voyer d'Argenson—proposed minor alternations in the Charter, whereas the Radicals, if they would accept a monarchy at all, demanded such changes as would make the king a mere figurehead. See, for example, Bertier de Sauvigny, *Bourbon Restoration*, pp. 142–46.

5. *Notice biographique sur M. Grégoire, ex-Sénateur.*

6. Mr. Chrétien of Blois has been studying Grégoire's election, and some of the relevant correspondence has not been available. When Mr. Chrétien's work is published, some of the following statements might require modification. See: Grégoire to Bérenger, 14 July 1819, *Mémoires*, 1:209–11; *Patriote des Alpes*, 11 Nov. 1847; Joseph Rey, "Appreciation des divers partis," BH Grenoble,

T 3939, fo. 82–84; *L'Independant*, 7 July 1819; Dumolard, "Stendhal electeur de l'abbé Grégoire," pp. 23–38; Paupe and Cheramy, *Correspondance de Stendhal*, 2:159–60.

7. Duke to Duchess de Broglie, 11 Sept. 1819, De Broglie Papers, "Extraits," (typed copies), p. 50; Lesur, *Annuaire historique pour 1819*, pp. 225–56; *La Quotidienne*, 13 July 1819; *Le Drapeau Blanc*, 4 Aug. 1819.

8. *Le Courier*, 22 and 25 July 1819; *Le Pilote*, 13 Aug. 1819; *Minerve français* 7 (1819): 191–92; *Journal des débats*, 30 Aug. 1819.

9. Brissot-Thivars, *Le guide électoral*, 1:304–5. Brissot-Thivars became very involved in Restoration politics. His cousin Anacharsis (J.-P. Brissot's son), feared that Louis-Saturnin eventually would suffer "if he always mixes in politics, where there is nothing to gain ꞏbut prison"; Anacharsis to Sylvain Brissot, 6 Feb. 1819, in Perroud, *Correspondance*, pp. 442–43.

10. *Le Drapeau Blanc*, 7 Aug. 1819. See also: *Le Pilote*, 13 and 17 Aug. 1819; *Journal des débats*, 5 Sept. 1819; Clausson, *Précis historique de la Révolution de Saint-Domingue*, p. 29n; *Histoire de l'Ile de Saint-Domingue*, pp. 126, 135, 136.

11. Lavaud, *Notice sur Henri Grégoire*, passim; Mazerat, *Notice biographique*, distributed with the *Journal libre de l'Isère*, 10 Sept. 1819—the electoral college opened on 12 Sept.; *L'echo des Alpes* (Grenoble), 2 (1819): 14.

12. De Broglie, ed., *Souvenirs*, 2:66; Duke to Duchess de Broglie, 16 Sept. 1819, De Broglie Papers, "Extraits," pp. 52–53; Lesur, *Annuaire pour 1819*, p. 6; *Minerve française* 7 (1819): 382; *L'echo des Alpes* 2 (1819): 73–74, 122–23; *La Renommée*, 19 Sept. 1819, p. 377; Rey, "Appreciation," BH Grenoble, T 3939, p. 82.

13. Clary to Grégoire, 16 Oct. 1819, Arsenal 6339, fo. 63–64; *La Quotidienne*, 18 Sept. 1819.

14. Italics in the original, *Le Drapeau blanc*, 24 Sept. 1819. See also *Le Défenseur des colonies*, published irregularly, and changed to the *Observateur des colonies, de la Marine, de la politique, de la littérature et des arts* with the third issue in Jan. 1820.

15. *Gazette de France*, 27 Sept. and 1 Oct. 1819, pp. 1152 and 1175; Hyde de Neuville, *Mémoires et souvenirs*, 2:418–19; *La Quotidienne*, 25 Sept. 1819; Mme de Necker to Duchess de

Broglie, 12 Oct. 1819, De Broglie Papers, "Lettres," p. 21 (typed copies).

16. Grégoire, *Lettre aux électeurs du département de l'Isère.*

17. Lavaud, *Appel aux contemporains,* p. 2; *Le Constitutionnel,* 30 Sept. 1819. Lavaud was referring to the following speeches and writings by Grégoire: his plea for imprisoned nonjuring priests, 4 Dec. 1794; for Jews, see Chaps. 1–2; against feudal survivals, 5 Feb. and 4 March 1790; Fribourg Swiss, 2 May 1790; Frenchmen imprisoned abroad, 2 July 1790; mulattoes, see Chaps. 3–5; letter to the Grand Inquisitor of Spain, 1798; *De la traite.* For other praise of Grégoire see: *Le Pilote,* 18 Nov. 1819; John Bowing to Grégoire, 16 Sept. 1819, anon. private collection in Paris.

18. De Staël to Grégoire, 2 Oct. 1819 in Grégoire's *Mémoires,* 1:217–23.

19. *Le Pilote,* 18 Nov. 1819.

20. Duchess de Broglie, diary printed in *Souvenirs,* 2:95, 98, 100–105; *Le Courier,* 2 and 13 Oct. 1819; D'Argenson to Grégoire, 7 Oct. 1819 in [Lallement], *Choix de rapports . . . 23. Session de 1819,* 50n; *Minerve français* 7 (1819), 574, ed. Benjamin Constant. Lanjuinais wrote Grégoire on 9 Oct. 1794 that it was "in part in your name, it was with the aid of your silence that the leaders of the vandals proscribed me"; anon. private collection in Paris.

21. *La Quotidienne,* 7, 10, and 30 Nov. 1819; Sapey, *Député de l'Isère, a ses collègues,* pp. 1–6; *Gazette de France,* 9 Nov. 1819, p. 1328; *La Renommée,* 16 and 19 Nov. 1819, pp. 606–7 and 618; *Gazette de Paris,* 27 Nov. 1819, p. 1403; *Le Constitutionnel,* 28 Nov. 1819; Lesur, *Annuaire pour 1819,* p. 2; Albertine de Broglie to Mme Abisson du Perron, 12 Nov. 1819, De Broglie Papers, "Lettres," p. 25.

22. Chamber of Deputies minutes, 2 Dec. 1819, AN, *C I, 210; *L'Independant,* 2 Dec. 1819; *La Quotidienne,* 4 Dec. 1819; Grégoire to Lambrechts, 6 Dec. 1819, in *Mémoires,* 1:230–31; Lafayette to anony., 10 Dec. 1819 in Lafayette, *Mémoires,* 6:56–57.

23. Chamber of Deputies minutes, 6 Dec. 1819, AN, *C I, 210; [Lallement], *Choix de rapports,* 23:7, 10–45, 49n; Lesur, *Annuaire pour 1820,* pp. 3–9; *Le Defenseur des colonies,* no. 1, p. 31; procureur général at Grenoble to garde des sceaux, 3 April 1820, AN, BB 18, 998, dr. 5624.

24. Cited in Dugast's introduction to Grégoire's *Histoire patriotique*, pp. 131–2.

25. The Charter forbade all investigation into past events. See: Grégoire, *Seconde lettre aux électeurs du département de l'Isère*; Audiguier, *Epitre à M. Grégoire*, p. 19n; Cousin D'Avalon, *Grégoriana*.

26. Mme Necker to Albertine, 12 Oct. 1819, De Broglie Papers, "Lettres," p. 21.

27. For the moderates' continued distrust of Grégoire, see Guizot, *Du Gouvernement de la France*, pp. 80, 234–35. The Radicals again resorted to conspiratorial activities; Bertier de Sauvigny, *Bourbon Restoration*, pp. 172, 181–82. A Société Grégoirienne supposedly survived in Grenoble as late as 1 July 1822; AN, F⁷ 3795, no. 58.

28. Laroche's offending pamphlet: *Lettres de M. Grégoire*. See also: John Bowing to Grégoire, 10 March 1821, Sir Charles Macarthy to Grégoire, 21 June 1821, and Laroche to Grégoire, 6 Sept. 1821, anon. private collection in Paris. Also; Lafayette to Clarkson, 15 Feb. 1821 in Kennedy, *Lafayette & Slavery*, p. 37; Grégoire to Marshal Etienne MacDonald, 19 Nov. 1822 in *Mémoires*, 1:240–46; Grégoire, *Abdication volontaire*; ministry of justice circular, 8 Dec. 1820, AN, BB 17, A 9, dr. 7.

29. Article by Joseph Rey in *Patriote des Alpes*, 13 Nov. 1847; Grégoire, *Mémoires*, 1:226; Duchess to Duke de Broglie, 7 Sept. 1819, De Broglie Papers, "Extraits," p. 48; Vastey to Clarkson, 29 Nov. 1819, Griggs and Prator, eds., *Henry Christophe*, p. 180.

30. Grégoire to Clarkson, 14 Dec. 1820, HEH, Clarkson Papers, CN 102; Grégoire's letters to Jennart in BM Nancy discuss his arrangements for secretly sending money to a nonjuring cleric who had bitterly criticized his revolutionary career.

12

The Patriarch of Haiti

Discouraged by his nullified election, Grégoire lost all hope for France. In Europe he was only interested in the Greek revolution and in the small international band of ecclesiastics who continued to resist the spread of ultramontane ideas. He paid scant attention to current French affairs except in so far as they related either to the church or to the Negroes.

Racial equality remained one of Grégoire's favorite causes. The abolitionist campaign actually had not changed very much since 1789. The three problems which had interested egalitarians in the National Assembly—procuring equal rights for mulattoes and free Negroes in the colonies, effectively outlawing the slave trade, and emancipating slaves—had remained unresolved, while one new one had been added, that of ensuring Haitian independence. Moreover, the experiences of the intervening thirty years had embittered the colonists and made the abolitionists less optimistic about the possibilities of success. Caution and moderation became their mottoes.

Aware that he would not help either the mulattoes or the free Negroes in the colonies by publicly pleading for their rights, Grégoire avoided discussing French imperial conditions. He privately intervened in a few cases where mulattoes were being persecuted,[1] but he doubted whether the legislature would either grant them complete equality or abolish slavery in the near future. Consequently he concentrated on combatting the obstacles which Africans faced either on their native continent or in the new nations of the Western Hemisphere.

Grégoire regarded Haiti as the most important of these new states. It was the only one where European settlers had lost control. In addition, it was the only black nation which had developed social and political institutions similar to, although not identical with, the European model. Haitian survival and prosperity would disprove the planters' supposedly scientific racial arguments and therefore would force them to recognize the Negroes' capacity for self-government. Once colonists accepted all races as innately equal, the other racial problems could be easily resolved. One did not enslave or sell one's brothers, after all.

Grégoire, moreover, regarded Haiti as the perfect laboratory for evaluating ideas. According to him, it was a new society whose institutions were still pliant in which republicanism, racial equality, and enlightened religious leadership might be put to the test. If the Haitian experiment succeeded, its lessons could be applied in other Caribbean islands, and perhaps they might be modified and adapted to such established countries as the United States and France.

Earnestly hoping that Haiti would prosper, Grégoire encouraged his correspondents there to prove themselves by developing western religious, educational, and scientific institutions. Free from white interference, he thought, Haiti could adopt the good features of European civilization without imitating its bad ones. Then Haiti would become a model for the rest of the world.[2]

Grégoire resumed his correspondence with Haiti as soon as communications between France and the Western Hemisphere were restored. He learned the details of the many changes which had taken place in the island since Dessalines declared Haitian independence in 1804, especially its division in 1807 into two hostile regimes, a Negro kingdom in the North under Henry Christophe, and a mulatto republic in the South and West under Alexandre Pétion. Civil war between the two parts had lasted through 1813, and their relations would remain tense for another decade.

In addition to the temporarily quiescent conflict between North and South, both Haitian regimes were menaced by the French landowners' determination to launch an expedition against the island. But various domestic and international complications made any attempt to reconquer Saint-Domingue impractical for the moment. Although England theoretically recognized French rights to the island and Louis refused to renounce his jurisdiction over the former colony, the British government unofficially opposed a French expedition while Louis retroceded to Spain all claim to the colony of Santo Domingo. The king, moreover, permitted French merchants to resume unofficial commercial relations with the island and sent ambassadors to both regimes. Negotiations soon collapsed, however, because neither side was willing to make sufficient concessions.[3]

France's refusal to recognize Haitian independence had serious consequences for the two regimes. The mother country's policy isolated the island from other European nations and cut it off from its potential markets. In addition, the Haitians could not find priests for their churches or schools because France and Spain insisted that the papacy must not recognize Negro or mulatto rulers anywhere in the world. Thus Haiti was culturally and economically isolated from Europe and only slowly recovered from the devastation left by prolonged civil wars.

Realizing that France would not recognize their independence in the near future, both Haitian governments asked private individuals in Europe to represent their interests and to provide cultural assistance. But the European abolitionists differed over which regime merited their attention. The French favored the republic while the English preferred the monarchy.

Along with the other French egalitarians, Grégoire automatically supported the republic. But shortly after the European war ended, Christophe's foreign secretary, Julien Prévost (the Count de Limonade), expressed the king's warm feelings toward Grégoire. Prévost praised the former bishop's *Littérature des Nègres* and requested copies of his future works. Calling Grégoire *"the new las-casas"* and *"defender of the cause of liberty and of unfortunate people,"* he sent various official documents which he thought would earn Grégoire's approval.[4]

Grégoire was too dogmatic a republican ever to accept a monarchy in Haiti. Nonetheless, he did not want the kingdom to be overthrown by whites, and he used the documents which Prévost provided as examples of the Haitians' capacity for self-government. Although he also sent some of his pamphlets to the Negro regime, he was not swayed by Christophe's flattery and refused to correspond directly with the king.[5]

Dismayed by Grégoire's silence, Christophe turned to the British abolitionists and asked them to intercede with the former bishop. But Grégoire again refused to correspond with the monarch, and the African Institute entrusted the kingdom's interests to Lafayette and Baron Jean de Turckheim of Alsace. Since the French were more interested in the republic, Christophe relied more and more upon the English. He appointed the abolitionists as his European agents and encouraged Wilberforce and Clarkson to send Methodist ministers who established a primary and technical school system. In return, he offered to adopt the English language and to convert his subjects to Protestantism.[6]

Born in the British colony of Grenada, Christophe lived there until he was ten, and he remained emotionally tied to England for the rest of his life. But these bonds only intensified the quiescent tension between North and South because the second president of the republic, Jean-Pierre Boyer, rejected English influence and expelled as spies all Protestant missionaries who crossed the border.[7] Thus European connections and growing confessional differences created additional friction between the mulatto and Negro regimes.

In some respects Boyer was in a less favorable position than was Christophe. Although Grégoire and other French abolitionists favored the republic, they could give it little more than moral support because they lacked political power and financial resources. Moreover, with the exception of Grégoire and Lafayette, the French devoted most of their attention to the slave trade and regarded Haitian independence as a secondary problem.

Resenting the abolitionists' disinterest, the republican deputies in France felt more comfortable with Grégoire, who, after all, was more familiar to them. Therefore, while the more respectable Negrophiles presented Haitian petitions to the king and the legislature, the deputies privately consulted Grégoire as to strategy. Although they did not necessarily follow his advice, they and their compatriots in Haiti respected the man who had tried so valiantly to assist the Negroes during the past quarter of a century, and they showed their appreciation in whatever ways they could.[8]

During the next decade Grégoire served as an unofficial advisor, sending books and counsel to the Republic of Haiti. He entertained a private correspondence with the president covering a wide range of topics but emphasizing religious and social questions. In 1818 Boyer offered Grégoire an opportunity to put his ideas into practice and invited him to resume his espiscopal functions in Haiti.

Despite Boyer's insistence that he needed a prelate of good character and his promise to care for any "interests" which Grégoire might have, the former bishop, now sixty-eight years old, refused to go because he feared he would not survive for very long in the inhospitable Caribbean climate. His brief experience in Blois discouraged him from assuming a bishopric under questionable circumstances. In addition, he apparently believed that he could better serve the Haitians if he stayed in France and maintained a close watch over the planters who were becoming increasingly incensed about British influence in the northern part of the island.[9]

Still, Grégoire took his obligations seriously, and the first book that he wrote specifically for Haiti was his *Manuel de piété à l'usage des hommes de couleur et des Noirs*. The epigram for this manual, *God makes exception of no one*, ran directly counter to the scripturally based racist arguments common during the early part of the nineteenth century.[10] As background to the book, he described the role which Catholicism had played in the struggle against slavery, using Cardinal Cybo's instructions to seventeenth-century missionaries as his key example.

But the manual was written for Negroes rather than whites, and Grégoire did not have to convince them about racial equality. Instead, he wished to persuade his readers to become Catholics. The Haitians, however, would not become practicing Catholics simply because two hundred years before one prelate had tried to stop the slave trade before it really began to flourish. Catholicism also had to help them with their current problems. Consequently, Grégoire focused upon the two areas in which he thought that Catholicism might prove useful, political and social organization.

Grégoire regarded the establishment of a stable political order as the Haitians' most pressing problem. For him, the family was the basic social unit. Without strong home ties, no state could educate its future citizens and therefore it could not develop a durable form of government. Unstable families were especially common in Haiti because slavery had destroyed all bonds by encouraging concubinage, prostitution, and common law marriages. Even though the slave owners had disappeared,

Grégoire argued that the Haitians would only overcome their past if they followed the stringent sanctions which Catholicism preached against temporary sexual unions. Thus, he concluded, only Catholicism would provide the foundation upon which a stable system of justice, morality, and social order might be created.

In this manual, Grégoire carried revolutionary ecclesiastical reforms one step further than the Constitutional church had gone. He simplified religion as much as he could, and, emphasizing morality above ritual, justified whatever doctrine he retained on practical rather than dogmatic grounds. For example, although his stand on marriage and divorce was Catholic, he avoided theological explanations and, instead, showed how strict marriage customs would combat the sexual laxity which slavery had fostered. The only peculiarly sectarian rite which he insisted upon retaining was the veneration of saints. Even this practice was useful, according to him, because it encouraged the worshipper to become virtuous by providing him with worthy models to emulate. He compiled a list of saints carefully selected either because they were black or because their martyrdom reflected problems relevant to Haitian conditions.

Grégoire insisted that Frenchmen would view Haitian independence more sympathetically if the blacks adopted an identifiable variety of an European religion—preferably Catholicism—as well as purified versions of European institutions. But he shared at least some of his contemporaries' prejudices. The Negroes whom he cited as examples in this manual and in other works were those who met European cultural standards. As in his *Littérature des Nègres*, he failed to find anything to admire in the civilization of nineteenth-century Africa. When he did praise that continent, he stressed the achievements of North African Christianity, which had been imported from abroad, and, along with most authors who discussed the continent, he ignored all of it south of the Sahara Desert.

Although Grégoire deprecated the Africans' native civilization, he expected their descendants in the new world to create a society which would serve Europe as an example. Indeed, as his disillusionment with France's urban life and culture mounted, he, along with Thomas Jefferson and others, dreamed of creating a peaceful egalitarian peasant state. Although such a utopia was unobtainable in Europe, Grégoire thought it might be realized in the Caribbean. But he was pursuing the myth of a self-sufficient nonindustrialized society which had never existed and certainly was unsuited either to African or to West Indian conditions.

It is easy to understand why eighteenth-century agrarians idealized primitive rural life even while they looked down upon the true culture of their favorite "noble savages." Despite the popularity of exotic themes in eighteenth-century literature, most Europeans firmly believed in their cultural if not their racial superiority over other civilizations. Even writers like Montesquieu, who praised Chinese or Persian life, did so out of ignorance or as a literary device, deliberately creating utopias against which they could criticize their own country. Since Grégoire's only contact with the outside world came through literature, he cannot be blamed for being as unsophisticated or as ignorant as his contemporaries were. His cultural bias, however, created frustrations and ill feelings because he expected the Haitians to model themselves upon a legend which contradicted both their cultural heritage and the realities of their environment.

The disparity between Grégoire's dreams and Haitian conditions did not become obvious for almost another decade. In the meantime Boyer renewed his invitation that Grégoire live "among [his] infants" where he could enjoy the fruits of his good deeds and, by his presence, "inspire in them the love for religious virtues which flows from [his] beautiful soul."[11]

Although Grégoire again refused to leave France, he continued to act as a guardian for Haitian interests and became concerned when, in 1821, Rome suddenly sent an apostolic

Jean-Pierre Boyer. Medallion by Pierre-Jean David d'Angers.

vicar to the island. This was the first official papal emissary to appear in the former French colony after the Legislative Assembly unilaterally abolished the office of apostolic vicar in 1792. Since the pontiff unquestionably had acted with French knowledge and approval, Grégoire's suspicions were aroused.

Yet Grégoire's scepticism about the pope's motives rested on more than simple distrust of Rome. The vicar-to-be, Pierre de Glory, Bishop of Macri, had originally served as a curé in Guadeloupe, but his strong pro-Bourbon sentiments had forced

Napoleon to deport him. Grégoire doubted whether Glory's royalist sympathies had been lessened by the Restoration, and, he assumed, the vicar probably would try to prepare for a white invasion by undermining Haitian loyalty to Boyer. Grégoire therefore advised the president to expel the vicar and suggested ways whereby Boyer might purify the existing church structure.[12]

Glory and Grégoire's letter of warning arrived in Haiti on the same ship. Although not a devout Catholic himself, Boyer was anxious to place the church in Haiti on firm foundations. Underestimating both papal animosity and the power of one individual priest, he not only permitted Glory to disembark, but he instructed his priests to recognize the vicar's authority. The vicar soon alienated the president by publicly flounting Boyer's decrees, and within a few weeks the president ordered him to leave.[13] Glory's Haitian career, brief as it was, left the church there even more shaken and conflict-ridden than before.

Following the failure of Glory's mission, Boyer tried to regularize Haitian Catholicism by asking the pope to extend the archbishop of Santo Domingo's jurisdiction over the entire island. The Catholic church remained adamant against such a move. It identified all republics, black or white, with the dechristianization policy of revolutionary France. Fully committed to the Bourbon cause in Spain as well as in France and probably annoyed by Boyer's expulsion of Glory, Rome would take no action which would imply recognition of the Haitian republic. Boyer finally admitted that he would never reach an agreement with the pontiff. Therefore, he abolished the episcopacy, named himself head of the church, and imported priests from Venezuela. Here matters would rest for another forty years, and no amount of encouragement from Grégoire could alter the situation.[14]

Because the Haitian church seemed condemned to permanent anarchy, Grégoire again directed his advice to all of the population, not only the president. Circumstances had changed since he had composed his first *Manuel de piété,* and in 1822 he revised this work to meet the new problems which had arisen in the meantime. He shifted his emphasis somewhat in the new edition. Although he still regarded the establishment of firm and stable family ties as Haiti's most urgent social problem, he also was dismayed about the antiwhite, anti-Protestant sentiment which was developing in the island. He urged the Haitians to forget past conflicts between mulatto, Negro, and white. Using the visual arts to reinforce his text, he added a series of illustrations to his manual which showed all three groups living together in harmony.[15]

Grégoire designed this manual to promote "the progress of piety, civilization, and good morals among our brothers of African origin." Within a year sixteen hundred copies were circulating in Haiti, and Americans reportedly were using both it and the manual of 1818 to instruct Negroes of Haitian descent who, along with their masters, had fled to North America during the revolutionary upheavals in the Caribbean.[16]

The strictly religious questions which he treated in his *Manual de piété* interested Grégoire more than anything else. Yet as spiritual advisor to Haiti, he also had to explain how, under a republican government, church and state defined their respective spheres of authority. Since laws governing marriage, divorce, and inheritance provided the greatest potential source of controversy in any predominantly Catholic country which had a significant non-Catholic minority, it was important for civil and religious officials to agree on marriage requirements. In Haiti, however, the Venezuelan priests imported by Boyer did not understand the problems created by the prevalence of voodoo worship as well as by Protestant missionary activities and past French colonial practices. Accustomed to the greater influence which ecclesiastics exerted in the Spanish empire, they tried to impose orthodox Catholic regulations and were reluctant to acknowledge any civil authority over marriage.

Grégoire understood the Haitian problem somewhat better

because, during the French Revolution, he had already been forced to accept secular jurisdiction over family law. Consequently, in his *Considérations sur le mariage* he modified the stand which he had taken in his first manual. Although he still believed that civil and religious institutions required stable families, he realized that many Haitians had little experience with European family law. Hence any attempt to introduce too rigid marriage restrictions and divorce prohibitions would be ignored by a large part of the population.

In his *Considérations sur le mariage*, Grégoire used as a guide the regulations drawn up by the post-Terror Constitutional church. Although he now placed greater emphasis on the sanctity of marriage, his underlying assumptions remained the same. According to him, the state, as a secular institution, had the right to impose conditions for marriage different from those established by the church. If the state included any significant number of non-Catholics, then it must permit divorce. Catholics should not take advantage of these laws, but the decision must be made by individuals rather than by the government.[17]

Altogether Grégoire believed that the church must remain subordinate to the state and must refrain from interfering in political affairs. Family law was only one area of potential conflict, albeit a delicate and fundamental one. During the 1820s a new problem arose which he felt compelled to discuss, the status of white Protestant missionaries and their converts. For many years he had studied racial and sectarian discrimination as separate questions. Now in Haiti the two problems merged because the Methodist pastors whom Wilberforce sent to the northern kingdom were complaining of racial and religious persecution.[18]

Grégoire's stand on anti-Semitic and anti-Catholic legislation in France and England was too well known for him to ignore the plight of Protestant missionaries in Haiti. Perhaps, he wrote in his *De la liberté de conscience*, Haitians disliked Methodist preachers because they distrusted all whites. Nonetheless, he insisted, no matter how justified religious or racial persecution might appear to be at any given moment, it was wrong. He reiterated his prerevolutionary belief that the state must not interfere in religious affairs (by expelling missionaries, in this case) but should only establish the environment in which men could follow their consciences.

Since most Haitians were at least nominally Catholic, Grégoire explained in simple terms the church's distinction between civil and religious toleration. As a Catholic he could not believe any other religion to be true. This, he said, was religious intolerance, and it was a characteristic shared by all confessions. Still, no man, be he layman, priest, or magistrate, had the right to use force because coercion in matters of faith led to hypocrisy and tyranny. The government must grant to each man "the natural right to exercise at his own risk that [religion] which he has chosen." As Catholics he advised Haitians to pray for eventual Protestant enlightenment, but as citizens he urged them to leave dissenters free to follow their own beliefs.[19]

Grégoire's discussion of Haitian social institutions in his *Considérations sur le mariage* and his criticism of racial and religious intolerance in his *De la liberté de conscience* contained some harsh statements. He blamed civil and religious officials for Haiti's slow rate of development and hoped that his remarks would encourage them to undertake essential reforms. Otherwise, he explained, French imperialists might take advantage of Haiti's problems and use discrimination against whites as a pretext for invading the former colony. "You know," he wrote, "he who addresses [these words]; his invariable attachment cannot hide the righteousness of his intentions." It was, he said, far better for him to advance these criticisms than for Haiti's enemies to make them.[20]

Grégoire provided the islanders with moral advice and, under his direction, the mulattoes organized a society for the propagation of Christianity. But, according to Grégoire, Haiti's social and moral problems would never be resolved unless the educational system were greatly improved. Convinced that good schools depended on traditional religious institutions, which, in turn, depended upon having enough ecclesiastics to serve the population, he urged Boyer to found a seminary even though the priests could not be canonically ordained.[21]

A few laymen trained in the Lancaster method volunteered for service in Haiti. Encouraged by their interest, Grégoire collected whatever books he could and, together with Lafayette, planned an ambitious educational system, including a medical school, for Haiti. But the two old abolitionists' projects came to naught. Grégoire and Lafayette lacked sufficient funds while the island's primary system was inadequate for either a medical school or a seminary. Like the former white rulers, Boyer feared the effect which education might have upon the mass of impoverished and exploited blacks under his rule. Consequently he made no effort to improve Haitian educational facilities, and he supposedly even hid the books which Grégoire had so painstakingly collected.[22]

While Grégoire was most interested in improving Haiti's religious and educational facilities, he also paid attention to the other difficulties which the republic faced. In so far as the Haitians were concerned, their most urgent problem was to achieve French recognition. In this respect, at least, Grégoire proved to be more of a liability than an asset.

In 1820 Boyer authorized a Haitian resident in France, Civique de Gastine, to act as his deputy. Encouraged by the abolitionists, Civique submitted to the Chamber of Deputies a petition for Haitian independence in which he also recommended the abolition of slavery in the French West Indies and denounced French involvement in the slave trade. But Civique's timing was unfortunate because France was in the depths of the reaction caused by de Berry's assassination, and the Chamber refused to discuss his appeal.[23]

Civique remained in France and, when for a brief period in 1821 the government relaxed restrictions on publications pertaining to Haiti and to the slave trade, he petitioned Louis XVIII to abolish slavery and to recognize Haitian independence. The king had sympathized with the abolitionists before the Restoration, but the Ultras exerted strong pressure on him. Civique, moreover, included a long eulogy of Grégoire in his petition and tactlessly castigated the Chamber for voiding Grégoire's election. "The blind hatred which you bear the man," he wrote, "makes you misunderstand, contest all of his virtues." Grégoire's historical record, Civique pointed out, would be judged by God; yet as a "writer on moral subjects, as philosopher, as benefactor of humanity, he belongs to the present and to future generations,"[24] Such ill-advised praise of an ostracized schismatic destroyed what little influence Civique's petition might have had.

Even while Civique was attempting to gain recognition from France, Boyer tried to strengthen his negotiating position by conquering the northern kingdom. As the president organized his forces, Christophe's subjects, alienated by the king's harsh labor policies, rebelled against the monarch. In August 1820 Christophe suffered a heart attack which left him paralyzed. Shortly thereafter his officers also revolted, and he committed suicide. The republican forces under Boyer then invaded and overthrew Christophe's generals, but Negro opposton to mulatto rule persisted for another half year.

In 1822 Boyer conquered the Spanish part of Hispaniola, and for the first time in over a hundred years, all of the island came under one rule. Still, unification intensified rather than simplified the president's problems because it added to a population already bitterly divided by racial and religious differences a sizeable number of hostile Spanish speaking subjects who hoped for French intervention.[25]

Pleased with Boyer's victories, Grégoire urged the Negroes to accept the new regime. Although the president did not overcome the last pockets of black resistance for several months, as early as June 1821 Grégoire congratulated him on his achievements. Republican successes, he commented, provided an "irrefutable reply to all of the lies about the children of Africa presently circulating in Europe."[26]

Unable to assist the Haitian quest for recognition directly, Grégoire advised Boyer to seek European respect by joining the fight against slavery and the slave trade. He thought that such a step would forestall French intervention because the planters were primarily interested in Haiti as a new source of labor. Hence the longer slavery lasted in the West Indies, the greater would be the temptation for French colonists to seize the island. Grégoire also urged Haiti to assist the Greek revolutionaries in their struggle against the pagan Ottomans. Such aid, he assumed, would improve Haiti's reputation among European liberals and radicals, who might then support the Republic more enthusiastically.[27]

Boyer was grateful for Grégoire's continued interest in his regime and for the Frenchman's attempts to reconcile the northerners to it. But the republic could do little more to follow his advice than it was already doing. Civique was still in Paris petitioning the legislature for recognition and for the abolition of slavery in the remaining colonies, while an antislave trade commission had been established in Haiti. Moreover, the republic could not spare money or arms for Greek rebels because the government still feared a French invasion.[28]

Although Boyer found Grégoire's recommendations impractical, he sent the former bishop a shipment of coffee as a token of his esteem. Boyer's gift touched but also embarrassed Grégoire. In the past he frequently had been accused of venality and of accepting bribes, even though in reality he had never received compensation for assisting various minority groups. He had no desire to change this practice now, but he feared insulting the Haitians. After some consideration, he sold most of the coffee and donated the proceeds to the Greek independence movement. He used the small remaining amount to entertain those among his friends who enjoyed savoring a beverage produced by free labor.[29]

At long last in 1825 the Haitians' hopes approached fulfillment. Much to everyone's surprise the new French king, Charles X, attempted to win moderate support. Ignoring the men whom he had led under his brother's regime, Charles firmly rejected the planters' demands for an expedition against Haiti, and his ministry unilaterally and conditionally relinquished all rights over Saint-Domingue. Still, France did not automatically resume amicable relations with her former colony but instead made formal recognition contingent upon receiving preferential trade rights and one hundred fifty million francs in compensation for the white landholdings confiscated during the Revolution.

At first Boyer hesitated, but finally he agreed to discuss the French terms. Fearing an indiscretion similar to that committed by Civique de Gastine five years before, Boyer forbade his agents in Paris to visit Grégoire. They obeyed his instructions until negotiations temporarily collapsed and they were recalled.

In the meantime, in Haiti Boyer honored the French ambassador with a premature celebration. In order to avoid embarrassing the envoy, he carefully removed a portrait of Grégoire from the banquet hall. Much to the president's consternation, however, a Haitian senator proposed a toast "to the venerable *Henri Grégoire*, the constant friend of Haitians and of all men of the black race!" The French ambassador refused to join the salute and shortly thereafter left Haiti. Grégoire's portrait then was restored to its place of honor.[30]

Although much antagonism remained, France renounced any intention of reconquering the Republic of Haiti, and de facto recognition soon followed. Thereafter trade between the two countries gradually increased. Several more years would pass, however, before all of the remaining difficulties were resolved, and negotiations with the papacy proved unsuccessful.

Grégoire realized the significance of French recognition, but he was embittered by Boyer's behavior during the negotiations. Perhaps overimpressed by the flattery which Haitians had lavished upon him and too convinced of his own importance for the island, he reacted strongly to the slights which the president had condoned.[31] What hurt him most was the Haitians' insistence upon gaining full recognition at any cost—even if it meant repudiating him. After one highly placed official reportedly made disparaging remarks about him, comparing him with a lemon from which all of the juice had been extracted, Grégoire lost his patience and voiced some of the disillusionment about Haitian developments which he previously had kept to himself. No longer limiting his remarks to condemning racial and religious discrimination, he criticized the island's economic and political institutions as well.

Grégoire's concern about Haiti was well founded. The country's inadequate administrative and military system collapsed as soon as the threat of invasion disappeared. Obliged to raise funds in order to pay the large indemnity which France demanded, Boyer reintroduced Toussaint's harsh rural code. The president, however, lacked the early leader's administrative genius. His laws, which reduced agricultural workers to a status resembling peonage, did not produce the anticipated increase in productivity. Fearing the dissatisfaction which spread rapidly throughout the island, Boyer closed the few remaining schools. In violation of everything that Grégoire had preached during the preceding decade, racial distinctions hardened into a new caste system, whites were expelled, and Haiti became a Negro republic ruled by a mulatto minority.

Convinced he no longer could help the Haitians, in October 1826 Grégoire composed a farewell letter, or an epistle, to his former protégés. In this last message to the Haitians, he confined himself to generalities, promising to prepare a detailed memorandum concerning the Haitian constitution for Boyer's private use.[32]

Rather sadly, Grégoire finally recognized how his hasty temper had limited his effectiveness. He attributed the decline of his influence to two factors: his blunt criticism of Haitian conditions, which he belatedly regretted, and the Haitians' desire for complete recognition. Convinced that France eventually would have recognized the republic whether or not Boyer met all of her demands, he regarded the Haitians' anxiety on that matter as unwarranted. But, not wanting to hinder their happiness in any way, Grégoire asked the Haitians to forget rather than despise him.

Grégoire's farewell epistle was the work of a querulous, disillusioned old man. Although he admitted his tactlessness, he could not understand where the real problem lay, in his failure to comprehend the cultural differences between himself and the Negroes in Haiti. In addition, he could not provide the services which the Haitians urgently required. They might have respected the moralistic preachings which he periodically sent them, and the few who knew of his efforts to provide them with books probably appreciated his intentions, but he could not advise Boyer on agricultural reconstruction nor could he facilitate negotiations with the papacy. Still, the Haitians regretted the former bishop's bitterness. They vowed neither to forget nor to despise his good deeds and regretted that the island's enemies finally had succeeded in driving a wedge between it and "the most faithful heart among [its] defenders."[33]

In his farewell to Haiti, Grégoire noted that "slavery weighs again over the entire [European] continent," and he offered his services to the victims of tyranny wherever they might live. He probably was referring to Greek revolutionaries who were still trying to win their independence from the Ottoman Empire. Shortly after the outbreak of the Greek revolution in 1821, Grégoire had asked the Haitians to assist the heirs of classical democracy, but President Boyer had been unable to send help. Now Grégoire decided to devote his failing strength to this noble cause.[34]

Despite this new project and despite his disillusionment with Haiti, Grégoire did not abandon the Negroes. He tried to trace the source of various malicious rumors about Haiti which circulated in Europe, and he continued to correspond with

English abolitionists.[35] In addition, he became increasingly interested in other countries in the new world. For many years he had expected future egalitarian progress to be made there, and such recent events as the Denmark Vesey plot in the United States convinced him that slavery would not survive for very long in the newly independent nations of the Western Hemisphere.

Grégoire thought that his predictions were being fulfilled in the early 1820s when most of the Spanish Latin American colonies achieved their independence. As they severed their ties with Europe, a few of the new states where slavery was insignificant emancipated the Negroes and moved in the direction of recognizing racial equality. But such important slave-owning states as Brazil and Cuba retained slavery until the 1880s, and in all of the countries save Haiti whites retained a disproportionate amount of influence.[36]

Grégoire also was interested in the Latin American churches. He was acquainted with one of the early ecclesiastical rebels against Spanish and papal authority in Mexico, Servando Teresa de Mier. Through his contacts with Mier and because of the praise and honors which several of the new states showered upon him, Grégoire saw an opportunity to promote the type of ecclesiastical reforms which he had failed to achieve in Haiti. Consequently, he advised the various governments to limit their relations with Rome and to establish national churches.[37]

Recent events confirmed Grégoire's suspicions concerning the pope who, in 1816, denounced all independence movements. Although the pope upheld Spanish jurisdiction over Latin America, Pius VII did send an apostolic mission. These officials met with little success, and in 1824 the pontiff issued a new encyclical condemning revolutions. During the following years, Rome gradually relented and tried to reestablish ties with Latin America, but Grégoire doubted whether these actions represented a significant retreat from the pontiff's desire to resurrect the two Bourbon empires. He therefore recommended that the new states establish autonomous churches which would help preserve their independence and perhaps might repair the ecclesiastical abuses which Rome had fostered during the preceding centuries.[38]

Grégoire regarded the United States as the most interesting new country in the Western Hemisphere. Convinced that the first colony to achieve independence should continue to serve other nations as a model, he was disillusioned because it not only showed no signs of abolishing slavery but actually was in the process of solidifying its racial caste system. Consequently, he tried to use what influence he had to encourage the American abolitionist movement.

The passage of time helped Grégoire renew his friendship with American philanthropists. After Barlow's death, bitterness among the poet's friends over Grégoire's critique of the *Columbiad* faded. As the traumatic events of the Terror receded into the distant past, the revolutionary bishop's reputation among American francophiles steadily increased. When they went to France, they generally visited with him. More important, the New York Historical Society admitted Grégoire to foreign membership, and he tried to enlist the "zeal and distinguished talents" of that society's president, Gulian Verplanck, in the fight against American participation in the trade. He made similar appeals to his other correspondents in the United States.[39]

By 1826 Grégoire realized that his efforts were futile and that the United States would not grant equal rights to persons of African descent in the near future. Still, he refused to generalize on this observation and continued to regard race prejudice as an outgrowth of aristocratic pride.[40] This conclusion reinforced what he had known before but had chosen to ignore for several years; the key to racial problems lay in European traditions rather than in the new world. It was at home that he must fight the roots of prejudice if he was ever to achieve any permanent improvement in the Negroes' status.

NOTES

1. Grégoire to Verplanck, 11 July 1823, NYHS; Grégoire to Blanchet, 29 Nov. 1824, BM Laon, autographes, 22 carton, no. 39, p. 7.

2. Grégoire to anon., 15 April 1815, BN, NAF 24,910, fo. 288.

3. Chanlatte, *Situation d'Hayti*; Saunders, *By Authority. Haytian Papers*, 1:84; Leborgne de Boigne, *Nouveau système de colonisation*, pp. 10, 70.

4. Italics and capitalization in the original; Comte de Limonade to Grégoire, 10 June 1814, Arsenal 6339, fo. 44–47 verso. See Grunebaum-Ballin, *Henri Grégoire*, p. 331.

5. Grégoire communicated indirectly with the kingdom through the English abolitionists; M.P. (Price?) to Grégoire, 3 March 1815, BPR, Rév. 171, no. 64.

6. Stephens to Grégoire, 7 Sept. 1815, Arsenal 6339, fo. 53–59 verso; Vastey to Clarkson, 29 Nov. 1819, Clarkson to Christophe, 24 Jan., 28 April, and 10 July 1820, Griggs and Prator, *Henry Christophe*, pp. 179–80, 187 and note, 197, 201.

7. Cole (p. 31) says that Christophe was not a slave. Clarkson to Boyer, 25 May 1825 [*sic* for 1821] and Boyer to Clarkson, 30 July 1821, Griggs and Prator, *Henry Christophe*, pp. 225, 229.

8. Colombel to Grégoire, 9 Nov. 1819, Arsenal 6339, fo. 79–80 verso, another copy, fo. 85–86 verso. See also: Duéveneaux to Grégoire, 12 Nov. 1819, Arsenal 6339, fo. 65–66 verso; *Le Télégraphe* (Port-au-Prince), 20 Dec. 1818; *L'Eclaireur haytienne ou la parfait patriote, journal politique, commercial et literraire* [*sic*], (Port-au-Prince), 27 Aug. 1818; *L'Abeille Heytienne*, 16 Sept. 1817, 1 Feb., and 1 March 1818, pp. 9, 11–13, and 4; Chanlatte, *Almanach republicain*, 1818, p. 33; Audiguier, *Epitre à M. Grégoire*, pp. 22–23.

9. Sabourin to his sister, 25 Sept. 1818, Arsenal 6339, fo. 60. Napoleon reportedly made a similar suggestion in 1816: Las Cases, *Mémorial de Sainte-Hélène*, 3:395 and 4:204–5. The planters failed to distinguish between the abolitionists, who encouraged and supported Christophe, and the British government, which did not yet recognize Haitian independence; Fladeland, "Abolitionist Pressures," pp. 364–65; Christophe to Clarkson, 18 Nov. 1816, Griggs

and Prator, *Henry Christophe*, pp. 101, 62, 72; Wilberforce to Macaulay, 7 Jan. 1815, 6 April 1816, and Christophe to Wilberforce 18 Nov. 1816, in Robert and Samuel Wilberforce, eds., *Correspondence of Wilberforce*, 1:353–54, 358–59; 2:147; Cole, *Christophe*, pp. 216–23.

10. Grégoire, *Manuel de piété, à l'usage des hommes de couleur et des Noirs*, p. 3; summarized in *Chronique religieuse* 1 (1819): 161–64. As early as 1815 a British abolitionist had urged him to send books of piety to Haiti: M.P. (Price?) to Grégoire, 3 March 1815, BPR, Rév. 171, no. 64. See also Grégoire's *Mémoires*, 1:204.

11. Ignac to Grégoire, 1 April 1820, Arsenal 6339, fo. 81–82.

12. Grégoire to Boyer, 20 Aug. 1821, Ardouin, *Etudes*, 9:68–69, 27; memo for Colombel, 14 Aug. 1821, Arsenal 6339, fo. 98–103; Clarkson to Boyer, 25 May 1825 [*sic* for 1821], and Boyer to Clarkson, 30 July 1821, Griggs and Prator, *Henry Christophe*, pp. 225, 229–30; *Revue encyclopédique* 9 (1821): 15; Gastine, *Lettre au roi*, p. 71.

13. Glory's pastoral letter, n.d., Arsenal 6339, fo. 38–43 verso.

14. Paul, "Bilan spirituel du Boyerisme," pp. 11–15; Mecham, *Church and State in Latin America*, pp. 285–86.

15. Grégoire, *Manuel de piété*, 1822.

16. Grégoire to Bowing, 31 Oct. 1822, anon. private collection in Paris; to Verplanck, 17 May 1823, NYHS; to Clarkson, 13 May 1823, HEH, CN 103; William Price to Roberts Vaux, 10 July 1818, Pennsylvania Historical Society.

17. Grégoire, *Considérations sur le mariage et sur le divorce*; Necheles, "The Abbé Grégoire," pp. 237–41. Marriage laws, of course, were a serious issue during the Revolution because the Legislative Assembly first, and subsequent regimes thereafter, tried to secularize family law. Nonetheless, most Frenchmen saw the need to legitimize their unions, either through the church or the state (or both), whereas slave conditions had discouraged formal unions among blacks in the colonies.

18. Leslie Jones to Grégoire, 27 Sept. 1824 and Bowing to Grégoire, 8 Jan. 1825, anon. private collection in Paris; *Revue encyclopédique* 27 (1825): 888–89.

19. Grégoire, *De la liberté de conscience et de culte à Haïti*, p. 14; *Chronique religieuse* 5 (1820): 333–34.

20. Grégoire, *Considérations sur le mariage*, p. 60.

21. Grégoire to Boyer, 20 Aug. 1821, Ardouin, *Etudes*, 9:68–69; Grégoire to Degola, 17 Feb. 1820, Gubernatis, *Degola*, p. 365; *Chronique religieuse* 4 (1820): 246–48 and 5 (1820): 331–34.

22. Lafayette to Grégoire, 7 and 23 July 1818, anon. private collection in Paris; Vaval, "Boyer," pp. 3–7.

23. Gastine, *Pétition à MM les Députés relative à l'abolition de l'esclavage*. It is unclear, but likely, that Civique was a mulatto. He always identified himself as a French citizen but died and was buried in Haiti: *Revue encyclopédique* 15 (1822): 611 and an invitation to the funeral sent to Grégoire, in Arsenal 6339, fo. 115. See also: Grégoire to Clarkson, 14 Dec. 1820, HEH, CN 102; Lafayette to Clarkson, 15 Feb. 1821, Kennedy, *Lafayette*, p. 37; *Chronique religieuse* 6 (1821): 155–58.

24. Gastine, *Lettre au roi*, p. 51; *Le Télégraphe*, 10 June 1821, p. 1 and the following issues, especially 1 July 1821, p. 3.

25. It had been united briefly during the Revolution. Bulletin of police générale, Nantes, 15 Nov. 1823, AN, F[7] 3795, no. 61.

26. Grégoire to Boyer, 22 June 1821; see also letter of 20 Aug. 1821: Ardouin, *Etudes*, 9:66, 68–69, 27–64.

27. Grégoire to Boyer, 22 June and 20 Aug. 1821, Ardouin, *Etudes*, 9:66–69. For Grégoire and Greece see: Lascaris, *L'abbé Grégoire*, pp. 10, 12, 72–73; Carnot's introduction to Grégoire's *Mémoires*, 1:205–7; Grégoire to Clarkson, 13 May 1823, HEH, CN 103.

28. Gastine, *Seconde pétition* and *Pétition à MM. les Députés sur la nécessité*.

29. Lescaris, *L'abbé Grégoire*, pp. 11–12; Grégoire to Boyer, 20 and 24 Aug. 1821, in Ardouin, *Etudes*, 9:68–69, 71–72. Shortly before this time a lack of funds had forced him to move into a smaller apartment; see Grégoire to Jennart, 4 April 1820, BM, Nancy, autographes.

30. Ardouin, *Etudes*, 9:370–71; de Salvandy, *De l'émancipation de Saint-Domingue*, pp. 7, 67.

31. But some French observers blamed Grégoire for the Haitians' fear and hatred of France; bulletin of police générale, 15 Nov. 1823, AN, F[7] 3795, no. 61.

32. Grégoire, *Epître aux Haïtiens*; notes for proposed revision of the Haitian constitution, n.d., Arsenal 6339, fo. 112–verso.

33. Editor's note, Grégoire's *Epître*, p. 12n.

34. Grégoire, *Epître*, pp. 12–13; Grégoire to Mustoxidi, 14 April 1820 and Dutrône to Coray, 1 Oct. 1829, Lascaris, *L'abbé Grégoire*, pp. 14–15, 3n, 5, 8, 14; Grégoire to Trongnon, 11 Jan. 1829, AD, L&C, F 592, fo. 87; to same, 14 May 1829, BM Lunéville, p. 149; "Visites de Weiss," 7 Oct. 1827, BPR, CD; note in Schomburg Coll. C–4.

35. Lafayette to Grégoire, 12 June 1828, Macaulay to Grégoire, 3 Feb. 1827, and Macaulay's correspondence with Grégoire through 1829 in anon. private collection in Paris.

36. Grégoire urged the Brazilians to abolish slavery: *Revue encyclopédique* 29 (1826): 297.

37. For Latin American churches see: *Revue encyclopédique* 31 (1826): 236; 33 (1827): 842; 36 (1827): 741; J. N. Gutierez to Grégoire, 3 Dec. 1826, anon. private collection in Paris. For Servando de Mier: letter to Grégoire, 22 April 1802, Arsenal, 6339, fo. 26–31; Grégoire, *Apologie*, p. 10; Arciniegas, *Latin America*, pp. 308–10, 344.

38. Arciniegas, *Latin America*, pp. 345–50 and Mecham, *Church and State*, pp. 61–77.

39. Grégoire to Verplanck, 17 May 1823, NYHS. See also his letters of 23 June 1822 and 26 March 1819, NYHS; Grégoire to Warden, 18 Oct. [1826], MHS. Grégoire was a vice-president of the American Colonization Society for Liberia, and he sent abolitionist material to Bishop Carroll; Grégoire to Carroll, 1 Feb. 1815, Baltimore Archdiocese, 4 B 7.

40. Grégoire, *Noblesse de la peau*, pp. 23–24.

13

The Nobility of the Skin: 1820–1830

While Grégoire waited for the new world republics to develop a utopian society, he continued to worry about Africans elsewhere. Hoping to assist Negroes in their homeland and in the remaining colonies, he established unofficial ties with the moderate and cautious French abolitionists. Although these men had opposed his election to the Chamber of Deputies and had hesitated to form a society because he might become a member, they found him a useful intermediary between themselves and the British philanthropists,[1] for even though he was a political outcast, he alone had the time and the desire to carry on an extensive correspondence and to compose antislavery tracts. Since abolition would never succeed in France until Frenchmen rejected slavery as an evil, and since the abolitionists were completely dependent upon their British colleagues, Grégoire continued to perform important functions for the movement.

During the decade of the 1820s, most of Grégoire's correspondence with his fellow egalitarians concerned France's failure to prosecute slave traders. This was the issue which linked the French and English philanthropists who, otherwise, were divided by their support for one or the other Haitian regimes.[2] The French needed English aid, while the English feared that their hard-won victory over British slave traders might be lost if foreigners sold large numbers of Africans. As long as some countries continued the trade, slaves would be smuggled into those parts of the Western Hemisphere where importation was illegal, including the British colonies. The abolitionists realized that English planters would argue that cheap labor in French and Spanish colonies was destroying their market. Thus foreign slave traders endangered the progress which the British philanthropists had made so far.

The British government faced a delicate diplomatic problem. It had the naval power to halt what, according to English law, was piracy, but it could not search suspect foreign ships in peacetime without permission from the appropriate governments.[3] Spain and Portugal granted limited right of search in 1818, but French authorities refused to permit another country to interfere with their merchant fleet, and they failed to act against the numerous slave ships of all nations which were using the French flag. Therefore, the British could neither enforce the 1815 treaty nor prevent the illegal use of the French flag unless the French ministry agreed to cooperate.

The egalitarians needed dramatic evidence and solid statistics to arouse both an apathetic public and passive officials against extensive French involvement in the slave trade. Eventually they found two witnesses, both former residents in the French colony of Senegal, one a retired official, Joseph Morénas, and the other a missionary, the Abbé Guidicelly. These men testified to the prevalence of illegal slave trading in Africa, and, in addition, Guidicelly charged French colonial officials with having hindered his efforts to convert the Senegalese.

The priest's complaints interested Grégoire very much. For two decades he had urged missionaries to preach against the trade and had denounced it as an obstacle to proselytization both in Africa and in the colonies. Now he had evidence to refute the planters' assertion that slavery helped spread Christianity among Africans. The British were not overly concerned about Catholicism, but they were just as anxious as Grégoire to use all available testimony against slave traders.[4]

Grégoire and his friends encouraged the two witnesses to publicize their information about slave trading in Senegal, but despite their avowed piety, the Ultras ignored Guidicelly's accusations. Moreover, in June 1820 when Morénas submitted a petition to the Chamber of Deputies, the landowners tried to discredit his charges. The former official, they insinuated, must have had personal reasons for criticizing his colonial superiors. Thereupon the minister of the navy decided to institute legal proceedings against Morénas.[5]

Since the minister's decision posed a grave threat to French abolitionism, Grégoire and his friends needed precise and detailed information to verify Morénas' statements. If the former official were to be convicted, they never again would persuade anyone connected with the colonies to testify against the slave traders.

Fortunately, Macaulay had come to Paris to help his colleagues with Morénas' petition. He was a leading member of the African Institute, which the British abolitionists had created in 1807 for the express purpose of ensuring enforcement of the English ban on slave trading. The society not only collected evidence of British violations, but after Napoleon outlawed the French trade in 1815, it also watched French merchant vessels and colonies. Thus when French officials threatened to prosecute Morénas, Macaulay procured the evidence necessary to substantiate the official's accusations, and the ministry dropped its charges.[6]

In the Morénas affair and in others, Macaulay chose Grégoire as his French agent because he personally preferred the former bishop to the other abolitionists. The religious outlook of the two men was remarkably similar, despite their confessional differences. One followed the evangelical millenarian tradition, the other sympathized with the neo-Jansenist millenarian heritage, and both believed that they had an obligation to prepare for the earthly utopia over which Christ eventually would rule.

Macaulay regarded Grégoire as one of the few men in France who had "spiritual religion—a sense of abiding responsibility, and a habit of communion with his God and Savior." He regretted that some persons lacked "the magnanimity ever to forgive" Grégoire's exaggerated statements made "during the effervescence of men's minds" in France. At a time when the continental abolitionists' antipathy for the former bishop was strongest, he wrote Grégoire: "We are not separated in those things which are the real distinguishing features of Christian character—the love of God and his son Jesus Christ, our Savior, and the express desire to suffer all his will."[7]

Since the French abolitionists still hesitated to form their own organization and therefore depended completely upon English financing and documentary evidence, Macaulay could force them to cooperate with Grégoire, at least privately. Thus, for example, even though he corresponded directly with other French philanthropists, he channeled information and funds for men who were being persecuted by slave owners through Grégoire, who, in turn, distributed the money and gave the information to the abolitionists in the legislature, Constant, de Broglie, Turckheim, and Lafayette.[8]

Once the ministry dropped its charges against Morénas, Macaulay urged him to submit a second petition. But fearing it would be as ineffective as the first, Macaulay also asked the English foreign office to support the continental abolitionists' demands for strict legislation against French slave traders. In addition, he approached the French ambassador, Elie Decazes, whose career in the ministry had been cut short by the controversy over Grégoire's election. Now, less than a year later, Macaulay advanced Grégoire's proposal to impose degrading penalties on men convicted of slave trading, but when Decazes showed no enthusiasm, Macaulay decided not to pursue the matter and advised Grégoire against publishing a pamphlet on the subject.[9]

Macaulay's advice probably was sound because the conservatives' victories in the 1820 elections temporarily paralyzed abolitionist activity. The new chamber enacted increasingly restrictive press laws which prevented Grégoire from printing even the documentary evidence which the British had sent to him. Consequently he gave the material to foreign journalists in the hopes that it might be published elsewhere in Europe. At the same time, Lafayette and Constant decided against resubmitting Morénas' petition.[10]

Obviously the French abolitionists needed some sort of association to devise strategy and to finance an active publicity campaign. Yet even in the midst of their panic over Morénas' petition when Macaulay again suggested that they form a society, the cautious liberals and moderates refused to follow his advice. During the summer of 1821 Lafayette and Grégoire contemplated taking the initiative themselves, and the guests at the dinner party at which Grégoire served Haitian coffee probably discussed the plans formulated by the two revolutionaries. Their schemes were impractical, however, because Constant, de Staël, and de Broglie—the men who would have to undertake the legislative work—still adamantly refused to risk any public association with Grégoire.[11]

Finally the French abolitionists discovered a way to coordinate their activities without risking identification with the old Amis des Noirs and specifically without including Grégoire and Lafayette. In 1821 they established an interfaith Société de la Morale Chrétienne which handled a broad series of humanitarian problems on an interdenominational basis.

This society's ecumenical nature was a thinly-veiled disguise for the evangelical Protestantism preached by the Paris synod under Pastor Marron. Although Grégoire had cooperated with Protestants, Jews, and avowed atheists in the past, he could not

join such a blatantly sectarian association. The society, moreover, encompassed within its program the entire field of nineteenth-century philanthropic activity and, at first, paying only
of its energies to educational and penal reform, paying only
scant attention to slavery and to slave trading. Even after the
members founded an antislave trade commission in April 1822,
they hesitated to publicize its existence and subordinated it to
their strongly sectarian activities until the July Revolution of
1830.[12]

Planters and conservatives attacked the Société de la Morale
Chrétienne for its obvious ties with England, but they could
not accuse it of contamination by Grégoire. Although many of
his friends were founding members, the leaders of the society
included his most irreconcilable critics among the moderates,
François-Pierre Guizot and the Duke de Broglie. For many
years it avoided mentioning the former bishop by name, even
when it used the material which he received from England. It
only broke this rule once in 1822 when its journal cited Grégoire's discovery of Cardinal Cybo's letter condemning the
slave trade. If Grégoire was hurt by his exclusion, he masked
his feelings and praised the society's work.[13]

The Société de la Morale Chrétienne confronted the same
dilemma which had long plagued all abolitionists. Since the
fall of the Gironde in 1793, philanthropists had avoided
identification with any specific political party, eschewed legislative activity as much as possible, and refused to make any
popular appeals. The fate of the various petitions submitted to
the Chamber of Deputies by Morénas and Civique de Gastine
only confirmed the abolitionists' reluctance to use the methods
which their predecessors had employed.

Yet the abolitionists felt called upon to act. Only the Chamber and the ministry had the power to enforce the ban on slave
trading, and if the Société de la Chrétienne Morale wished to pro-
cure effective penalties for slave traders, it had to deal directly
with the government. Lacking the power which an aroused public

might have given them, the philanthropists resorted to political intrigues and tried to achieve the desired legislation by threatening to prevent passage of the budget.[14]

The abolitionists were afraid to attack slavery directly. For example, Talleyrand called one of Constant's speeches against slave traders "a passport to England."[15] Anxious to avoid a repetition of the Morénas affair, the egalitarians now linked abolitionism with the liberals' and moderates' general opposition to the conservative ministry. They used violations of the ban on slave trading as grounds for criticizing the regime, just as the Ultras had used the question of Haitian independence as a pretext for attacking the Radicals. Besides a few committed members, neither party really regarded imperial issues as very important, and both employed them as convenient tools. Still, in the face of conservative electoral victories, the liberal-moderate coalition hesitated to pursue the slave trade question very vigorously, and despite their new organization, the abolitionists remained dependent upon English assistance.

The abolitionists gradually attracted public support and expanded their activities. Their accomplishments during the final years of Louis XVIII's reign were meagre, however, amounting to little more than publicly appealing for strict enforcement of antislave trade laws, sponsoring essay contests on abolishing the trade, and petitioning the Chamber of Deputies to repeal discriminatory legislation against free mulattoes in the colonies. Macaulay again supported their efforts, but the ministry ignored their pleas.[16]

Despite the society's failure to achieve any of its goals, Grégoire was emboldened by its increased publicity and, for a time, even thought that the Chamber might assist the West Indian mulattoes.[17] Barred from more fruitful activity by his exclusion from the legislature and the Société de la Morale Chrétienne, he vowed to use the only weapon which remained to him—his pen—to fight against racial prejudice and slave trading.

N. Maurin del.

Bénédiction Nuptiale.

*Nuptial benediction; illustration from the 1822
edition of Grégoire's* Manual de piété.

For a while Grégoire's journalistic ties provided him with an outlet, and he again tried to arouse religious sentiment against the slave traders. For example, in a series of articles which he published in the *Chronique religieuse* he argued that the contemporary church should imitate the early Christians who had vigorously opposed slavery. He once again appealed to devout men of all faiths who agreed that "the nobility of color, invented by European pride, is as absurd as that of parchment."[18]

As his pleas remained unanswered, Grégoire became increasingly shrill and, resuming the hyperbolic tone common in his revolutionary publications, he portrayed the members of the proslavery coalition as assassins and perverts. But the *Chronique* had a very small circulation and could not provoke a widespread reaction against slave trading.

After 1821 even the *Chronique* was no longer available to him, and Grégoire had no alternative but to pay for his own publications. By selling part of his library and by other means, between 1822 and 1826 he accumulated sufficient funds to publish a series of pamphlets. Armed with documents provided by the African Institute and with information gleaned from his private correspondence, he pleaded all the egalitarian causes at the same time. He expressed his concern over racism in almost all of the works which he wrote during the second half of the Restoration. When he had nothing of his own to print, he translated and edited the English abolitionists' tracts. Not surprisingly, he frequently denounced French apathy, pusillanimity, and ignorance, while he praised Anglo-American philanthropists for having "more character, more civil courage" than their continental colleagues.[19]

Not afraid for his personal safety, but unwilling to interfere in a delicate situation, Grégoire refrained from commenting on conditions within the French empire. Instead he reverted to the question of slave trading which absorbed his abolitionist colleagues but which he had only incidentally discussed after

1814. At one point he had planned to write a pamphlet advocating harsher penalties for slave traders, but his English friends, after consulting the French ambassador in London, had advised against making such a proposal. The French public, they had warned, was not yet ready to accept degrading penalties, or "peines infamantes," for slave traders.[20]

By 1822 Grégoire no longer cared whether his countrymen were ready. Determined to arouse Frenchmen from their apathy, he blamed the contemporary Catholic clergy for having failed to spread egalitarian ideas, and he pointed to the role that the English dissenters had taken in awakening widespread proAfrican sympathy. This he contrasted with Cardinal Fontana's refusal to adopt an official stand against slave trading. Only if priests condemned the sale of human flesh, Grégoire asserted, would all of France realize how hideous and how infamous slave trading actually was. Only then would the government be forced to take such effective measures as instituting a slave registration system in the colonies and granting England the right to search French vessels for contraband Africans.[21]

But slave trading was merely one symptom of a more fundamental evil, and in his last significant publication on racial questions, his *Noblesse de la peau,* Grégoire discussed the relationship between Christian ideology, slave trading, and the entire problem of social inequality. Broadening his attack, he castigated all forms of stratification, whether founded on political power, social caste, religious affiliation, hereditary characteristics, noble birth, or racial features.

Grégoire advanced some interesting insights in his *Noblesse de la peau.* Pointing to the rapid increase in anti-European sentiment among the Haitians, he observed that race prejudice was not only a white phenomenon. Instead, he asserted, it must reflect some deepseated instinct in human nature.

Still, Grégoire regarded white racism as the most harmful form. Rather than trying to explain the general phenomenon of race prejudice, he focused on antipathies towards Negroes

which he attributed to a variety of factors, including aristocratic sentiment—or what he called the aristocracy of the skin
—and the financial interests of a coalition composed of merchants, slave traders, and plantation owners. Glossing over the
economic aspects of slavery and failing to pursue his more
expanded definition of egalitarianism, he expounded a narrow,
doctrinal interpretation of French racism. Rather simplistically,
he linked racial pride with the religious hypocrisy which, according to him, characterized the Restoration. A truly religious
man who knew that the soul has neither sex nor color, he
admonished his readers, would never make arbitrary distinctions
among men, no matter what his financial interests might be.
Thus, as so often before, Grégoire posed an interesting question, the universality and multisided nature of inequality, but
refused to follow his ideas to their logical conclusions.

In this work Grégoire mixed his old revolutionary optimism
with his more recently acquired pessimism. Convinced that the
Haitian experiment would convert white supremacists, he predicted that "the nobility of the skin will suffer the same fate
as that of parchment." But, recognizing that racial prejudice
called forth more elemental and brutal passions than political
controversies did, he questioned whether whites would peacefully relinquish their rights. The Revolution had left its mark
on him, and he feared that future egalitarian progress would
come only through violence. Reverting to his earlier apocalyptic
visions, he warned those who refused to recognize the trend of
the future: "You are sleeping on a volcano."[22] Yet an element
of hope remained. Although he thought that the impending
struggle would be even more bitter than the revolutionary
conflagration, he thought it might lay the foundation for universal freedom.

By 1826 Grégoire had come a long way from his naive enlightenment faith in man's goodness. Always more charitable
towards individuals than groups, he now despaired about
humanity as a whole and found that the longer he studied

his fellow creatures, the less he loved them. After all, he had been progressively disillusioned by the French, the Haitians, and the Americans. But because he believed that God's sun shone on both the wicked and the good, he tried to accept men as they really were and vowed to help them as best he could.

Grégoire's persistent support for Negro rights did not pass unnoticed. Whenever censorship regulations permitted, his friends publicized his pamphlets in the *Revue encyclopédique* and in the reports of the African Institute. Towards the end of the 1820s the *Revue encyclopédique* published a few articles and reviews bearing his name. Grégoire arranged for English and American editions of his *Noblesse de la peau* while his *Apologie de Las Casas* was reprinted as an introduction to a multivolume edition of the Spanish bishop's works. This same essay served as the basis for an article in the *Retrospective Review*.[23]

As Grégoire's prestige slowly revived in Europe and America, one of his friends petitioned the Chamber of Deputies to restore the pension due to him as a member of the Royal Institute. But the time was not yet ripe. The representatives, who had not forgiven his assault on their sanctuary, refused even to consider this request.[24]

Conservatives still felt strongly about Grégoire. Anticipating the day when they would achieve complete revenge on their revolutionary enemies, they again focused their attacks on him. The Ultra planters, especially, could not forget his role in the Saint-Dominguean disaster, and following the colonists' example, the conservative journal, the *Ami de la religion et du roi*, failed to find any merit in his recent publications about the island. Thus, the editor regarded Grégoire's concern over Haitian morality as belated and blamed him for current French difficulties with the island.[25]

The conservatives had good reason for optimism because, as Louis XVIII neared his end, he became increasingly incapable of resisting their demands. During the years immediately preceding his death, real authority passed into the hands of his brother, Charles d'Artois. Frightened by the Ultras' increased power, liberals and moderates retreated even further into silence. The Ultras' victory seemed assured when Louis XVIII died in September 1824, and the leading conservative ascended the throne as Charles X.

Expecting the worst, Grégoire commemorated the beginning of Charles' reign by publishing an *Histoire des confesseurs des rois*. The subject was suggested by the monarch's reputation for devout Catholicism and by his early attempts to revive certain medieval rituals and laws. Thus, in this book, Grégoire tried to define the proper relationship between church and state and, in general, criticized the clergy for meddling in political questions. Still, he bitterly attacked those seventeenth-century religious advisors who had failed to use their influence to protect Africans and, instead, had justified slavery as a way to convert the Negroes to Catholicism.[26]

Grégoire's *Histoire des confesseurs* did not explicitly condemn the institution of monarchy, but his opinion of the new king was obvious. Under the preceding regime the book probably would have been banned, but surprisingly enough Charles, after a decade of irresponsibly denouncing all liberal or even moderate policy, at first tried to govern through a right-center rather than an Ultra majority. His first actions were conciliatory, and he temporarily eased censorship laws. Thus Grégoire's works circulated freely.

The French abolitionists were pleasantly astonished when, among other things, Charles unilaterally recognized Haitian independence. Not only was the island now secure, but, as Grégoire had predicted, once the colonial landowners could no longer hope to regain Saint-Domingue, they ceased opposing imperial reform, and the deputies finally were free to reorganize France's colonial system. At last the Chamber heeded the philanthropists' protests about discrimination against free mulattoes in the West Indies, and it extended metropolitan criminal and civil codes to the colonies.[27]

By 1826 the minister of the navy promised to help the oppressed mulattoes and to step up enforcement of existing antislave trade laws. The abolitionists' gains were less significant than they at first appeared to be, however. Slave trading continued to flourish while the reorganized imperial system reinforced the power of the planter oligarchy and did not greatly improve conditions of slavery. Nonetheless, by the end of the Bourbon Restoration, the slave trade committee of the Société de la Morale Chrétienne had managed to arouse limited public enthusiasm for further change. This committee became less cautious as abolition tracts circulated freely, and the authors attributed much of their recent success to the efforts of Grégoire and of the late Auguste de Staël.[28]

Immediately following the July Revolution of 1830, the slave trade commission became a public organization independent of the Société de la Morale Chrétienne. This was an important step, and the members had reason to be proud of their progress. But their victories seemed insignificant when compared with either the abolitionists' dizzy successes in 1794 or the accomplishments of their English colleagues. Such older men as Grégoire, Lafayette, and Macaulay were too disillusioned to admit that the abolitionists had made any substantial gains during the past decade and a half.

NOTES

1. Lafayette, for example, asked him to provide material for a speech that Constant was preparing; undated letter (June 1821?), anon. private collection in Paris.

2. The British feared either that the mulattoes might reenslave the blacks or that the defeat of the Negro kingdom by mulatto

forces would reduce Negro prestige in Europe; James Stevens to Grégoire, 7 Sept. 1815, Arsenal 6339, fo. 53–59 verso; Duke de Broglie to Duchess, 26 May 1822, De Broglie Papers, "Extraits," p. 75.

3. In the *Louis* judgment, an English court had ruled that the right of search must be explicitly granted by treaty: Lloyd, *The Navy and the Slave Trade*, p. 44.

4. Grégoire had been in contact with officials in Senegal since 1815 and knew Guidicelly personally; see Grégoire to anon., 15 April 1815, BN, NAF 24,910, fo. 288; Grégoire to Antoine Métral, 10 March 1819, AD, L&C, F 353.

5. Martin, *Histoire de l'esclavage*, p. 260; *Chronique religieuse* 5 (1820): 327–31; Clarkson to Grégoire, 20 Nov. 1820, Arsenal 6339, fo. 67–67 verso.

6. Macaulay to Grégoire, 20 Oct. and 14 Nov. 1820, Arsenal 6339, fo. 73–74 verso and 72–72 verso; Grégoire to Clarkson, 14 Dec. 1820, HEH, CN 102; Knutsford, *Life of Macaulay*, pp. 359–60.

7. Macaulay to wife, 19 Dec. 1823, Knutsford, *Life of Macaulay*, p. 409; Macaulay to Grégoire, 2 Oct. 1820, Arsenal 6339, fo. 68–68 verso. Remarks attributed to Grégoire: Macaulay to wife, 27 Dec. 1823, Knutsford, op. cit. p. 415.

8. Clarkson to Grégoire, 20 Nov. 1820, Arsenal 6339, fo. 67–67 verso; Grégoire to Clarkson, 14 Dec. 1820, HEH, CN 102; Macaulay to Grégoire, 30 March 1821, anon. private collection in Paris.

9. Macaulay to Grégoire, 14 Nov. 1820, Arsenal 6339, fo. 72–72 verso; Macaulay to Grégoire, 16 March 1821, anon. private collection in Paris.

10. Grégoire to Clarkson, 14 Dec. 1820, HEH, CN 102; *Chronique religieuse* 6 (1821): 155–58.

11. See Chapter 12; *Patriote des Alpes*, 13 Nov. 1847; Grégoire, *Mémoires*, 1:226; Duchess to Duke de Broglie, 7 Sept. 1819, De Broglie Papers, "Extraits," p. 48; Lafayette to Grégoire, n.d. and 1 Aug. 1821, anon. private collection in Paris; Macaulay to Grégoire, 20 Oct. 1820, Arsenal 6339, fo. 73–74 verso; Knutsford, *Life of Macaulay*, p. 359; Vastey to Clarkson, 29 Nov. 1819, Griggs and Prator, *Henry Christophe*, p. 180.

12. *Journal de la Société de la Morale Chrétienne* 1 (1822):

17–19, 68–69; *Revue encyclopédique* 10 (1821): 271–75 and 482–94; Kennedy, "Suppression of the Slave Trade," pp. 71–72. The leading Protestant members included Guizot, Pastor Oberlin, Pastor Marron (president of the Paris synod), and Auguste de Staël.

13. *Journal de la Société de la Morale Chrétienne* 1 (1822): 237; *Revue encyclopédique* 13 (1822): 494; Grégoire to Julien, 15 June [1824], Arsenal 14,043, fo. 3. His correspondence with Warden shows his interest in the society's educational schemes; Warden papers in MHS and LC.

14. Duchess de Broglie, "Journal politique," entries for 5 (?) Jan. and 2 April 1822, De Broglie Papers (typed copy); Duke to Duchess de .Broglie, 30 May 1822, loc. cit. "Extraits," p. 79; Lafayette to Grégoire, n.d. (June 1821?), anon. private collection in Paris; Lafayette to Clarkson, 15 Feb. 1821, in Kennedy, *Lafayette*, pp. 37–38.

15. Duchess de Broglie, however, did not take Talleyrand's remarks seriously; her "Journal politique," entry for 2 April 1822, De Broglie Papers.

16. Macaulay to wife, 27 Dec. 1823, Knutsford, *Life of Macaulay*, p. 415; ibid., pp. 413, 327. Grégoire to Verplanck, 17 May and 11 July 1823, NYHS; *Le Pilote*, 8 Nov. 1823; *Revue encyclopédique* 14 (1822): 442 and 15 (1822): 417; Grégoire's testimony for an accused mulatto: letter to Blanchet, 29 Nov. 1824, BM, Laon, autographes, carton 22, no. 39, p. 7; Kennedy, "The Suppression," p. 108.

17. Grégoire to Verplanck, 11 July 1823, NYHS.

18. *Chronique religieuse* 2 (1819): 121, 39.

19. Grégoire, *Observations préliminaires*, p. 3. This is a reprint from Clarkson's *Histoire du commerce*; the English edition, *The Cries of Africa*. See also: Macaulay to Grégoire, 30 March 1821 and Laroche to Grégoire, 12 Feb. 1822, anon. private collection in Paris; Grégoire, *De l'influence du Christianisme sur la condition des femmes*.

20. Macaulay to Grégoire, 14 and 27 Nov. 1820, Arsenal 6339, fo. 70–72 verso; Macaulay to Grégoire, 16 March 1821, anon. private collection in Paris; Grégoire to Clarkson, 14 Dec. 1820, HEH, CN 102.

21. Grégoire, *Peines infamantes,* passim.

22. Grégoire, *Noblesse de la peau,* p. 51.

23. The English version has not been located. His articles in the *Revue encyclopédique* 17 (1823): 268; 18 (1823): 351. See also: *Sixteenth report of the African Institution,* pp. 22, 28; *Revue encyclopédique* 16 (1822): 349; Grégoire to Bowing, 31 Oct. 1822, anon. private collection in Paris; Llorente, *Oeuvres de don Barthélemi de las Casas,* 2:336–67 and comment in 1:vii; *Retrospective Review,* 1822, pp. 262–66; *Journal de la Société de la Morale Chrétienne* 7 (1826): 126; some of the reviews by Grégoire: *Revue encyclopédique* 29 (1826): 279, 744–45; 31 (1826): 117, 412–13, 681–83.

24. Barthélemy, *Pétition à la Chambre des Députés.*

25. *Ami de la religion et du roi* 33 (1822): 333, and 34 (1823): 393–94.

26. Grégoire, *Histoire des confesseurs,* pp. 430–31; *Revue encyclopédique* 24 (1824): 757.

27. *Extracts from the 18th & 19th reports of the African Institution,* p. 25; *Revue encyclopédique* 29 (1826): 524; Lafayette to Clarkson, 8 May 1829, in Kennedy, *Lafayette,* pp. 43–44; Société de la Morale Chrétienne, *Nouveaux faits relatifs à la traite des noirs; Revue encyclopédique* 48 (1830): 595–644.

28. Morénas, *Précis historique,* p. 416; Isambert, *Mémoire pour le président,* p. 70; Lafayette to Grégoire, 9 March 1830, anon. private collection in Paris.

PART FOUR

Conclusion

14

The Apotheosis of Grégoire:
An Evaluation

During the last years of the Restoration, Grégoire once again gathered a coterie of young admirers who used his ostracism as an example of why they disliked the Bourbon regime. As the most notorious republican of his era, Grégoire had symbolic importance for the opposition. Still, his followers were more interested in his reputation than in his current opinions, most of which they regarded as anachronistic.

While Grégoire's young friends admired one or another of his beliefs separately—his republicanism, his egalitarianism, or his supposed Gallicanism—they failed to see the assumptions which underlay and provided a link between these apparently disparate doctrines. As far as Grégoire was concerned, republicanism, abolitionism, and ecclesiastical purity were but different applications of the same principle, the equality of all men before God. Egalitarian ideals, in fact, permeated all of his writings and were among the cardinal tenets of his unique version of Catholicism. Until the end of his life, he continued to explore the various facets of this doctrine, and he unsuccessfully searched recent church history for others who shared his convictions and who, therefore, might lend authority to his views.[1]

During the Restoration, Grégoire expounded his religious ideas in a series of books. At first his works did not win many converts to his ideal of an egalitarian, republican church. But as the years passed and Charles abandoned his conciliatory policy, an ever larger number of Frenchmen became dissatisfied with the monarchy. Liberals and Republicans adopted as their favorite issues two causes with which Grégoire was closely identified, Philhellenism and Gallicanism. Grégoire had discussed these subjects long before the revolutionaries of 1830 had become aware of their existence—his interest in Greek independence, for example, dated back to 1809. Towards the end of Charles' regime, therefore, members of the opposition showered praise on Grégoire's writings, even if they did not always agree with their contents.[2]

Some of the dissidents founded a journal, the *Gazette des cultes*, which preached religious toleration for Protestant, Jew, and heterodox Catholic alike. Naturally, the editors idolized Grégoire, and, not satisfied with praising him in the pages of their paper, they published a separate pamphlet, a *Première et dernière réfutation*, which answered the Ultras' charges against the old revolutionary and characterized him as a "man whose steadfast character highlights the perpetual variations of so many *honorable* men."[3]

Despite the praise which his young friends lavished upon him, Grégoire realized that they resented advice from the *gérontocracy*. He was, indeed, confused and bewildered by their theories. He found the liberal ultramontanism preached by Félicité-Robert de Lammenais to be incomprehensible, while he privately defended Christianity against Claude-Henri de Saint-Simon's onslaughts. Yet he basically approved of Lammenais' desire to sever the church's ties with the monarchy, and he certainly agreed with Saint-Simon's criticism of castes, slavery, and inherited nobility.[4]

Shortly after the July Revolution of 1830, some of Grégoire's supporters urged him to write a pamphlet denouncing the new constitution and advocating the complete abolition of slavery. In a rare flash of political insight, he demurred because he was still *sous la remise* among the gang of emigrés, Jesuits, and "sad debris of our political assemblies," who in the past had followed all flags, worn all colors, and professed all faiths, and who now dominated French politics.[5] The new ministry, composed of both 1819 Liberals and his accusers of that date, would probably be antagonized rather than persuaded by his suggestions. Since several of the influential cabinet members were already committed to enforcing the ban on slave trading, they would be more likely to act if he remained silent.

Grégoire judged the new ministry correctly. Guizot, a leading abolitionist and a member of Louis-Philippe's ministry who had attacked Grégoire in 1820, insisted on maintaining his ostracism and refused to reinstate him as a member of the Royal Institute.[6] Thus, while Grégoire refrained from commenting on the race problem, the king publicly supported abolitionism, and in March 1831 other egalitarians, both young and old, achieved passage of a strong law against the trade.

Perhaps Grégoire remained silent because he disapproved of Louis-Philippe's government. In any case, in August 1830 he withdrew to the country to avoid the numerous visits from his admirers which overtaxed his failing health. Within a few weeks, however, he could no longer contain his indignation. In his *Considérations sur la liste civile*, for the first time in sixteen years he explicitly condemned the institution of monarchy. He realized that France still was not ready for a republic, and he feared that any attempt to establish one would lead to anarchy. Nonetheless, he criticized the revolutionaries for having failed to create the democratic monarchy which they had promised and recommended drastic alterations in the new constitution. When his proposals were ignored, his disillusionment intensified. At first his friends regretted his hostility towards the new regime, but they soon would share his disdain for Louis-Philippe's bourgeois monarchy.[7]

Six months after the July Revolution, Grégoire fell mortally ill with cancer. During his final weeks he tried to make his peace with the Catholic hierarchy. In his correspondence with Archbishop Hyacinthe Quélan of Paris, Grégoire pointed to his long struggle to achieve the "imprescriptible rights of suffering humanity without distinction of color, climate, or race." The archbishop, more interested in theology than in service to mankind, demanded that Grégoire renounce the Civil Constitution of the Clergy and admit that he had sinned by supporting the revolutionary reforms.[8]

Grégoire could not accept Quélan's terms, and his arguments failed to sway the prelate. Yet Louis-Philippe still hoped to appease anticlerical Liberals and did not want to provide them with a martyr. His minister of the interior urged Quélan to relent, but the prelate remained adamant. Newspapers learned of the quarrel when Quélan warned the curés under his jurisdiction against giving Grégoire final rites unless the Constitutional bishop formally abjured. Fearing a scandal among Liberals, the king personally intervened and instructed the queen's confessor, the Abbé Marie-Nicolas-Silvestre Guillon, to give Grégoire extreme unction.[9]

Grégoire's condition steadily declined, and he knew nothing of the controversy which raged around his sickbed. Shortly before he died he told his companion:

> For eight days I have been tormented. I see a Negro population locked up on an island serving it as refuge against tyranny and which is about to die of starvation! . . . I have been told that Protestants and Jews have come to see me; although they are not of my faith inform them of my gratitude. . . . I would like theological works to be sent to Haiti. Poor Haitians! . . .

That very day he lapsed into incoherency, and on 28 May 1831 his long and troubled life came to an end.[10]

Controversy followed Grégoire to the grave. When Quélan forbade any of the Paris clergy to officiate at his funeral, Louis-Philippe requisitioned a church and persuaded a priest who was not under the archbishop's jurisdiction to perform the ceremony. Grégoire's old colleague from the Convention, Antoine-Claire Thibaudeau, pronounced the funeral oration, and a young Jewish lawyer who had handled several of Grégoire's legal cases during the Restoration also spoke. A number of Jews, including entire classes of school children, attended services for the former Catholic cleric. A few minor disorders occurred, but at last Grégoire's earthly remains were laid to rest.[11]

Grégoire's former protégés honored his memory from time to time after his official funeral. The Haitians mourned his passing in September 1831 when Boyer ordered solemn masses throughout the island, and the entire population undertook a subscription to erect a statue of their long-time benefactor. One hundred years later, Haitian delegates participated in centenary ceremonies in Paris. In addition, Jews in the Northeast built a statue of their former champion which was destroyed by the Nazis during World War II. Its successor today dominates a tranquil square in Lunéville, the intellectual capital of his native province.[12]

Grégoire's interest in underprivileged people of all colors and creeds survived his death. In 1838 the prize which he had established for the best essay on the regeneration of Africa was awarded to Victor Schloecher who, ten years later, would propose the abolition of slavery in a new revolutionary assembly. In addition, Grégoire's executrix and long-time friend donated funds, which he had provided in his will, to the hospital in Blois under the express condition that it must serve invalids of color.[13]

In the new world, Americans ignored Grégoire's advice during his lifetime, and his correspondent, Bishop John Carroll of Baltimore, failed to take a public stand against slavery. Yet Grégoire's *Littérature des Nègres* continued to be read and

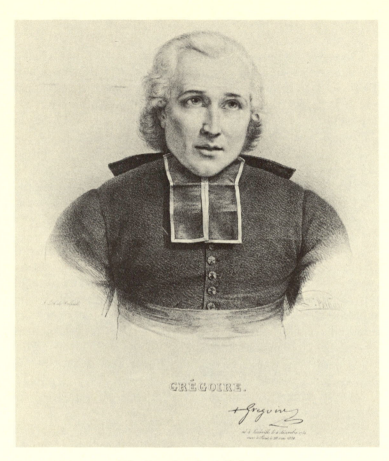

GRÉGOIRE.

The Apotheosis of Grégoire;
posthumous portrait.

discussed there. Some slavery apologists denounced the book well after his death, while the aged abolitionist, Charles Sumner, called the author a "hero of humanity."[14] Still, the trend which Grégoire had noted towards the development of a racial caste system continued in the United States, and it remains one of America's greatest problems today.

At the time of Grégoire's death, his life appeared futile because, of all his goals, only Jewish emancipation had been realized. His ineffectiveness can be attributed partly to his personality, partly to the unusual and anachronistic character of his religious ideology which alienated potential supporters and detracted from his secular theories, and partly to the deeply entrenched opposition to his radical program.[15]

Grégoire's personality hampered his legislative career. Such traits as dogmatism, hasty temper, and refusal to pursue power for its own sake antagonized even those deputies who accepted his principles, and prevented him from marshalling a loyal following. Yet these same characteristics—save, of course, his temperament—eventually created a legend which depicted him as a martyr to the struggle for social justice. In later life friends and enemies alike forgot his political ineffectiveness and attributed to him legislation which he had not actually introduced but for which he had long pleaded.

A propagandist rather than a lawmaker, Grégoire wished to provide Frenchmen with a transcendant morality upon which his other reforms might rest. His concern was valid. As we have since seen, mechanistic political and economic reforms are meaningless. Universal manhood suffrage and technical independence have become licenses for exploiting weak although theoretically free peoples. Unless the values of progress and power are qualified by a universally accepted definition of justice, scientific advances serve only to intensify inequality and suffering.

But Grégoire picked a weak vessel, a schismatic church which alienated intellectuals by adhering too closely to discredited forms. In addition, orthodox condemnation prevented practicing Catholics from heeding his sermons. His words influenced only those who cared too little about Catholicism either to follow or to hate it, a group whose political power declined rapidly after 1792.

Thus Grégoire's influence as spokesman and propagandist

was limited by his unique and anachronistic religious concepts. During the first part of the Revolution he subordinated his theology to his secular philosophy and thereby avoided antagonizing secular-minded deputies, but after 1795 his Christianity became increasingly apparent and could not be ignored. By 1814 he was "a tainted outsider" who could not marshall religious sentiment behind him. His identification with schism was unfortunate because Christian appeals remained the strongest basis for mass propaganda until the later part of the nineteenth century. Thus, because he refused to renounce the Constitutional church, neither Rome nor the French hierarchy would answer his pleas that they take a stand against slavery until after he died.[16]

Grégoire's religious theories also muddled and oversimplified his secular program. Although he recognized environmental influences on human behavior, he nonetheless saw the roots of all evil in the corrupt nature of existing religious institutions. According to him, if only the church were reformed, the environment could be improved and men would cease being greedy, selfish, and unjust. And yet he knew better. In his writings on people outside the range of Christianity, like Jews and West Indian Negroes, he observed the deleterious effects of poverty, poor diet, degrading labor, and social discrimination. He thought both groups would be uplifted by exposure to Christianity, but he regarded social and economic reforms as prerequisites either for significant improvement or for proselytization.

In attempting to resolve European problems, Grégorie overemphasized the need for moral regeneration and neglected to devise solutions for the economic and social problems which he clearly saw. Hence he fell back on his unworkable religious schemes and failed to use his influence to guide others into fruitful fields of investigation. The only exception occurred in 1796 when he brought together men like Wadstrom and Lanthénas, but he could not sustain the Société des Amis des

Noirs et des Colonies after these two men died. Since Grégoire's thought led to a dead end, he could not have any disciples except in the most general sense.

Still, Grégoire did have intellectual heirs. Stripped of its religious overtones, much of Grégoire's program coincided with what became the nineteenth-century Radical ideology. Like the Radicals, he favored nonbelligerent nationalism, independence of church and state (in actuality, subordination of church to state), constitutionalism, equal civil, social, and political rights for all residents of a country, universal public education including vocational training, and regulation of the economy in the interest of social justice. Both he and the Radicals disliked the still nascent industrial revolution and, wishing to retard its development, rejected the Liberals' rigid economic individualism.

Since the Radicals fought valiantly for their ideals during the nineteenth century, Grégoire's program was finally implemented despite his personal failure. But the history of this struggle— the century-long delay in enacting his recommendations and the numerous reversals marked by increasing cynicism concerning the reformers' motives—illustrates Europe's failure to adjust to rapid social and economic changes. Compared with both revolutionary and Restoration statesmen, Grégoire stood at the threshold between two eras and even between two worlds. Bound by his religious, cultural, and economic ideas to an outdated past, he nonetheless tried to hasten the transition from a stratified to an egalitarian society as well as from a European-centered to an Atlantic-oriented world. Perhaps he could not have provided complete answers, but the prolonged refusal of European statesmen to consider seriously the questions which he raised aggravated existing conflicts.

If Grégoire's personality and unusual theories contributed to his ineffectiveness as a politician, the entrenched forces of opposition did so even more. Many of our current difficulties can be traced to the intransigence of continental conservatives until after the 1848 upheavals. By the time that even the Liberals came to power, their program was inadequate, their reforms were too late, and they could not combat the acute tensions created by belligerent nationalism, industrialism, and, eventually, revived imperialism.

On the whole, historical speculation is futile, but occasionally it reveals the roots of contemporary problems by identifying the beginning of decisive trends. The period between 1815 and 1848, for all its drab politics, is just such a crucial era when some of the problems which Grégoire saw could still have been peacefully resolved. Unquestionably, postponing reforms only intensified subsequent social and political upheavals.

The Catholic church, as a leading conservative force, was one of the chief offenders. Many of Grégoire's theories depended upon an enlightened clergy, but when he died in 1831 the church appeared to be even further than ever from his ideals, and it has only begun to liberalize during the past decade. Most of the changes which he proposed during the eighteenth century—the translation of the liturgy, the convocation of national and local councils, and the reduction of episcopal control over the lower clergy—were adopted, at least in theory, by Vatican Council II.

If the Catholic church had instituted even some of the reforms which Grégoire and his friends had proposed during and after the Revolution, if it merely had proved more responsive to demands for change, it would be in a far stronger position today. Instead, for a century it rejected all innovations because they were identified with the Revolution and permitted itself to be used by selfish private interests rather than serve as the guardian of Europe's conscience. When liberalism finally penetrated, it proved unable to modify the strengthened centralization which Grégoire had always opposed and which now threatens to tear the church apart.

Although the church is now closer and more responsive to the needs of the common man, it is less capable today than it was in 1831 of assuming a commanding role in creating the moral foundation for social justice. Its obstinacy at first encouraged secularism by antagonizing intellectuals. Then the church contributed to the spread of agnosticism, if not anticlericalism, by condemning the competing ideologies of nationalism and socialism and by failing to respond to the disruptive forces of the industrial revolution.

Because it remained European-centered for too long, the church also failed to recognize changing needs in the outside world, and newly emancipated peoples have been attracted to the same secular ideologies which captivated European minds. Even if these peoples have joined any of the established churches, they usually have superficially adhered to the most prestigious confession among their former masters.[17]

Bound by conservatism and ethnocentrism, the church could not reap any advantage from the temporary religious revivals which accompanied various crises during the past century. For example, religiosity was intensified during the late nineteenth-century controversy over militant anti-Semitism, during the holocaust of World War II, and now during the intense cultural nationalism brought on by the struggle against colonialism in its various forms. In each case the victims have returned to and tried to recast their traditional faiths to meet new challenges and serve as symbols of identity. Because the Catholic church—indeed Christianity as such—failed to act during any of these crises, it lost potential followers, and, instead of playing a decisive role today, it is merely one voice among many pleading for racial reconciliation, social responsibility, and international understanding.

Grégoire's ideas about nationalism were also frustrated by Restoration conservatism. He regarded the nation as the essential unit for reform and advocated democratization and centralization so that the state might better serve the popular will. Recognizing that political reforms depended upon national independence, he insisted that each group of people had the right to its own identity. Consequently he supported the aspirations of suppressed European nationalities and criticized the territorial arrangements of the Congress of Vienna.[18]

Unquestionably, the Allied Powers' attempts to stabilize Europe in 1814, the frustrations, and then the process whereby various nations achieved independence and unity during the nineteenth and twentieth centuries unleashed the passions of belligerent, xenophobic nationalism. Grégoire was the spokesman for an enlightened, tolerant, and reforming nationalism, which was a casualty of the barricades and battlefields of nineteenth-century Europe, and which has not been resurrected.

The fight for human equality has proven even more elusive than that for religious reform and national identity. The broad definition which Grégoire presented in his *Noblesse de la peau* has now become commonplace. But as the nobility of parchment faded into oblivion, a different basis for stratification, which was just becoming evident in revolutionary France and America, has perpetuated new and perhaps deeper divisions between men. Unfortunately, it is not as easy to legislate against privileges founded on the still meaningful distinctions in education, wealth, and political connections as it was to abolish outdated aristocratic prerogatives.

True egalitarianism depends not only on mechanical political devices but also on economic institutions. But Grégoire had only the most vague and general understanding of economics, and he always subordinated it to morality. Nonetheless, he made a few pregnant suggestions. He regarded the state as ultimately responsible for the welfare of all citizens and thought that free public education with adequate vocational instruction would provide the foundation for a prosperous, although not necessarily absolutely egalitarian, society. Like many social critics, he tended to regard education as a panacea, but, in addition, he believed in direct government assistance for such socially useful projects as draining swamp lands and promoting agricultural improvements. He never proposed appropriate legislation, but he seemed convinced that the state must be the employer of last resort.[19] His ideas, on the whole, were more similar to those held by the Radicals than the pre-Marxian socialists, and he never supported any scheme for equalizing wealth.

The Liberals' economic theories were the most influential part of their entire program. Compared to them, Grégoire's concept of state responsibility might be considered a definite improvement. If his theories had been implemented, however, they would have retarded rapid industrialization by increasing taxation and imposing additional restrictions upon manufacturers. But perhaps we are now ready to admit that material progress is not the only criterion for judging the past or the present.

The fight for racial equality encompasses all the other reforms which Grégoire championed, and the survival of race prejudice is intimately connected with the reluctance of the major churches to assume moral leadership, the frustrations engendered by retarded national aspirations, and the failure to extend the principles of economic and political justice to the outside world.

The unjust treatment of the non-European world by the Atlantic countries has had innumerable consequences. It has contributed to the decline in Christian influence and has aggravated the problem of belligerent nationalism by extending it over the entire world. The legacy of white racism has also created grave domestic problems in the former colonies. An earlier termination of slavery, for example, would have drastically altered the history both of Africa and of those countries in the Western Hemisphere whose entire economic development probably would have been retarded and certainly would have been different if the slave trade had been effectively halted in 1814. European technical assistance, as Grégoire requested for Haiti, rather than the foreign exploitation, which occurred throughout the non-European world in the later part of the nineteenth century, would probably have provided greater political stability and less glaring social inequality than exists today in formerly colonized territories. His schemes, therefore, would have delayed but humanized the development of Latin America, Africa, and the Far East.

As propagandist for racial, religious, social, and political equality, Grégoire desired to, and succeeded in embodying the enlightened conscience, the so-called "general will" of revolutionary France. It is difficult to assess his role, however. He cannot be compared with the men who have come to symbolize his era—the Mirabeaus, Robespierres, Talleyrands, and Napoleons—because the same values and terms do not apply. All of these men had far more influence over the course of the Revolution, and hence of future history, but none represented the more desirable human characteristics. France and the world have suffered from too many Mirabeaus and Napoleons. Although a world composed of Grégoires undoubtedly would not survive for very long, occasionally a man who will not compromise, who is satisfied with modest personal achievements, and who is willing to dedicate his life to the welfare of others is needed. Grégoire may have lacked the charisma of either a Napoleon or a Robespierre, but he was the best that his age had to offer.

The egalitarian movement in France needed a hero, and Grégoire was the only serious candidate. Although his stand on the judgment of Louis XVI and the persecution of Roman Catholics could be and has been questioned, his career was not flawed either by identification with the Terror, as was Robespierre's, or by responsibility for questionable diplomatic and domestic policies, as was Brissot's. Having missed the benefits of political leadership, Grégoire also escaped its liabilities. His position was more similar to Voltaire's, with the significant difference that Voltaire never had Grégoire's opportunity to translate his theories into action and, consequently, was never expected to devise a concrete program. As propagandists, both men disinterestedly campaigned for persecuted minorities and came to symbolize these causes forever after. For all Grégoire's shortcomings, Sumner's eulogy still appears valid. "In all history," the abolitionist wrote in 1876, "no hero of humanity stands forth more conspicuous for instinctive sympathy for the Rights of Man and constancy in their support."[20]

NOTES

1. "Supplément au Bréviaire de Blois, à l'usage de M. Grégoire, ancien sénateur et ancien évêque de ce siège," 1825, pp. 34, 57, Arsenal, 2166.

2. Grégoire's *Histoire des sectes*, revised and expanded edition in six volumes published by Baudouin between 1828 and 1845, the original, confiscated edition was reprinted by Potey in 1814; his *Essai historique sur les libertés de l'Eglise gallicane et des autres églises de la catholicité, pendant les deux derniers siècles* (Paris: Bureau du Censeur, 1818) was reprinted several times. See, for example, the "Correspondance privée," a circular reproduced by a very simple, so-called bauduche technique used to evade the censorship laws. It dealt with revolutions abroad, French politics, and other similar topics; BPR, Rév. 172, no. 1–21, 22 Oct.–11 Nov. 1827. Grégoire made his last public attack on ultramontanism in Jan. 1830 when he published an *Appel à la raison, par un proscrit*, also printed in the *Gazette des cultes*, 9 Jan. 1830.

3. Italics in the original, *Première et dernière réfutation*, p. 4, reprinted from *Gazette des cultes*, 20 Oct. 1829, p. 2. See also ibid., 16 June, 4 Aug., 29 Sept. 1829, 23 Jan., 23 and 27 Feb. 1830.

4. Manuscript notes by Grégoire, 1 Nov. 1830 and n.d., Schomburg Coll. C–4. The term, "gerontocracy," was popularized in an 1828 pamphlet by the Genevan, James Fazy; Bertier de Sauvigny, *Bourbon Restoration*, p. 238.

5. Grégoire to Constacino, 6 Aug. 1830, *Mémoires*, 1:255–58; Bowing to Grégoire, 28 Aug. 1830, anon. private collection in Paris.

6. Guizot, *Du Gouvernement*, pp. 80, 234–36.

7. Grégoire, *Considérations sur la liste civile*; Grégoire to Pappenheimer, 13 Sept. 1830, AD, L&C, F 592, fo. 65.

8. Grégoire to Archbishop Quélan, 7 May 1831 in *Recueil de Pièces*, p. 4; documents in AD, L&C, F 721.

9. Baradère, *Derniers momens*, p. 13; *Journal des villes et des campagnes*, 15 May 1831; *L'Echo français*, 16 and 18 May 1831; *La Quotidienne*, 1 June 1831, p. 4.

10. Ellipsis in the original; Baradère, *Derniers momens*, p. 21.

11. Baradère to Ph. Desjardins, 27 May 1831, Lacoste statement, 29 May 1831, and prefect of police (Casimir-Pierre Périer) to curé, 29 May 1831 in AD, L&C, F 721; Carnot's introduction to *Mémoires*, 1:294–96.

12. Boyer's decree of 22 Aug. 1831 in Linstant [de] Pradine, ed., *Recueil général*, 5:386–87; *Le Télégraphe*, 31 July and 11 Sept. 1831; Vaval, "L'abbé Henri Grégoire," p. 21; *Résurrection du souvenir de l'abbé Grégoire, promoteur de la lutte contre l'esclavagisme et le racisme* (1750–1831) (Paris-Lunéville, n.p., 1956); conversation with E. Morse-Lévy, director of the Bibliothèque Israélite in Paris, July 1967.

13. *Intermédiaire des chercheurs et curieux* 11 (1878): 632; "Programme des prix," *Mémoires de la Société Royale de Nancy*, 1837, pp. cxi–cxiii; ibid., 1838, lxxxlv–xciii; Sainville, *Victor Schoelcher*, pp. 42–43, 130.

14. Sumner, *Prophetic Voices*, p. 151. One proponent of slavery wrote: "he has ransacked history to prove [the Negroes'] equality of intellect & has signally failed—This book would afford a good text for a sermon," J. C. Nott to J. H. Hammond, 25 July 1845, LC, J. H. Hammond Papers. Grégoire to Archbishop Carroll, 1 Feb. 1815, Baltimore Archdiocese, 4 B 7.

15. See E. J. Hobsbawm, *The Age of Revolution: 1789–1848* (New York: Mentor Books, 1962), pp. 292–98, for nineteenth-century radicalism.

16. See chapter 10, fn. 18.

17. Genovese, "Slave Revolts."

18. Grégoire, *De la traite*, p. 77.

19. On swamps: *Patriote françois*, 6 April 1790, p. 4; *Chronique de Paris*, 22 Feb. 1790, p. 209. Agricultural improvement: *Journal du citoyen*, 29 Prairial year 6 (17 June 1798), p. 539; [Grégoire,

et. al], *Rapport fait à la Société d'Agriculture du département de la Seine sur la nécessité de conserver l'Etablissement rural de l'ancienne Ménagerie de Versailles* (Paris: Imprimerie de Ballard, [year 8 (1799–1800)]); J.-L. Lefebvre, *Compte rendu à la Société d'Agriculture de Paris, de ses Travaux faits, commencés et projetés, depuis le 30 Mai 1788 jusques et compris le 30 Septembre 1793, an 3 de la République Française; et de l'emploi des fonds qui ont été mis à sa disposition pendant cet espace de temps* (Paris: Bureau de la Feuille Cultivateur, year 7 [1798–99]), pp. xxxi–xxxiii, 4, 122, 242.

20. Sumner, *Prophetic Voices*, p. 151.

Bibliography

MANUSCRIPT COLLECTIONS

PARIS

Archives Nationales:
Lettres et pièces diverses, sieur Dubois: AA54, 1509.
Secrétariat: AB XIX 3195.
Armoire de fer et Musée: AE II 1077.
Secrétariat d'Etat Impérial: AF^4 1213.
Archives privées: 29 AP 101, Roederer; 138 AP 100, Daru, used with permission; 154 AP II 136, de Tocqueville, used with permission.
Ministère de la Justice: BB^3, BB^{17}, BB^{18}.
Procès-verbaux des Assemblées nationales et pièces annexes: C 37 and *C I 210.
Comité des domaines: DXVIII C 115.
Comité des colonies: DXXV 3, 11, 38, 46, 56–58, 68, 69, 71, 72, 81, 82, 86, 88–91, 110, various papers collected in 1794 and 95 for the Colonial Commission's hearings, including "La conviction des faux principes de la Société des Amis des Noirs et des défenseurs des gens de couleurs," n.d., in 88, no. 840.
Administration communale: F^3 126, colonies; 195–99, colonies, 202, colonies. Moreau de Saint-Méry collection, mostly copies.

Police générale: F⁷ 3449, 3795, 3830, 4443, 6707.
Cultes: F¹⁹ 6200, 6201.
Parquet, Tribunaux Révolutionnaires: Barnave, W 12; Massiac Club, W 15; Affaire des Girondins, W 292; Affaire Barnave et Duport Dutertre, W 298.

Bibliothèque de l'Arsenal:
Grégoire's "Mémoires," draft, with letters on verso, MS 5290.
Grégoire's breviaries and handwritten supplements, 2164–166.
Grégoire's papers relating to Haiti, 6339 (photocopies available from the Library of Congress).
Autographs, 13,990.
Miscellaneous letters, 14,043.

Bibliothèque de l'Institut:
Papers of Chevalier Huzard, 1806–1830, MS 1976.
Papers of Buache de la Neuville, MS 2325.

Bibliothèque de Port-Royal:
Cartons of letters received by Grégoire organized alphabetically by department. Special cartons for the Council of 1797 and the Council of 1811. Includes the minutes of the Société des Amis des Noirs et des Colonies (TUVWXYZ) and a manuscript life of Grégoire (Loir-et-Cher II).
Bound volumes of pamphlets and letters: Rév. 168, 171, 172, 177, 180, 181. Includes: Grégoire's "De l'influence du christianisme sur l'abolition de l'esclavage," (177) and "Correspondance privée," 22 Oct.–11 Nov. 1827 (172).

Bibliothèque Nationale:
Masonic collection.
Manuscrits françaises 8986 I and 12,104 (both available on LC photocopies).
Roland papers, Nouvelles acquisitions françaises: 9533–34; Bixo autographs, NAF 22,737; Sonthonax letter, NAF 22,819; Joseph Reinach papers, NAF 24,910.

De Broglie Papers:
"Extraits des lettres de mon père et ma mère [le duc et la duchesse de Broglie]," typed.

"Copie du Journal politique de la duchesse de Broglie. Albertine Ida Gustavine de Staël Holstein, 1817–1823," typed.

"Lettres de Mme de Necker de Saussure à Albertine de Stael, d'esse de Broglie, 1817–1821," typed.

Anonymous private collection:

Grégoire's political correspondence, most original, some copies.

Grégoire, "Notes sur les Etats Généraux et specialement sur ce qui s'est passé dans la chambre du clergé avant la réunion des ordres. par M. l'abbé Grégoire Député de nancy [sic]," typed copy.

"Journal historique de la Société Libre et Littéraire de Philosophie Chrétienne," original and typed copy.

PROVINCIAL COLLECTIONS

Besançon, Bibliothèque Municipale:

Grappin Papers, MS 622, microfilm loaned by Dr. Chérest, Paris.

Blois, Archives Départementales of Loir-et-Cher:

Autographs, F 353; Grégoire, miscellaneous letters, F 592; Grégoire's death and funeral, F 721.

Registers of the Administrative Assembly of Loir-et-Cher, L 106; "Assemblée Directoire Loir-et-Cher," Feb. and March 1791, L 118.

Blois, Bibliothèque Municipale:

"Procès-verbaux des societés populaires."

Blois, Evêché:

"Registre des actes de despenses du conseil épiscopal de Loir et Cher," 1D 7 A.

Grenoble, Bibliothèque Historique de la ville de:

J. Rey, "Appreciation des divers partis," T 3939, microfilm loaned by Alan B. Spitzer, University of Iowa.

Laon, Bibliothèque Municipale:

Grégoire letters, Autographs, carton 22.

Lunéville, Bibliothèque Municipale:

Grégoire letter, MS 52.

Nancy, Bibliothèque Municipale:
Grégoire letters, Autographs.
Manuscript of Grégoire's "Promenade dans les Vosges" with letters addressed to him on verso, MS 532; "Notes biographiques sur des Lorraines," letters on verso, 957 (533); "Titres et diplomes," 1134 (536).

Nancy, Grand Séminaire:
Guilbert correspondence, vol. 2, MB 17; "Procès-verbaux des élections aux Etats-généraux, 1789," MB 123.
[Chatrian], "Calendrier historique de Nancy pour 1789," MC 121.

Strasbourg, Bibliothèque Universitaire:
Grégoire, "Recherches sur la domesticité; où l'on examine les moyens d'améliorer les moeurs des domestiques et de former en leur faveur des caisses de prévoyance," manuscript and German trans., MS 3901.

FOREIGN COLLECTIONS

Italy:
Florence state archives, Ricci papers; Vatican secret archives, Degola papers.

Netherlands:
The Hague, Allgemeen Ryksarchief, OBC 3458, Grégoire-Mouton correspondence, microfilm loaned by the Abbé J. Matha.

United States:
Baltimore, Archdiocese: Grégoire's letters to Bishop Carroll, 4 B 7.
    Maryland Historical Society: David Bailie Warden Papers.
Cambridge, Harvard Library: Joel Barlow Papers, AM 1468.
New Haven, Yale Library: Pequot Collection, Joel Barlow papers, M 981.
New York City, Historical Society: Gulian Verplanck Papers; John W. Francis, "Reminiscences. Extended to thirteen volumes by the addition of drawings, engravings and autographs" (New York, 1895).
————, Public Library, the Schomburg Collection, "Correspondence, L'Abbé Grégoire," C–4.

Philadelphia, American Philosophical Society: Benjamin Vaughn Papers, BV 46; Pennsylvania Historical Society: Roberts Vaux. San Marino, Calif., Henry E. Huntington Library: Thomas Clarkson Papers, CN 101–104. Washington, D.C.: Library of Congress, J. H. Hammond Papers (microfilm loaned by Thomas Stirton, Long Island University); Thomas Jefferson Papers, 33,125 and 33,511; Roume Collection; David Bailie Warden Collection, I and II.

CONTEMPORARY PRINTED SOURCES

Adresse à l'Assemblée Nationale, pour les citoyens-libres de Couleur, des Isles & Colonies Françoises. N.p., 1789.

Adresse de l'Assemblée provinciale de la partie du Nord de Saint-domingue, [sic] à l'Assemblée nationale. [Paris? Imprimerie de Demonialle, 1790]. AN, AD⁷ 25, Colonies.

Adresse de l'Assemblée Provinciale de la Partie du Nord de Saint-Domingue, à l'Assemblée Nationale. Notes des Membres du Comité de Rédaction de l'Assemblée générale sur cette Adresse. Port-au-Prince: Imprimerie de Mozard, 1790. AN, DXXV 86, no. 829.

African Institution. *Extracts from the 18th & 19th reports of the directors of the African Institution, read at their annual general meetings, held in London on the 11th day of May, 1824, & on the 13th day of May, 1825.* Philadelphia: Joseph R. A. Skerrett, 1826.

———. *Ninth report of the directors of the African Institution, read at the annual general meeting on the 12th of April, 1815.* London: Ellerton and Henderson, 1815.

———. *Sixteenth report of the directors of the African Institution, read at the annual general meeting, held on the 10th day of May, 1822.* London: Ellerton and Henderson, 1822.

Audiguier. *Epitre à M. Grégoire, ancien évêque de Blois.* Paris: Delaunay et Mongie, 1820.

Baradère, [Jean-Henri]. *Derniers momens de M. Grégoire.* Paris: Delaunay Libraire, 1831.

Barbé-Marbois, [François]. *Réflexions sur la colonie de Saint-Domingue*. Paris: Garnery, 1796.

Barlow, Joe. *Letter to Henry Gregoire [sic], Bishop, Senator, Compte of the Empire and Member of the Institute of France, in reply to his letter on the "Columbiad."* Washington: Roger Chew Weightman, 1809.

Barnave, [Antoine-Pierre-Joseph-Marie]. *Rapport fait à l'Assemblée nationale, le 8 Mars 1790, au nom du Comité des Colonies*. Paris: Imprimerie Nationale, 1790.

Barruel, [Augustin de]. *Abrégé des mémoires pour servir à l'histoire du Jacobinisme*. 2 vols. Hamburg: P. Fauche, 1801.

Barthélemy, [Pierre]. *Pétition à la Chambre des Députés, par . . . à l'effet d'obtenir la réintegration à l'Institut de MM. Grégoire, Arnault et Etienne*. Paris: [Mme. Veuve J.-L. Schertt], 1822.

Berr, Michel. *Appel à la justice des nations et des rois, ou Adresse d'un Citoyen français au Congrès qui devait avoir lieu à Lunéville, au nom de tous les habitans de l'Europe qui professent la Religion juive*. Strasbourg: L'Imprimerie de Levrault, Frères, X [1802].

Bertrand de Moleville, [Antoine-François]. *Histoire de la Révolution de France pendant les dernières années du règne de Louis XVI*. 8 vols. Paris: Giguet et Michaud, 1801–1802.

———. *Mémoires particuliers pour servir à l'histoire de la fin du règne de Louis XVI*. 2 vols. Paris: L. G. Michaud, 1816.

Bourdon de l'Oise, [François-Louis]. *Rapport fait par . . . au nom de la Commission des colonies composée des représentants du peuple Vaublanc, Tarbé, Hélot, Villaret-Joyeuse. Séance du 3 messidor an V* (21 June 1797). Paris: Imprimerie Nationale, 1797.

Brissot, [Jacques-Pierre]. *Lettre de . . . a M. Barnave, sur ses rapports concernant les colonies, les décrets qui les ont suivis, leurs conséquences fatales; sur sa conduite dans le cours de la révolution; sur le caractère des vrais démocrates; sur les bases de la constitution, les obstacles qui s'opposent à son achèvement, la nécessité de la terminer promptement, etc.* Paris: Desenne, 1790.

———. *Réplique de . . . à la première et dernière lettre de Louis-*

Marthe Gouy, Défenseur de la Traite des Noirs et de l'Esclavage. Paris: Belin, 1791.

Brissot-Thivars, L[ouis-Saturnin]. *Le guide électoral, ou biographie législative de tous les députés, depuis 1814 jusques et y compris 1818 à 1819.* 2 vols. Paris: Librairie Constitutionnelle, 1819.

[Chabanon, Charles de]. *Le dénonciation de M. l'abbé Grégoire, et de sa lettre du 8 juin 1791, adressé aux Citoyens de couleur & Nègres libres de Saint-Domingue, & des autres Iles Françaises de l'Amérique, &c.* Paris: Feuille du Jour, 1791.

Chanlatte, F[rançois] Desrivieres. *Almanach republicain, Pour l'année commune, 1818.* Port-au-Prince: Imprimerie du Gouvernement, n.d.

————. *Situation d'Hayti à l'égard de la France, et réflexions survenues à l'occasion de l'arrivée de M. le Général Dauxion de Lavaysse, Député de S. M. T. Ch. le Roi de France & de Navarre, Près le Président d'Hayti.* Port-au-Prince: de l'Imprimerie du Gouvernement, 1814.

[Chastenet-Desterre, Gabriel]. *Considérations sur l'état présent de la colonie française de Saint-Domingue.* N.p., 1796.

Clarkson, Thomas. *The Cries of Africa to the inhabitants of Europe; or, a survey of that bloody commerce called the slave-trade.* London: Harvey & Darton, n.d.

————. *Histoire du commerce homicide appelé traite des Noirs, ou cri des Africains contre les Européens, leurs oppresseurs, par . . . avec des observations préliminaires, par M. Grégoire, ancien évêque de Blois.* [Translated by Benjamin Laroche]. Paris: Imprimerie de Gueffier, 1822.

————. *The History of the Rise, Progress and Accomplishment of the Abolition of the African Slave-Trade by the British Parliament.* London: Longman, Hurst, Rees and Orme, 1808.

Clausson, L. J. *Précis historique de la Révolution de Saint Domingue. Réfutation de certains ouvrages publiés sur les causes de cette révolution. De l'état actuel de cette colonie, et de la nécessité d'en recouvrer la possession.* Paris: Pillet Aîné, 1819.

Clavière, Etienne. *Adresse de la Société des Amis des Noirs, à l'Assemblèe nationale, à toutes les Villes de Commerce, à toutes les Manufactures, aux Colonies, à toutes les Sociétés des Amis* de la Constitution; Adresse dans laquelle on approfondit les relations politiques et commerciales entre le Métropole et les Colonies, etc. Paris: Desenne, 1791.

Clermont-Tonnerre, Stanislas de, Comte. Opinion de M. . . relativement aux persécutions qui menacent les juifs d'Alsace. Versailles: Baudouin, 1789.

Cocherel, [Nicolas] de. Observations de M. . . Député de Saint-Domingue, à l'Assemblée Nationale, sur la demande des Mulâtres. Paris: Clousier, 1789.

Conspiration découverte par le représentant du peuple Creuset-Pascale, ou préceptes des évangélistes selon Saint-Marc. Paris: Imprimerie de Pain, (1793?). AN, AD⁷ 30.

La contre-révolution démontrée nécéssaire par les Jacobins de Paris, dans le Testament politique de la Souveraineté expirante de M. l'Abbé Grégoire, qu'ils ont adopté. Paris: n.p., 1792.

Cournand, [Antoine] de. Réponse aux observations d'un habitant des colonies, SUR le Mémoire en faveur des Gens de couleur, ou sang-mêlés, de Saint Domingue, & des autres Iles françoises de l'Amérique, adressé à l'Assemblée Nationale, par M. GREGOIRE, Curé d'Embermenil, Député de Lorraine. N.p., n.d.

Cousin D'Avalon, C[harles]-Y[ves]. Grégoriana, ou résumé général de la conduite, des actions et des écrits de M. le comte Henri Grégoire. Paris: Plancher, 1821.

Creuzé, Michel-Pascal. Lettre de . . . Membre du Conseil des Anciens, à Jean-Philippe Garan, député du Loiret. Paris: Maret, V [1797].

Le cri de l'innocence révolutionnaire. Paris: L. Potier de Lille, 1793. AN, DXXV 56.

de Curt, [Louis]. Motion de M. . . . député de la Guadeloupe, au nom des Colonies réunis. Paris: Baudouin, 1789.

Découverte d'une conspiration contre les intérêts de la France. N.p., n.d., [1789–90]. AN, DXVIII C115, no. 13.

[Delbare, François-Thomas]. Histoire des deux chambres de Buonaparte depuis le 3 Juin jusqu'au 7 Juillet 1815. Paris: Gide Fils, 1815.

Delmas, Antoine. Histoire de la révolution de Saint-Domingue, depuis le commencement des troubles, jusqu'à la prise de

Jérémie et du Môle S. Nicolas par les Anglais. 2 vols. Paris: Mame Frères, 1814.

Dernières observations des citoyens du couleur des isles et colonies françoises, du 27 Novembre 1789. N.p., 1789.

Dillon, [Henri]. *Mémoire sur l'esclavage colonial, la nécessité des colonies et l'abolition de la traite des Nègres.* Paris: J. J. Blaise, 1814.

Dugast, Charles M., ed. *Histoire patriotique des arbres de la liberté par Grégoire, membre de la Convention nationale; précédée d'un essai sur sa vie et ses ouvrages par M . . ., et d'un introduction par M. A. Havard.* Paris: Adolphe Havard, 1833.

M. Dumouchel; soi-disant évêque du département du Gard, et tous les autres défenseurs de la religion constitutionnelle de France, Convaincus d'ignorance, de mauvaise foi et d'hérésie, par les Catholiques du département du diocèse de Nîmes. Paris: Dufresne, n.d. BPR, Rév. 55.

[François, Louis-Joseph]. *Mon apologie.* N.p., [1791].

Garran [de Coulon, Jean-Phillippe]. *Rapport sur Julien Raimond, Fait au nom de la Commission des Colonies et des Comités de Salut public, de Législation et de la Marine réunis, le 24 floréal de l'an 3 de la République.* (13 May 1795). Paris: Imprimerie Nationale, year 3 (1795).

————. *Rapport sur les troubles de Saint-Domingue, fait au nom de la Commission des Colonies, des Comités de Salut Public, de Législation et de Marine, réunis.* 4 vols. Paris: Imprimerie Nationale, years 5–7 [1797–99].

Gastine, Civique de. *Lettre au roi, sur l'indépendance de la République d'Haïti, et l'abolition de l'esclavage dans les colonies françaises.* Paris: Marchands de Nouveautés, 1821.

————. *Pétition à MM. les Députés des départemens relative à l'abolition de l'esclavage dans les colonies françaises.* Paris: Marchands de Nouveautés, 1820.

————. *Pétition à MM. les Députés des départemens sur la nécessité où se trouve la France de faire une traité de commerce avec la république d'Haïti et sur les avantages qu'en retireraient les deux nations.* Paris: Marchands de Nouveautés, 1822.

————. *Seconde pétition adressée à MM. les Députés des départemens sur l'abolition de l'esclavage et des règlemens incon-*

stitutionnels qui privent les hommes de couleur de leurs droits politiques dans les colonies françaises. Paris: Marchands de Nouveautés, 1822.

Gaterau. *Réponse aux libelles séditieux publiés à Philadelphie contre les Hommes de couleur de Saint-Domingue.* Philadelphia, n.p., 1796. (AN, AD⁷ 29).

Gouly, B[enoît]. *Opinion et reflexions morales, physiques et politiques par . . . sur le rapport de la Commission des onze, relatif au regime constitutionnel des Colonies françaises.* Paris: Imprimerie Nationale, year 3 [1795].

Grégoire, Henri-Baptiste. *Abdication volontaire et motivée du titre de Commandeur dans la Légion d'Honneur.* New ed. Paris: Fain, 1822.

———. *Adresse aux députés de la seconde législature.* Nantes: Guimar, 1791.

———. *Apologie de las-Casas [sic], évêque de Chiappa, Par le citoyen Grégoire. Lu à l'Institut national le 22 floréal an 8.* (12 May 1800). Paris: Baudouin, 1802.

———. *Appel à la raison, par un proscrit.* Paris: Imprimerie de Piran Delaforest, Morinval, 1830. Reprinted from *Gazette des cultes,* 9 January 1830. BM Nancy: 80.192⁵.

———. *Compte rendu par le citoyen . . . au Concile national, des travaux des évêques réunis à Paris.* Paris Imprimerie-Librairie Chrétienne, 1797.

———. *Considérations sur la liste civile. Se vende au profit des blessés dans les journées des 27, 28, et 29 juillet.* Paris: Imprimerie de Decourchant, 1830.

———. *Considérations sur le mariage et sur le divorce, adressées aux citoyens d'Haïti.* Paris: Baudouin Frères, 1823.

———. *De la Constitution française de l'an 1814.* 2d ed. Paris: A. Egron, 1814.

———. *Critical observations on the poem of Mr. Joel Barlow, THE COLUMBIAD.* Washington: Roger Chew Weightman, 1809.

———. *De la domesticité chez les peuples anciens et modernes.* Paris: A. Egron, Imprimeur-Libraire, 1814.

———. *Epître aux Haïtiens.* Port-au-Prince: Imprimerie du Gouvernement, 1827.

Grégoire, Henri-Baptiste, et al. *Epître des évêques réunis à Paris aux pasteurs et aux fidèles des colonies françaises*. Paris: Imprimerie-Librairie Chrétienne, 1799. Reprint from *Annales de la religion* [1799], 49–76.

————. *Essai historique sur l'état de l'agriculture en Europe, au XVIe siècle*. Paris: Imprimerie de Mme Huzard, year 12 [1804].

————. *Essai sur la régénération physique, morale et politique des juifs*. Metz: Claude Lamort, 1789.

————. *Histoire des confesseurs des empereurs, des rois et d'autres princes*. Paris: Baudouin Frères, Libraires, 1824.

————. *Histoire des sectes religieuses qui, depuis le commencement du siècle dernier jusqu'à l'époque actuelle, sont nées, se sont modifiées, se sont éteintes dans les quatre parties du monde*. 2 vols. Paris: Potey, 1810. Reprint 1814 and 2d ed. in 6 vols. Paris: Baudouin Frères, 1828–45.

————. *De l'influence du Christianisme sur la condition des femmes*. Paris: Baudouin Frères, 1821.

————. *Lettre aux citoyens de couleur et Nègres libres de Saint-Domingue et des autres iles françoises de l'Amérique*. Paris: Patriote François, 1791.

————. *Lettre aux électeurs du département de l'Isère, Par M. . . . ancien évêque de Blois*. Paris: Baudouin Frères, 1819.

————. *Lettre aux philanthropes sur les malheurs, les droits et les réclamations des gens de couleur de Saint-Domingue et des autres îles françoises de l'Amérique*. Paris: Belin, 1790.

[————, et.al.] *Lettre pastoral des évêques réunis à Paris pour ordonner des prières en actions de graces des victoires remportés par les Armées de la République*. Paris: Imprimerie-Librairie Chrétienne, 1796.

————. *De la liberté de conscience et de culte à Haïti*. Paris: Baudouin Frères, 1824.

————. *De la littérature des Nègres, ou Recherches sur leurs facultés intellectuelles, leurs qualités morales et leur littérature; suivies de notices sur la vie et les ouvrages des Nègres qui se sont distingués dans les sciences, les lettres et les arts*. Paris: Maradan, 1808.

Grégoire, Henri-Baptiste. *An Enquiry concerning the intellectual & moral faculties, & literature of Negroes; with an account of the life & works of 15 Negroes & Mulattoes, distinguished in science, literature & the arts.* Translated by D[avid] B[ailie] Warden. Brooklyn: Thos. Kirk, 1810. Reprint. College Park, Md.: McGrath Publishing Co., 1967.

————. *Manuel de piété, à l'usage des hommes de couleur et des Noirs.* Paris: Baudouin Frères, 1818. Rev. ed. Paris, Baudouin Frères, 1822.

————. *Mémoire en faveur des gens de couleur ou Sangmêlés de St.-Domingue, & des autres Iles françoises de l'Amérique, adressé à l'Assemblée Nationale.* Paris: Belin, 1789.

————. *Motion en faveur des Juifs, par M. Grégoire, Curé d'Embermenil [sic], Député de Nancy; précédé d'une Notice Historique, sur les persecutions qu'ils viennent d'essuyer en divers lieux, Notamment en Alsace, & sur l'admission de leurs Députés à la Barre de l'Assemblée Nationale.* Paris: Belin, 1789.

————. *De la noblesse de la peau ou du préjugé des blancs contre la couleur des Africains et celle de leurs descendans noirs et sang-mêlés.* Paris: Baudouin Frères, 1826.

————. *Notice sur la Sierra-Leona, et sur une calomnie repandue à son sujet contre le gouvernement français; lue par le citoyen Grégoire, membre du Corps législatif et de l'Institut national, dans une séance de la classe des Sciences politiques et morales, le 2 pluviôse an 4.* (22 January 1796). N.p., year 4 [1796].

————. *Observations nouvelles sur les juifs, et spécialement sur ceux d'Allemagne.* N.p., [1806].

————. *Observations nouvelles sur les juifs, et spécialement sur ceux d'Amsterdam, et de Francfort; par . . . ancien évêque de Blois, Sénateur, etc.* N.p. [1807]. Extract from the *Revue philosophique, littéraire et politique*, 1807.

————. *Observations préliminaires sur une nouvelle edition d'un ouvrage intitulé: Histoire du Commerce homicide appelé Traite des Noirs.* N.p. [1822].

————. *Des peines infamantes à infliger aux négriers.* Paris: Baudouin Frères, 1822.

Grégoire, Henri-Baptiste. *Plan d'association générale entre les savans, gens de lettres et artistes, pour accélérer les progrès des bonnes moeurs et des lumières.* N.p. [1815–16?].

[————]. *Première et dernière réponse aux libellistes.* Paris: Adrien Egron, [1814].

————. *Réflexions de M. Grégoire, ancien évêque de Blois, sur l'Exposition des Prédictions et des Promesses faites à l'Eglise pour les derniers temps de la gentilité: par le P. Lambert.* N.p., [1806?].

————. *Réflexions générales sur le duel, par . . . curé d'Embermesnil & Député [sic] à l'Assemblée Nationale, en réponse à un ami.* Paris: Imprimerie de l'Auteur du "Courrier dans les 83 départemens," n.d. Extract from *Courrier de Provence,* 14 August 1790, pp. 176–80.

————. *Seconde lettre aux électeurs du département de l'Isère, par M. . . ., ancien évêque de Blois.* Paris: Baudouin Frères, 1820.

————. "Sur la littérature des juifs." *Correspondance sur les affaires du temps* 3 (1797): 88–91.

[————]. *De la traite de l'esclavage des noirs et des blancs; par un ami des hommes de toutes les couleurs.* Paris: Adrien Egron, Imprimeur, 1815.

————. *On the slave trade & on the slavery of the blacks & of the whites. By a friend of men of all colours.* Translated by Thomas Clarkson. Paris: Josiah Conder, 1815.

M. Grégoire député à l'assemblée nationale, et évêque constitutionnel du département de Loir et Cher, Dénoncé à la Nation. Paris: Crapart, [1791].

Guizot, [François-Pierre-Guillaume]. *Du Gouvernement de la France depuis la restauration, et du ministère actuel.* 2d ed. Paris: Librairie Française de Ladvocat, 1820.

Histoire de l'Ile de Saint-Domingue, depuis l'époque de sa découverte par Christophe Colomb jusqu'à l'année 1818. Paris: Delaunay, Louis Janet, Mongie, l'Aîné, Ladvocat, 1819.

Histoire du serment à Paris. Paris: Marchands de Nouveautés, 1791.

Isambert, François-André. *Mémoire pour S. Ex. le président de la République d'Haiti, contre Me. Blanchet, Avocat, sur la question morale de ce procès.* Paris: E. Duverger, 1827.

Lacroix, [François-Joseph] Pamphile [de]. *Mémoires pour Servir à l'Histoire de la Révolution de Saint-Domingue.* 2 vols. Paris: Pillet Aîné, 1819.

Lamoureux, [Jean-Baptiste] Justin. *Mémoire pour servir à l'histoire littéraire du département de la Meurthe, ou table statistique du progrès des Sciences, des Lettres et des Arts dans ce Département, depuis 1789, jusqu'en l'an XI* (1803). Nancy: J. R. Vigneulle, 1803.

Lanjuinais, J[ean] D[enis]. *Notice de l'ouvrage de l'évêque et sénateur Grégoire, intitulée De la littérature des nègres.* Paris: Maradan, 1808.

Laroche, Benjamin. *Lettres de M. Grégoire, ancien évêque de Blois, adressées l'une à tous les journalistes, l'autre à M. de Richelieu; précédées et suivies de considérations sur l'ouvrage de M. Guizot, Intitulé: du Gouvernement de la France depuis la restauration, etc.* Paris: Mad. Jeunehomme-Cremière, 1820.

Lavaud, J. *Appel aux contemporains, à la postérité, et plus particulièrement aux électeurs de l'Isère; sur l'élection d'Henri Grégoire.* Paris: Corréard, 1820. BM Nancy, 313.269[1].

Lavaud, J. *Notice sur Henri Grégoire.* Paris: Corréard, 1819.

Leborgne de Boigne, [Claude-Pierre-Joseph]. *Nouveau système de colonisation pour Saint-Domingue, combiné avec la création d'une compagnie de commerce pour rétablir les relations de la France avec cette isle.* Paris: Dondey-Dupré, 1817.

Lettre adressée à M. Grégoire, Curé d'Emberménil, Député de Nancy, par les Députés de la Nation Juive Portugaise de Bordeaux, 14 août 1789. Versailles: Baudouin, 1789.

Lettre des citoyens de couleur des isles et colonies françoises à MM. les membres du Comité de Vérification de l'Assemblée Nationale. Paris: Lottin & Lottin, 1789.

Limochel, F. *La France demandant ses colonies, ou réclamations de l'Agriculture, du Commerce, des manufactures, des artistes & des ouvriers de tous les départements, adressées au Corps Législatif, au Directoire, & à tous les Autorités Constituées de la République Françoise.* Paris: Volland, 1797.

Llorente, J[uan] A[ntonio], ed. *Oeuvres de don Barthélemi de las Casas, évêque de Chiapa, défenseur de la liberté des naturels de l'Amérique; précédées de sa vie, et accompagnés de notes*

historiques, additions, développemens, etc. 2 vols. Paris: A. Eymery, 1822.

Malenfant, Col. *Des colonies, et particulièrement de celle de Saint-Domingue; Mémoire historique et politique.* Paris: Audibert, 1814.

Mazerat, *Notice biographique.* Grenoble: Veuve Peyronard, 1819. BM Nancy, 311.635[23].

Moreau de Saint-Méry, [Médéric-Louis-Elie]. *Considérations présentées aux vrais amis du repos et du bonheur de la France, à l'occasion des nouveaux mouvemens de quelques soi-disant Amis-des-Noirs.* Paris: L'Imprimerie Nationale, 1791.

[————]. *Observations d'un habitant des colonies, sur le Mémoire en faveur des Gens de couleur, ou Sang-mêlés, de Saint-Domingue & des autres Isles Françoises de l'Amérique, adressé à l'Assemblée Nationale, par M. Grégoire, Curé d'Embermênil, Député [sic] de Lorraine.* N.p., 1789.

Morénas, J[oseph]. *Précis historique de la traite des noirs et de l'esclavage colonial, contenant; l'origine de la traite, sa progrès, son état actuel, et un exposé des horreurs produites par le despotisme des colons; ouvrage dans lequel on prouve qu'on a exporté d'Afrique, depuis 1814 jusqu'à présent, plus de 700,000 esclaves, dont un grand nombre sous pavillon français.* Paris: Firmin Didot, 1828.

Morgan, Lady [Sydney]. *France.* 4th rev. ed. 2 vols. London: Henry Colburn, 1818.

Le Mot du vrai législateur, sur la révolte & les incendies arrivés à Saint-Domingue, au mois d'août 1791. N.p., n.d. AN, AD[7] 25, colonies.

Moyse P. . . de Bordeaux. *Réponse à un article sur les juifs, de M. de Bonald, inséré dans le Mercure de France, du 8 Février 1806.* Bordeaux: Laivalle Jeune, 1806. BPR, Rév. 131.

Notice biographique sur M. Grégoire, ex-Sénateur. Metz: Lamort, [1818].

Observations très-essentielles, pour l'objet de la question à l'ordre du jour, adressées à NOSSEIGNEURS de l'Assemblée Nationale. N.p., n.d.

De l'opinion de M. Grégoire, ancien évêque de Blois et sénateur, dans le Procès de Louis XVI. N.p. 1810.

Page, [Pierre-François, and Brulley, Augustin-Jean]. *Développement des causes des troubles et désastres des colonies françaises, présenté à la Convention Nationale, par les Commissaires de Saint-Domingue, sur la demande des Comités de Marine & des Colonies, réunis, après en avoir donné communication aux Colons résidens à Paris, & convoqués à cet effet, le 11 juin 1793, l'an 2e de la République.* N.p., n.d.

Page, [Pierre-François], Brulley, [Augustin-Jean], and LeGrand, [Jean-Baptiste]. *Adresse à la Convention Nationale.* Paris: Laurens, Aîné, year 2 [1794].

Pellerin, [Joseph-Michel]. *Réflexions sur la traite des noirs.* Paris: Imprimerie Nationale, 1790.

Première et dernière réfutation de la calomnie éternelle de l'Ami de la Religion et des Jésuites. Paris: Piran Delaforest, Morinval, 1829. Extract from *Gazette des cultes,* 20 October 1829.

Programmes de la Société des philanthropes. N.p., n.d. BPR, Rév. 68.

Raimond, Julien. *Correspondance de . . . avec ses frères, de Saint-Domingue, Et les pièces qui lui ont été adressées par eux.* Paris: Imprimerie du Cercle Social, year 2 [1794].

———. *Lettre au citoyen D*** député à la Convention nationale, par . . . colon de Saint-Domingue, sur l'état des divers partis de cette colonie, et sur le caractère des déportées.* Paris: n.p., 1793.

———. *Lettre de . . . mulâtre, créole d'Aquin, et habitant de Jacmel, datée de Paris, rue Meslée, no. 33, le 4 Mars 1791.* Cap-François: Dufour de Rians, [1791?].

[———]. *Lettre d'un Citoyen, détenu pendant quartorze mois, et traduit au tribunal révolutionnaire, au citoyen C.B.***, représentant du peuple, en réponse sur une Question importante.* Paris: Imprimerie de l'Union, year 3 [1795].

———. *Réponse aux considérations de M. Moreau, dit Saint-Méry, député à l'Assemblée nationale, sur les colonies.* Paris: Imprimerie du Patriote François, 1791.

Rallier, [Louis-Anne-Esprit]. *Suite des observations sur Saint-Domingue. Paris Baudouin,* year 5 [1797].

Recueil de Pièces relatives aux obsèques de M. Grégoire et à la nomination de M. Guillon à l'évêché de Beauvais, publié par l'Agence générale pour la Défense de la Liberté religieuse. Paris: Bureau de l'Agence Générale, 1831.

Saladin, [J. B. Michel]. *Rapport fait par . . . au nom d'une commission spéciale, composé des représentants Grégoire, Chappey, Louvot, Beyts et Saladin, sur les pétitions des juifs de Metz et d'Avignon. Séance du 7 fructidor an V.* (24 August 1797). Paris Imprimerie Nationale, year 5 [1797].

de Salvandy, N[arcisse]-A[chille]. *De l'émancipation de Saint-Domingue dans ses rapports avec la politique intérieure et extérieure de la France.* Paris: Ponthieu, Delaunay, Dentu, 1825.

Sapey, Charles. *. . . Député de l'Isère, à ses collègues, Membres de la Chambre des Députés des Départemens.* Paris: Cit. Bailleul, 1819.

Saunders, Prince. *By Authority. Haytian Papers. A collection of the very interesting proclamations and other official documents; together with some account of the rise, progress, and present state of the Kingdom of Hayti.* London: W. Reid, 1816.

[Schottlander]. *Les premiers pas de la nation juive vers son bonheur sous les auspices du grand monarque Napoléon.* Paris, n.p., n.d.

Société de la Morale Chrétienne, Comité pour l'abolition de la traite des noirs. *Nouveaux faits relatifs à la traite des noirs.* Paris: Servier, 1826.

Tarbé, Charles. *Réplique à J. P. Brissot, Député de Paris, par . . . sur les troubles de Saint-Domingue.* Paris: Imprimerie Nationale, 1792. AN, AD⁷ 26.

Tonnelier, Jacques. *De la nécessité d'envoyer promptement à Saint-Domingue, trois Agens, conformément à la Loi du 12 Nivôse an VI.* (1 January 1798). Paris: Baillo, 1799.

[Tussac, Fr.]. *Cri des colons contre un ouvrage de M. l'évêque et Sénateur Grégoire, ayant pour titre de la littérature des nègres, ou réfutation des inculpations calomnieuses faites aux Colons par l'auteur, et par les autres philosophes négrophiles, tels que Raynal, Valmont de Bomare, etc.* Paris: Delaunay, 1810.

Venault de Charmilly, Col. *Lettre à M. Bryan Edwards, membre du Parlement d'Angleterre, et de la Société Royale de Londres, colon propriétaire à la Jamaïque, en réfutation de son ouvrage, intitulé Vues historiques sur la colonie française de Saint-Domingue, etc., etc. Publié en Mars dernier.* London: T. Baylis, 1797.

Wadstrom, Charles Bernhard. *Adresse au Corps législatif et au Directoire exécutif de la République français.* Paris: Imprimerie des Sciences et des Arts, 1795.

——. *[Note présentée à la Société des amis des noirs].* N.p., year 6 [1798].

COLLECTED DOCUMENTS AND MEMOIRS

Anderson, Frank Maloy. *The Constitutions and other select documents illustrative of the history of France, 1789–1907.* 2d rev. ed. Minneapolis: H. W. Wilson Co., 1908.

Archives parlementaires de 1787 à 1860. Recueil complet des débats législatifs et politiques des chambres françaises. Première série (1787 à 1799). 88 vols. to date. Paris: various publishers, 1867 to date.

Aulard, F[rançois Victor] A[lphonse], ed. *Recueil des Actes du Comité de salut publique avec la correspondance officielle des représentants en mission et le registre du Conseil exécutif provisoire.* 27 vols. Paris: Imprimerie Nationale, 1889–1933

——, ed. *La Société des Jacobins. Recueil des documents pour l'histoire du club des Jacobins de Paris.* 6 vols. Paris: Librairie Jouaust, 1889–97.

Bancal-des-Issarts, Henriette, ed. *Lettres autographes de Madame Roland, adressées à Bancal-des-Issarts, Membre de la Convention.* Brussels: J. P. Meline, 1836.

Bérenger de la Drôme, [Alphonse-Marie], ed. *Oeuvres de Barnave.* 2 vols. Paris: Jules Capelle et Guiller, 1843.

Brethé, J. J., ed. *Journal inédit de Jallet, curé de Chérigné, député du clergé du Poitou, aux Etats-Généraux de 1789.* Fontenay-le-Comte: Robuchon, 1871.

de Broglie, C. J. V. A., ed. *Souvenirs, 1785–1870.* 4 vols. Paris: Calmann Lévy, 1886.

Carnot, H[ippolyte], ed. *Mémoires de Grégoire, ancien évêque de Blois.* 2 vols. Paris: Ambrose Dupont, 1838.

Caron, Pierre, ed. *Paris pendant la Terreur, rapports des agents secrets du ministre de l'Intérieur.* 6 vols. to date. Paris: A. Picard, 1910 to date.

Cook, Mercer, ed. "Document: A Letter from a Haitian to Abbé Grégoire." *Journal of Negro History* 38 (1953): 438–39.

"Correspondance de Guillaume Mauviel, évêque des Cayes (Saint-Domingue), avec l'abbé Grégoire (4 novembre 1800–16 janvier 1804)." *Revue de la Révolution* 8 (1886): 27–32, 49–57.

Correspondance de Napoléon Ier publiée par ordre de l'Empereur Napoléon III. 32 vols. Paris: Henri Plon, 1858–70.

Cosson, Henri, ed. *Lettres de l'abbé Grégoire.* Paris Université, Centre d'etudes de la Révolution Française. Vol. 2, *Documentation.* Paris: Recueil Sirey, 1936.

Ford, Paul Leicester, ed. *The Writings of Thomas Jefferson.* Vol. 9, *1807–1815.* 10 vols. New York: G. P. Putnam's Sons, 1892–99.

[Garran de Coulon, Jean-Philippe]. *Débats entre les accusateurs et les accusés, dans l'affaire des colonies, imprimés en exécution de la Loi du 4 pluviose [sic].* (23 January 1795). 9 vols. Paris: de l'Imprimerie Nationale, year 3 [1795].

Ginsburger, [Moses], ed. "Zwei unveröffentliche Briefe von Abbé Grégoire." In *Festschrift zu Simon Dubnows siebzigsten Geburtstag (2. Tischri 5691).* Edited by Ismar Elbogen, Josef Meisl, Mark Wischnitzer, pp. 201–6. Berlin: Jüdischer Verlag, 1930.

Griggs, Earl Leslie and Prator, Clifford H., eds. *Henry Christophe, Thomas Clarkson, a correspondence.* Berkeley: University of California Press, 1952.

Hautrive, Ernest d', ed. *La police secrète du premier empire, bulletins quotidiens adressés par Fouché à l'Empereur.* 4 vols. Paris: Perrin et Cie., 1908–63.

Herold, J. Christopher, ed. *The Mind of Napoleon: A Selection From His Written and Spoken Words.* New York: Columbia University Press, 1955.

Hyde de Neuville, Baron [Jean-Guillaume]. *Mémoires et souvenirs du . . . .* 3 vols. Paris: Librairie Plon, E. Plon, Nourrit, et Cie., 1888.

Ingold, A. M. P., ed. "Lettres de Blessig à Grégoire," *Revue d' Alsace* 11 (1910): 478–90; 12 (1911): 58–67, 210–22.

Knutsford, Viscountess [Margaret Jean]. *Life and Letters of Zachary Macaulay.* London: Edward Arnold, 1900.

Koch, Adrienne and Peden, William, eds. *Life and Selected Writings of Thomas Jefferson.* New York: Modern Library, 1944.

Lafayette, Marie-Joseph-Paul-Roch-Yves-Gilbert-Motier, Marquis de. *Mémoires, correspondance et manuscrits. Par sa famille.* 6 vols. Paris: H. Fournier Aîné, 1837–38.

[Lallement, Guillaume N.], ed. *Choix de rapports, opinions et discours prononcés à la Tribune Nationale, recueillis dans un ordre historique, et imprimés d'après les pièces originales.* 23 vols. Paris: Alexis Emery, Libraire, 1818–23.

Las Cases, E[mmanuel]. *Mémorial de Sainte-Hélène, ou journal où se trouve consigné, jour par jour, ce qu'a dit et fait Napoléon durant dix-huit mois.* 8 vols. Paris: L'Auteur, 1823–24.

Lesur, C[harles] L[ouis]. *Annuaire historique universel, pour 1819.* Paris: Fantin, 1820.

———. *Annuaire historique pour 1820–1842.* 23 vols. Paris: Fantin, 1821–43.

"Letters of Toussaint-L'Ouverture and of Edward Stevens, 1798–1800." *American Historical Review* 16 (1910): 64–101.

"Lettres inédites." *Archives israélites de France, Revue mensuelle religieuse, historique, biographique, bibliographique et littéraire* 5 (1844): 415–17.

Linstant [de] Pradine, [Bon. A], ed. *Recueil général des lois et actes du gouvernement d'Haïti depuis la proclamation de son indépendance jusqu'à nos jours. Vol 5, 1827–1833.* 6 vols. Paris: Auguste Durand, 1860–81.

Montrol, F[rançois Mongin] de, ed. *Mémoires de Brissot.* 4 vols. Paris: Ladvocat, 1832.

Paupe, Ad[olphe] and Cheramy, P.–A., eds. *Correspondance de Stendhal (1800–1842).* 3 vols. Paris: Charles Bosse, 1908.

Perroud, Claude, ed. *J. P. Brissot, Correspondance et papiers.* Paris: Alphonse Picard & Fils, 1912.

Perroud, Claude, ed. *J. P. Brissot: Mémoires* (1754–1793). 2 vols. Mémoires et documents relatifs aux XVIII et XIX siècles. Paris: Librairie Alphonse Picard & Fils, n.d.

Pingaud, Léonce, ed. *Correspondance de Lecoz et de Grégoire* (1801–1815). Besançon: Dodiviers, 1906.

Sadler, Thomas, ed. *Diary, Reminiscences, & Correspondence of Henry Crabb Robinson, Barrister at Law.* 3 vols. London: Macmillan and Co., 1869.

Stewart, John Hall, ed. *A Documentary Survey of the French Revolution.* New York: Macmillan, 1951.

Wilberforce, R[obert] I[saac] and Samuel, eds. *The Correspondence of William Wilberforce.* 2 vols. London: John Murray, 1840; Philadelphia: Henry Perkins, 1846.

―――. *The Life of William Wilberforce.* 5 vols. London: John Murray, 1838.

SECONDARY SOURCES

Aimes, Hubert S. *A History of Slavery in Cuba, 1511 to 1868.* 1907. Reprint. New York: Octagon Books, 1967.

Anchel, R[obert]. *Napoléon et les juifs.* Paris: Presses Universitaires de France, 1928.

Arciniegas, Germán. *Latin America: A Cultural History.* New York: Alfred A. Knopf, 1967.

Ardouin, Alexis Beaubrun. *Etudes sur l'histoire d'Haiti, suivies de la vie du Général J. M. Borgella.* 11 vols. Paris: Dezobry & E. Magdeleine, 1853–55.

Berthe, Léon. "Grégoire, élève de l'abbé Lamourette." *Revue du Nord* 44 (1962): 39–46.

Bertier de Sauvigny, Guillaume de. *The Bourbon Restoration.* Translated by Lynn M. Case. Philadelphia: The University of Pennsylvania Press, 1966.

Boissonnade, P[rosper-Marie]. *St. Domingue à la veille de la Révolution et la question de la représentation coloniale aux Etats-Généraux (Janvier 1788–Juillet 1789).* Paris: Geuthner, 1906.

Bradby, E[liza] D[orothy]. *Life of Barnave.* 2 vols. Oxford: Clarendon Press, 1915.

Brette, A[rmand]. "Les Gens de couleur libres et leurs députés en 1789." *La Révolution française* 29 (1895): 326–45, 385–407.

Brunot, Ferdinand. *Histoire de la langue française des origines à nos jours.* 13 vols. 1905–53. Vol. 9, pts. 1, 2. Reprint. Paris: Librairie Armand Colin, 1967.

Byrnes, Robert Francis. *Antisemitism in Modern France.* Vol. 1, *The Prologue to the Dreyfus Affair.* New Brunswick, N.J.: Rutgers University Press, 1950.

Cabon, A[dolphe]. *Notes sur l'histoire religieuse d'Haïti, de la Révolution au Concordat* (1789–1860). Port-au-Prince: Petit Séminaire Collège Saint-Martial, 1933.

Cahen, Abraham. "L'émancipation des juifs devant la Société royale des sciences et des arts de Metz en 1787 et M. Roederer." *Revue des études juives* 1 (1880): 83–96.

Cahen, Léon. "La Société des Amis des Noirs et Condorcet." *La Révolution française* 50 (1906): 481–511.

Chassin, Ch[arles] L[ouis]. *Les cahiers des curés.* Paris: Charavay Frères, 1882.

Cobban, Alfred. *Aspects of the French Revolution.* New York: Georges Braziller, 1968.

Cohn, Norman. *The Pursuit of the Millennium.* Fairlawn, N.J.: Essential Books, 1957.

Cole, Hubert. *Christophe, King of Haiti.* New York: Viking Press, 1967.

Davis, David Brion. *The Problem of Slavery in Western Culture.* Ithaca, New York: Cornell University Press, 1966.

Debien, Gabriel. *Les colons de Saint-Domingue et la Révolution. Essai sur le Club Massiac (Août 1789–Août 1792).* Paris: Librairie Armand Colin, 1953.

Deschamps, Léon. *La Constituante et les colonies. La Réforme coloniale.* Paris: Perrin et Cie., 1898.

Dobson, Paul. "The Philosophe and the Negro Question." Paper read at the Southern Historical Association, New Orleans, 7 November 1968.

Dumolard, H[enri]. "Stendhal electeur de l'abbé Grégoire." In *Pages stendhaliennes.* Grenoble: Editions J. Rey, 1929.

Ellery, Eloise. *Brissot de Warville, A Study in the History of the French Revolution.* Boston: Houghton Mifflin, 1915.

Fladeland, Betty. "Abolitionist Pressures on the Concert of Europe, 1814–1822." *The Journal of Modern History* 38 (1966); 355–73.

Gazier, Augustin. *Etudes sur l'histoire religieuse de la Révolution française d'après des documents originaux et inédits.* Paris: Armand Colin et Cie., 1887.

————. *Histoire générale du mouvement janséniste depuis ses origines jusqu'à nos jours.* 2 vols. 5th ed. Paris: Librairie Ancienne Honoré Champion, 1924.

Genovese, Eugene. "Slave Revolts in the New World." Paper read at the Southern Historical Association, New Orleans, 8 November 1968.

Gottschalk, Louis R. *Lafayette Between the American and the French Revolution* (1783–1789). Chicago: University of Chicago Press, 1950.

Griggs, Earl Leslie. *Thomas Clarkson, The Friend of Slaves.* Ann Arbor: University of Michigan Press, 1938.

Grosclaude, Pierre. *Malesherbes, témoin et interprète de son temps.* 2 vols. Paris: Librairie Fischbacher, 1961.

Grunebaum-Ballin, Paul. *Commémoration du centenaire de la mort: L'abbé Grégoire et les juifs.* Paris: Imprimerie Française, 1931.

————. *Henri Grégoire, l'ami des hommes de toutes les couleurs: La lutte pour la suppression de la traite et l'abolition de l'esclavage, 1789–1831.* Paris: Société d'Editions Françaises et Internationales, 1948.

Gubernatis, Angelo de. *Eustachio Degola, il clero constituzionale e la conversione della famiglia Manzoni spogli da un carteggio inedito.* Florence: G. Barbera, 1882.

Hanke, Lewis. *Bartolomé de Las Casas: Bookman, Scholar & Propagandist.* Philadelphia: University of Pennsylvania Press, 1952.

Hardy, Charles Oscar. *The Negro Question in the French Revolution.* Menasha, Wisconsin: George Banta Publishing Co., 1919.

Hertzberg, Arthur. *The French Enlightenment and the Jews.* New York: Columbia University Press, 1968.

Hyslop, Beatrice. *French Nationalism in 1789 According to the General Cahiers.* 1934. Reprint. New York: Octagon Books, 1968.

James, C. L. R. *The Black Jacobins*. 2d rev. ed. New York: Vintage Books, 1963.

Jérome, L[éon]. *Les élections et les cahiers du clergé lorrain aux états-généraux de 1789*. Paris: Berger-Levrault et Cie., 1899.

Jordan, Winthrop. *White Over Black: American Attitudes Towards the Negro, 1550–1812*. Baltimore: Penguin Books, 1969.

Kahn, Léon. *Les juifs de Paris pendant la Révolution*. Paris: Paul Ollendorff, 1898.

Kennedy, Melvin D. *Lafayette & Slavery, from his letters to Thomas Clarkson & Granville Sharp*. Easton, Pennsylvania: The American Friends of Lafayette, 1950.

————. "The Suppression of the African Slave Trade to the French Colonies and Its Aftermath, 1814–1848." Ph.D. dissertation, University of Chicago, 1947.

Krieger, Leonard. "Nationalism and the Nation-State System: 1789–1870. In *Chapters in Western Civilization*. 3d ed. New York: Columbia University Press, 1962.

Lascaris, M. *L'abbé Grégoire et la Grèce*. Paris: A. Maretheux & L. Pactat, 1932.

Laurent, Gerard M. *Toussaint Louverture à travers sa correspondance (1794–1798)*. Spain: Industrias Graficas España, 1953.

Leconte, Vergniaud. *Henri Christophe dans l'histoire d'Haïti*. Paris: Editions Berger-Levrault, 1931.

Lefebvre, Georges. *La Révolution Française*. Peuples et Civilizations, vol. 13. Paris: Presses Universitaires, 1957.

Leyburn, James G. *The Haitian People*. New Haven: Yale University Press, 1941.

Liber, [Maurice]. "Les juifs et la convocation des Etats-Généraux, (1789)." *Revue des études juives* 63 (1912):185–210; 64 (1912):89–108, 244–77; 65(1913): 89–133; 66(1913):161–212.

Lionnois, J[ean] J[oseph]. *Histoire des villes vieilles et neuves de Nancy depuis leur fondation jusqu'en 1788*. 3 vols. Nancy: Haener Père. 1805–11.

Lloyd, Christopher. *The Navy and the Slave Trade: The Suppression of the African Slave Trade in the Nineteenth Century*. London: Longmans, Green and Co., 1949.

Macinnes, Charles Malcolm. *England and Slavery*. Bristol: Arrowsmith, 1934.

McCloy, Shelby T. *The Negro in the French West Indies.* N.p., University of Kentucky Press, 1968.

Maggiolo, [J. L. Adrien]. "L'abbé Grégoire, (1750–1789), Discours de réception." *Mémoires de l'Académie de Stanislas,* 4th series, vol. 5 (1872).

Malvezin, Théophile, *Histoire des juifs à Bordeaux.* Bordeaux: Charles Lefebvre, 1875.

Martin, Gaston. "La Doctrine coloniale de la France en 1789." *Cahiers de la Révolution française* 3(1935):7–44.

——. *Histoire de l'esclavage dans les colonies françaises.* Colonies et Empires. 1st series: Etudes Coloniales, vol. 4. Paris: Presses Universitaires de France, 1948.

Matinée, A. *Anecdotes de la révolution de Saint-Domingue racontées par Guillaume Mauviel, Evêque de la colonie (1799–1804).* St. Lô: n.p., 1885.

Maurel, Blanche. *Saint-Domingue et la Révolution française. Les représentants des colons en France de 1789 à 1795.* Paris: Presses Universitaires de France, 1943.

Mecham, J[ohn] Lloyd. *Church and State in Latin America: A History of Politico-Ecclesiastical Relations.* Rev. ed. Chapel Hill: University of North Carolina Press, 1966.

Meyer, Michael A. *The Origins of the Modern Jew: Jewish Identity and European Culture in Germany, 1749–1824.* Detroit: Wayne University Press, 1967.

Necheles, Ruth F. "The Abbé Grégoire and the Constitutional Church: 1794–1802." Ph.D. dissertation, University of Chicago, 1963.

Palmer, R[obert] R. *Twelve Who Ruled: The Year of the Terror in the French Revolution.* 1941. Reprint. New York: Atheneum, 1965.

Parisot, Robert. *Histoire de Lorraine (Duché de Lorraine, duché de Bar, Trois-Evêchés).* 2 vols. Paris: Auguste Picard, 1922.

Parkes, James. *A History of the Jewish People.* Rev. ed. Baltimore: Penguin Books, 1964.

Paul, Emmanuel C. "Bilan spirituel du Boyerisme." *Revue de la Société Haïtienne d'Histoire, de Géographie et de Géologie* 23(1952):1–15.

Perroud, Cl[aude]. *La proscription des Girondins (1793–1795).* Toulouse: Edouard Privat, 1917.

Perroud, Cl[aude]. "La Société française des Amis des Noirs." *La Révolution française* 69 (1916):122–47.

Pfister, Christian. *Histoire de Nancy.* 3 vols. Paris: Berger-Levrault, 1908.

———. "Les préliminaires de la Révolution à Nancy. L'élection aux Etats Généraux et le cahier de la ville de Nancy." *Mémoires de la Société d'Archéologie Lorraine et du Musée Historique Lorraine,* 4th series, vol. 10 (1910), pp. 5–106.

Pietri, François. *Napoléon et les israélites.* Paris: Berger-Levrault, 1965.

Posener, S. *Adolphe Crémieux: A Biography.* Translated by Eugene Golob. Philadelphia: The Jewish Publication Society of America, 1940.

Préclin, E[dmond]. *Les Jansénistes du XVIII siècle et la Constitution civile du Clergé: Le développement du richérisme. Sa propagation dans le Bas Clergé, 1713–1791.* Paris: Librairie Universitaire J. Gamber, 1929.

"Prix proposés en 1787 par la Société Royale des Sciences et des Arts de Metz." *Revue des études juives* 1(1880):97–102.

Ravitch, Norman. "Liberalism, Catholicism, and the Abbé Grégoire." *Church History* 36(1967):419–39.

Roberts, W[alter] Adolphe. *The French in the West Indies.* New York: The Bobbs-Merrill Company, 1942.

Sagnac, Ph[ilippe]. "Les juifs et la Révolution française (1789–91)." *Revue d'histoire moderne et contemporaine* 1(1899): 5–23, 209–34.

Saint-Rémy des Cayes, [Joseph]. *Pétion et Haïti: Etude monographique et historique.* 5 vols. Paris: n.p., 1854–57.

Sainville, Léonard. *Victor Schoelcher (1804–1893).* Paris: Fasquelle, 1950.

Seeber, E[dward] D[erbyshire]. *Antislavery Opinion in France During the Second Half of the Eighteenth Century.* The Johns Hopkins Studies in Romance Literature and Language, extra vol. 10. Baltimore: John Hopkins Press, 1937.

Soboul, Albert. *La France à la veille de la Révolution.* Vol 1, *Economie & société.* Paris: Société d'Edition d'Enseignement Supérieur, 1966.

Stein, Stanley J. and Barbara H. *The Colonial Heritage of Latin*

America: Essays in Economic Dependence in Perspective. New York: Oxford University Press, 1970.

Stoddard, T. Lothrop. *The French Revolution in San Domingo*. Boston: Houghton, Mifflin, 1914.

Sumner, Charles. *Prophetic Voices Concerning America. A Monograph*. Boston: Lee and Shepard, 1874.

Sydenham, M. J. *The Girondins*. London: Athlone Press, 1961.

Szajkowski, Zosa. *The Economic Status of the Jews in Alsace, Metz and Lorraine (1648–1789)*. New York: Editions Historiques Franco-Juives, 1954.

Taveneaux, René. *Le Jansénisme en Lorraine, 1640–1789*. Paris: Librairie Philosophique J. Vrin, 1960.

Thiry, Jean. *Le Sénat de Napoléon (1800–1814)*. Paris: Editions Berger-Levrault, 1949.

Touchard-Lafosse, [Georges]. *Histoire de Blois et de son territoire depuis les temps les plus reculés jusqu'à nos jours*. Blois: Imprimerie Felix Jahyer, 1841.

Vaval, Duraciné. "L'abbé Henri Grégoire dans ses rapports avec Saint-Domingue et Haïti." *Revue de la Société d'Histoire et de Géographie d'Haïti*, November 1931, pp. 16–34.

———. "Boyer." *Revue de la Société Haïtienne d'Histoire, de Géographie et de Géologie* 23 (1952):1–16.

Index

The Abbé Grégoire, 1787–1831
was composed in linotype Electra with
Optima display type. The entire book was printed
by offset lithography by The Book Press,
Brattleboro, Vermont.